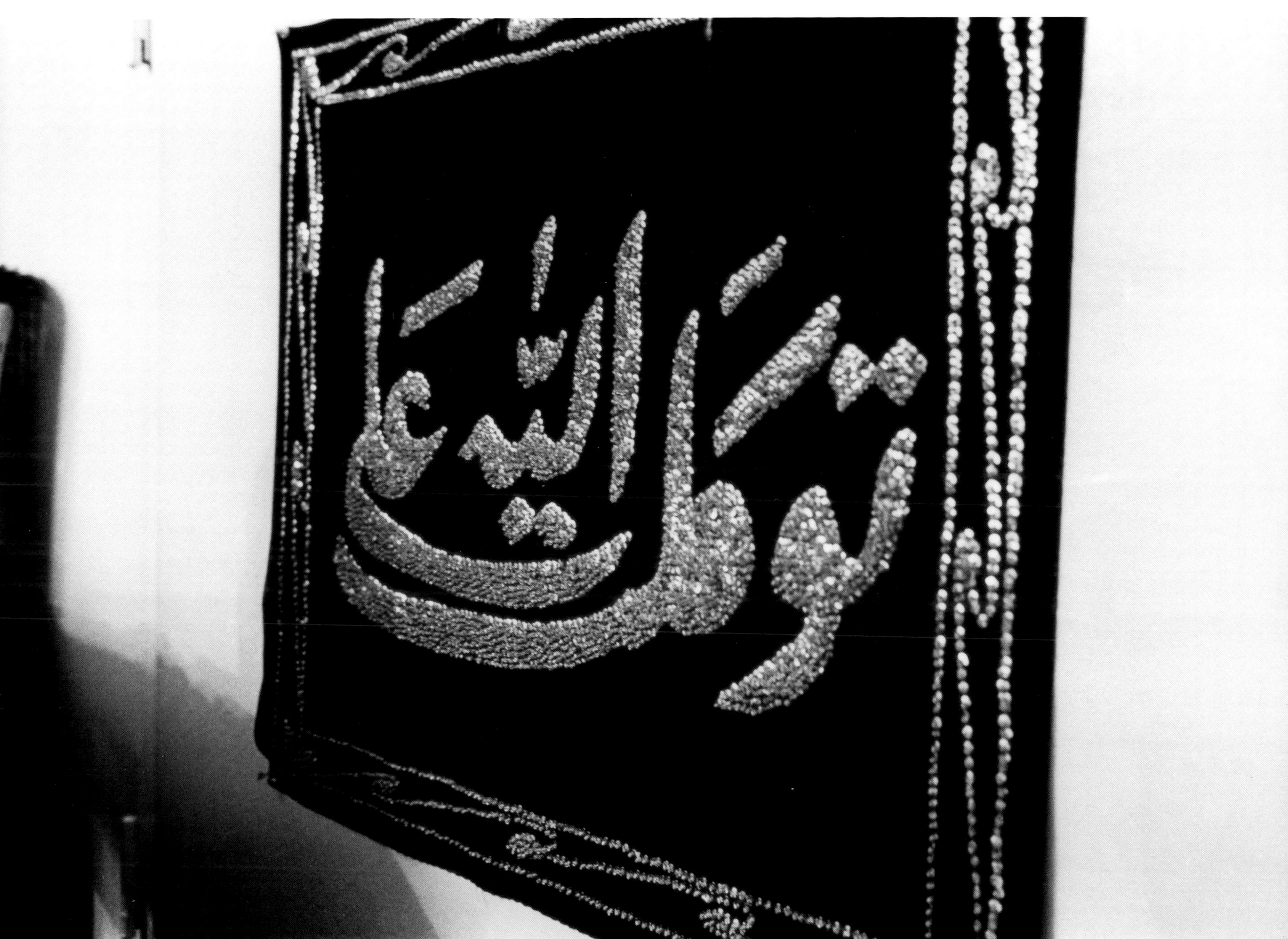

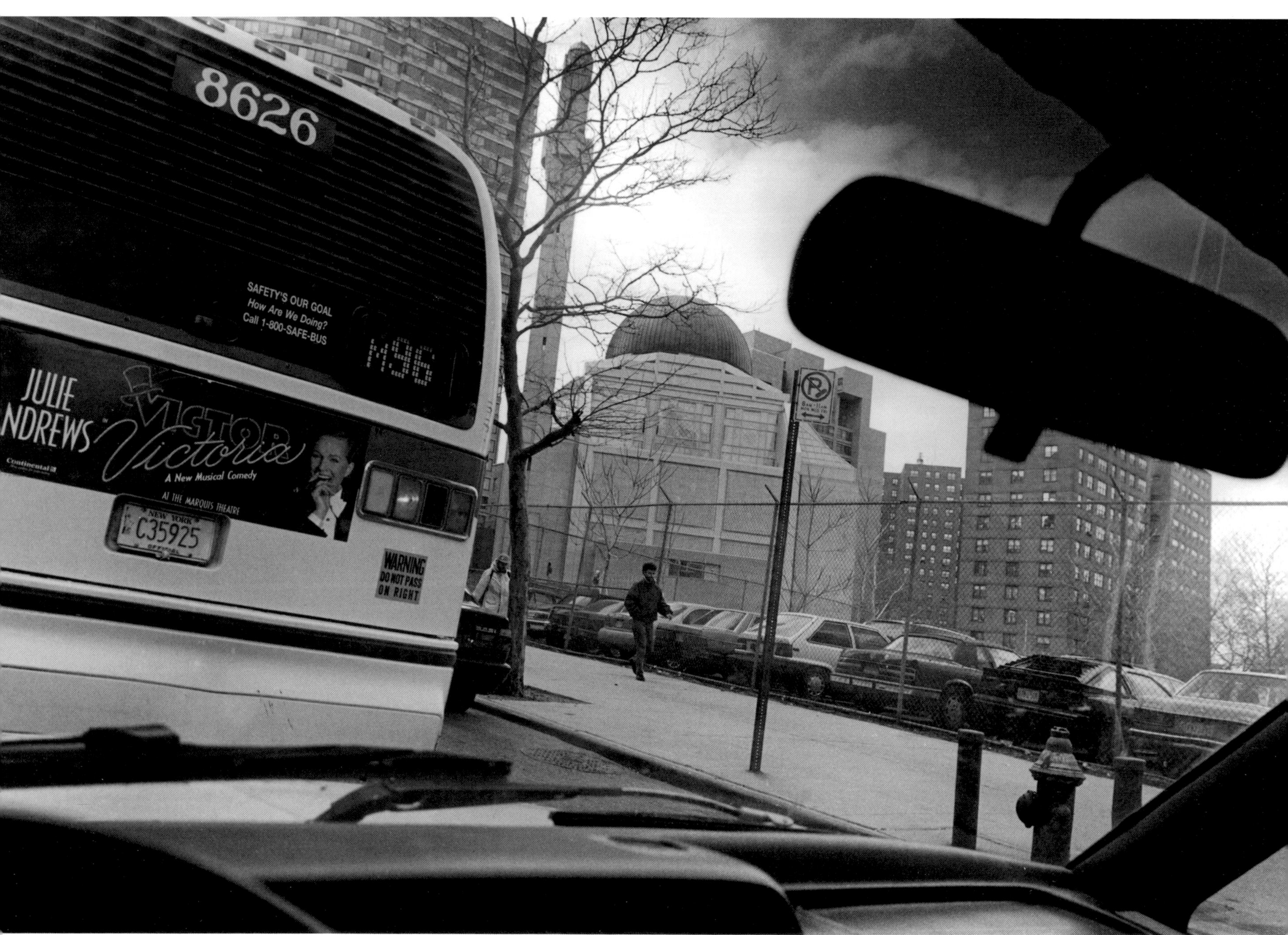

Islamic cultural center, Manhattan

NEW YORK MASJID

Going to Friday prayers, 31st Street, Astoria, Queens

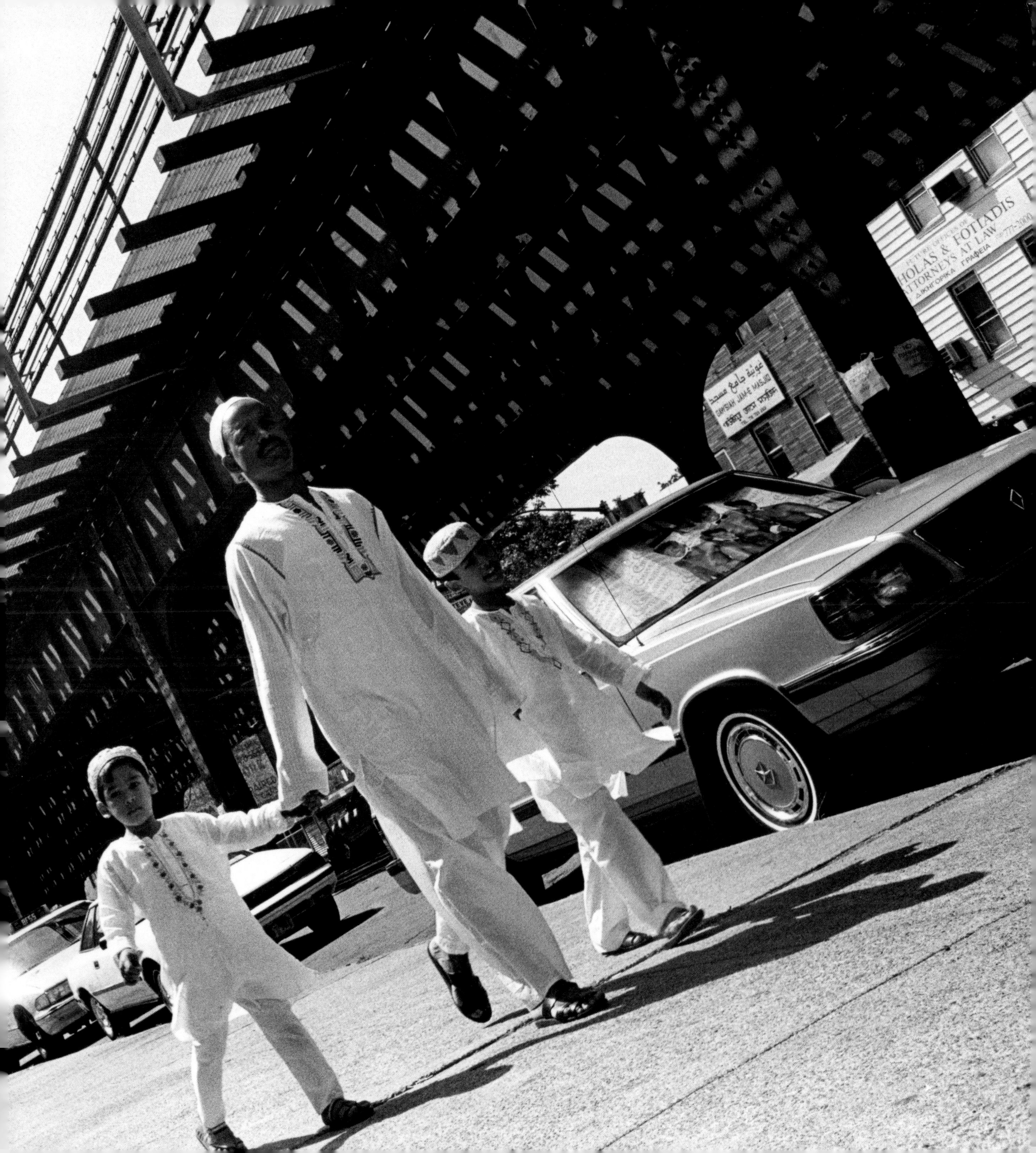
HOLAS & FOTIADIS
TTORNEYS AT LAW
ΓΡΑΦΕΙΑ
JAM-E MASJID

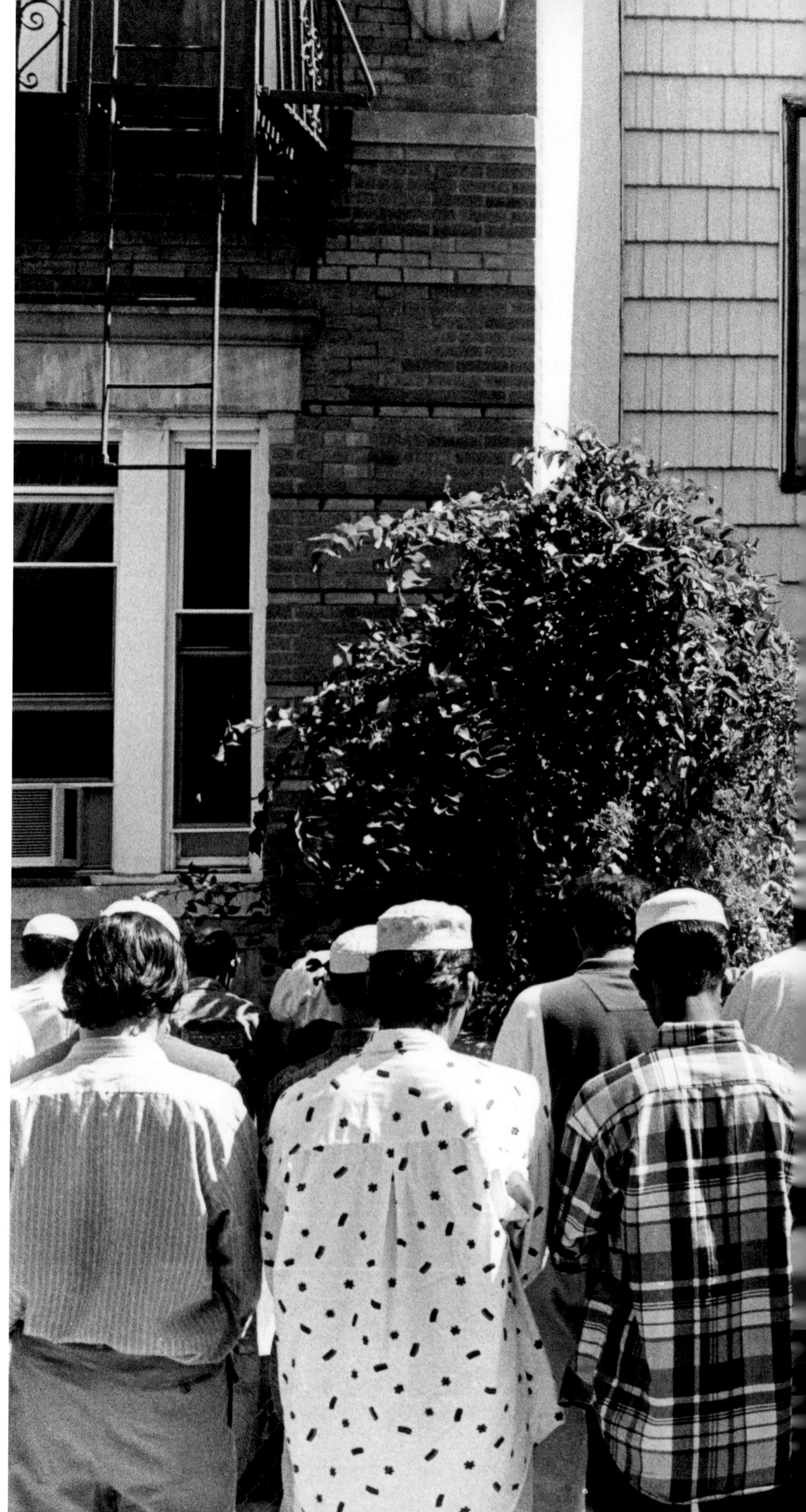

Shah Jalal Masjid, Queens

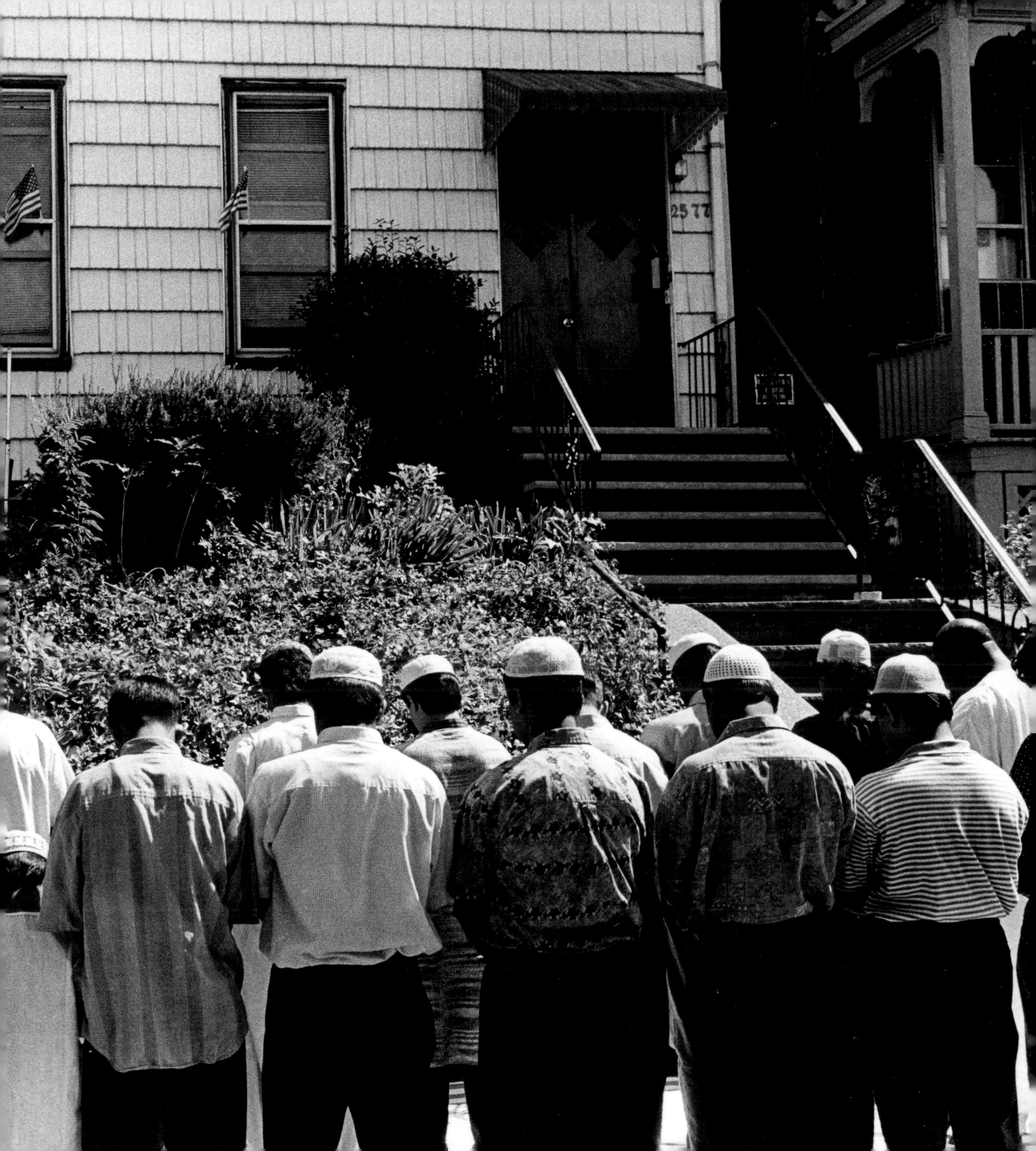
2577

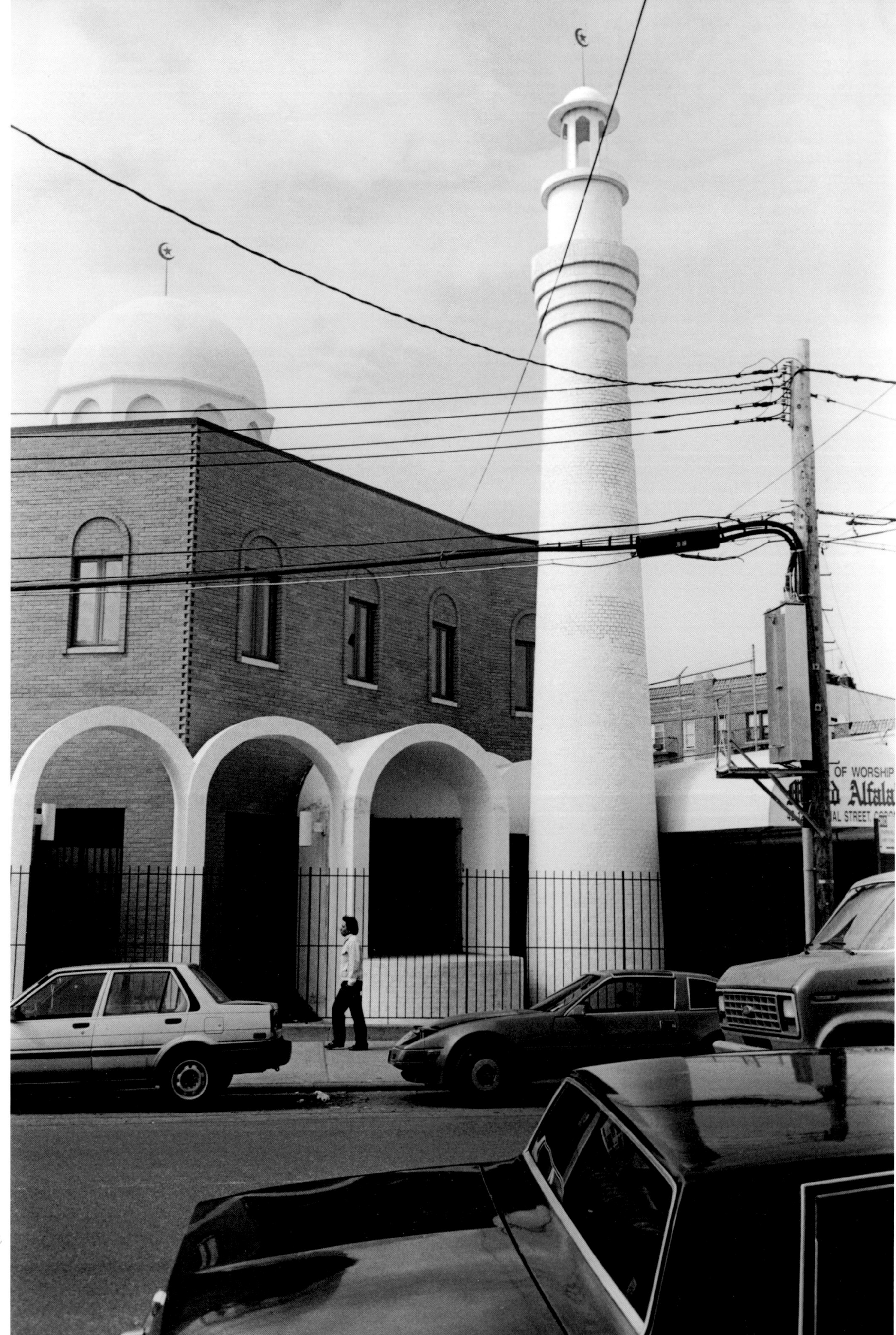

Masjid Alfalah,
queens

NEW YORK MASJID

THE MOSQUES OF NEW YORK CITY

powerHouse Books NEW YORK, NY

JERRILYNN D. DODDS TEXT EDWARD GRAZDA PHOTOGRAPHS

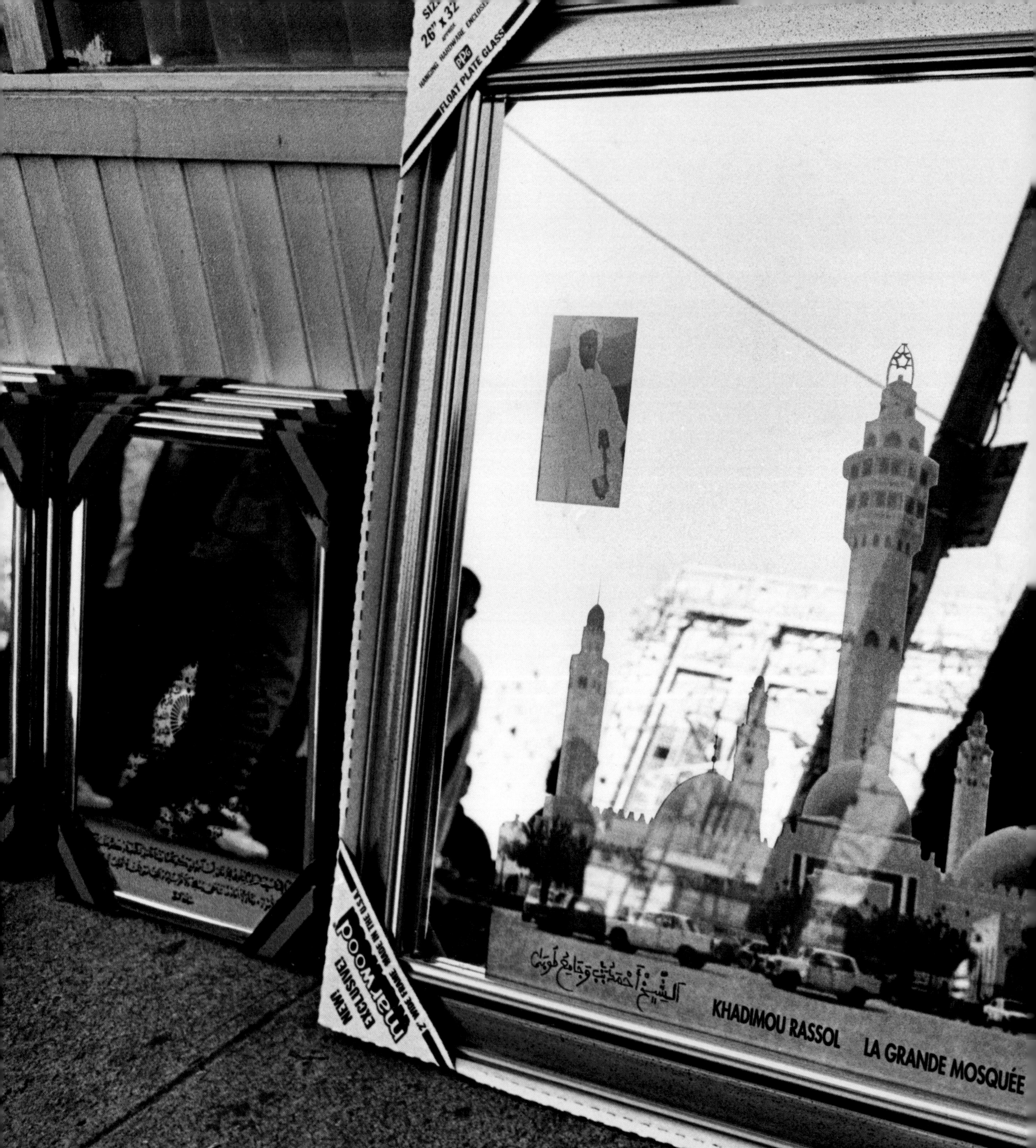
26" x 32"
FLOAT PLATE GLASS
KHADIMOU RASSOL
LA GRANDE MOSQUÉE

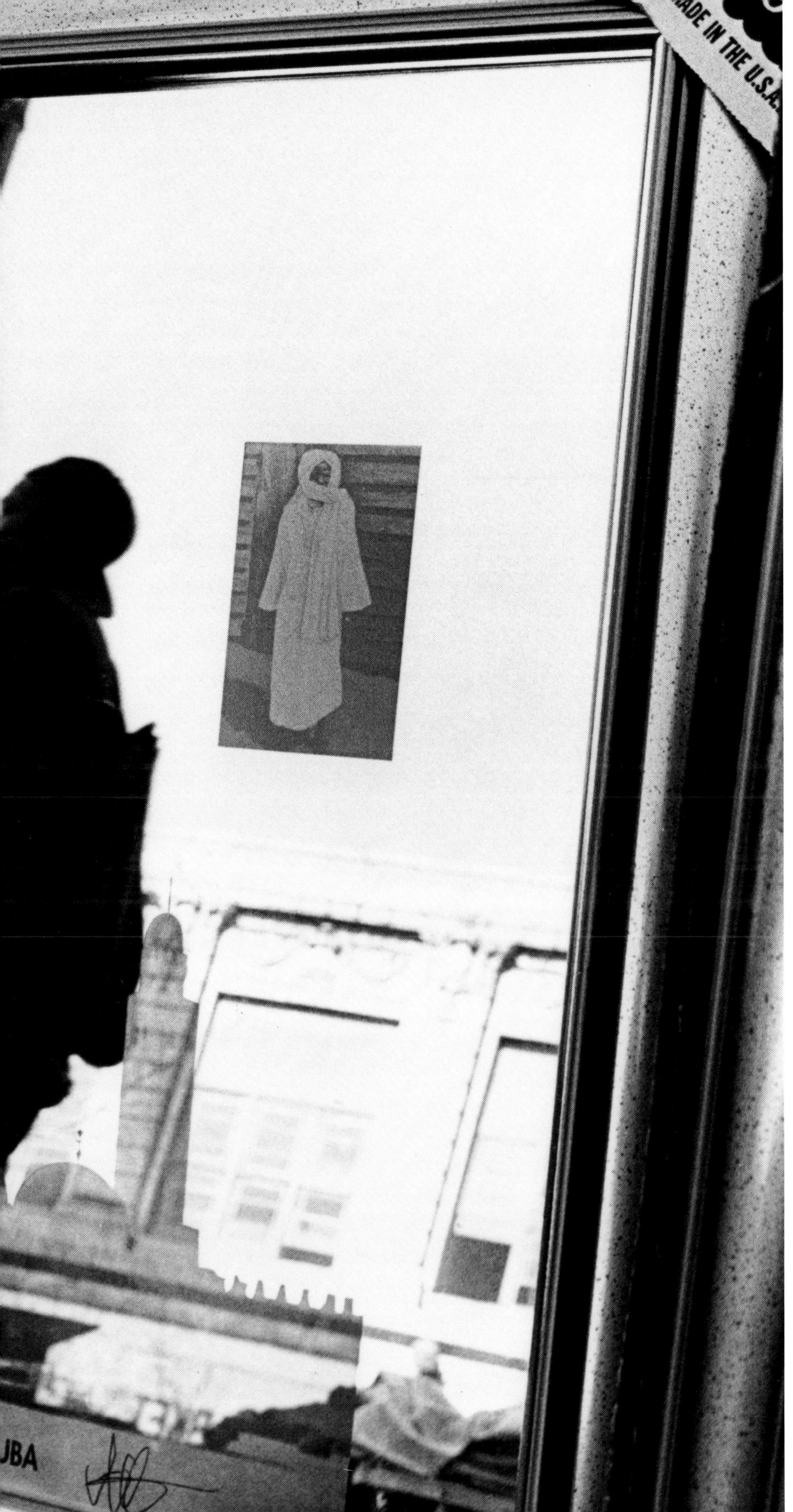

contents

Masjid Malcolm Shabazz, Manhattan

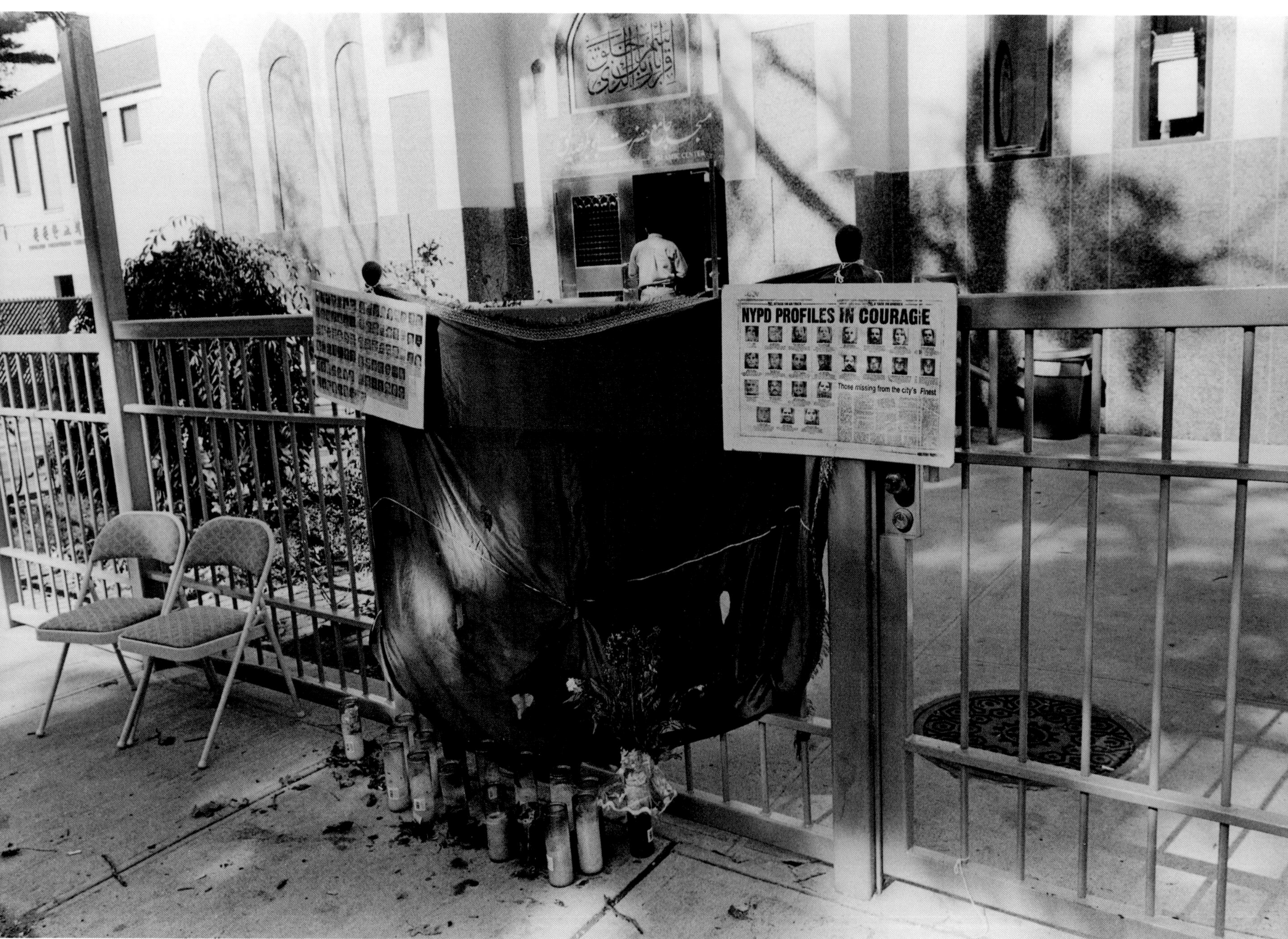

shrine to victims of 9/11 attacks, Masjid Hazrat-i-abu Bakr, Queens

FOREWORD: SEPTEMBER 2001

The chronology of this book, by virtue of a grievous and bitter coincidence, is framed by two attacks, a symmetry that is ruefully antithetical to its goal. *New York Masjid: The Mosques of New York City* was meant to chronicle searches for visual identity among diverse Muslim communities who were often ill understood and reductively represented after the first terrorist attacks on the World Trade Center in 1993. At the heart of this project was a desire to bear witness to the building up of New York's urban fabric by American Muslims; to articulate an answer to the polarized media image of the "Muslim Terrorist" embraced in the early 1990s. This book represents, then, research conducted throughout the last decade. The final manuscript was submitted for publication in August 2001, a month before the horrific events of September 11.

We lament terribly that the story we tell here will now seem framed by these two attacks, in which the communities whose emergence we chronicle are unimplicated, except in terms of the deep loss and pain they share with other New Yorkers. We hope, nevertheless, that this study might participate in the emerging public discourse concerning American Islam. The mosques themselves remind us that it is impossible to isolate ourselves from something which is already part of us; that we need now to make a place for Islam in a vital and transforming American identity.

Jerrilynn Dodds and Edward Grazda

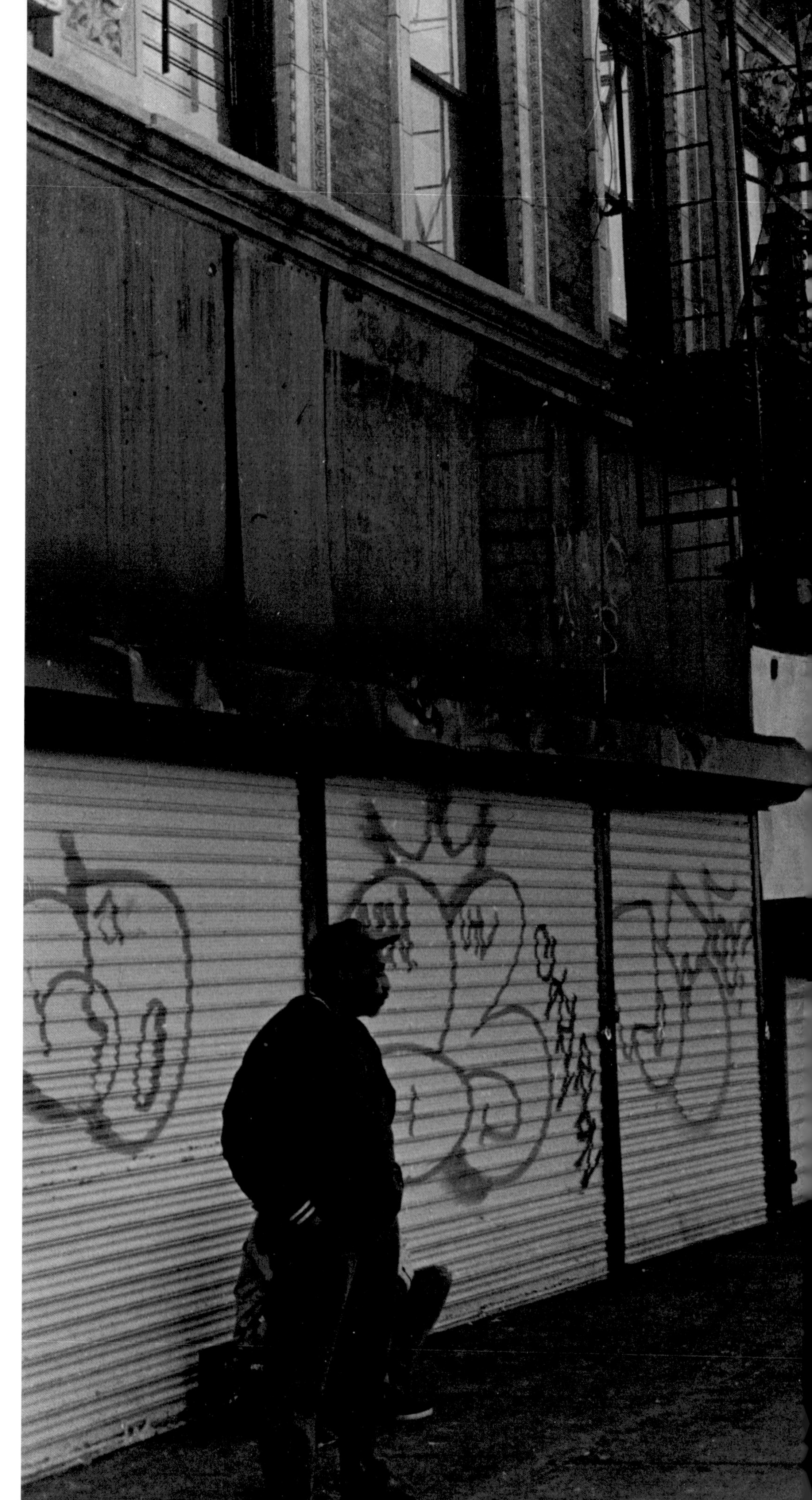

Masjid Malcom Shabazz, Manhattan

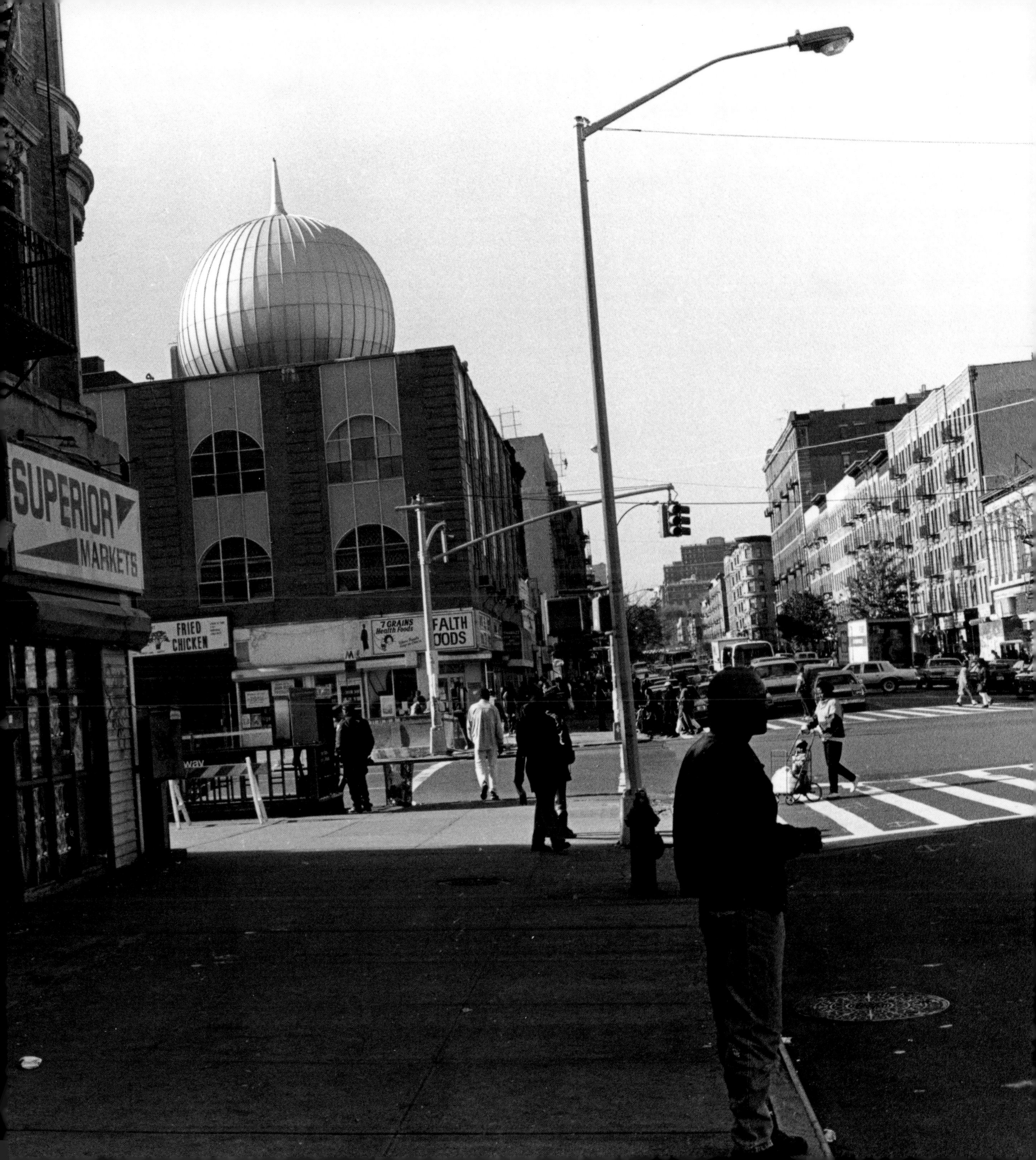
SUPERIOR
MARKETS
FRIED
CHICKEN
7 GRAINS
Health Foods

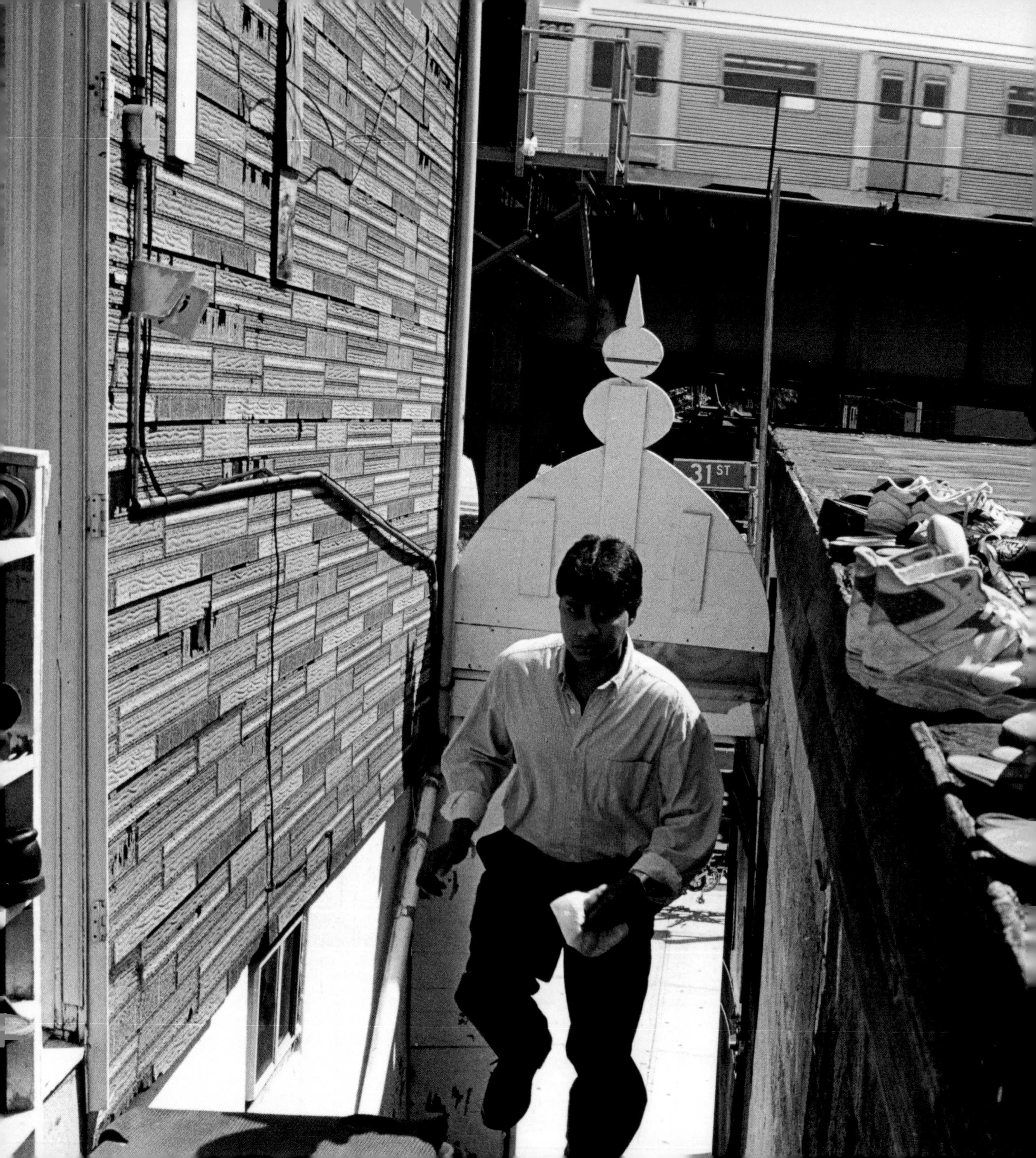
31 ST

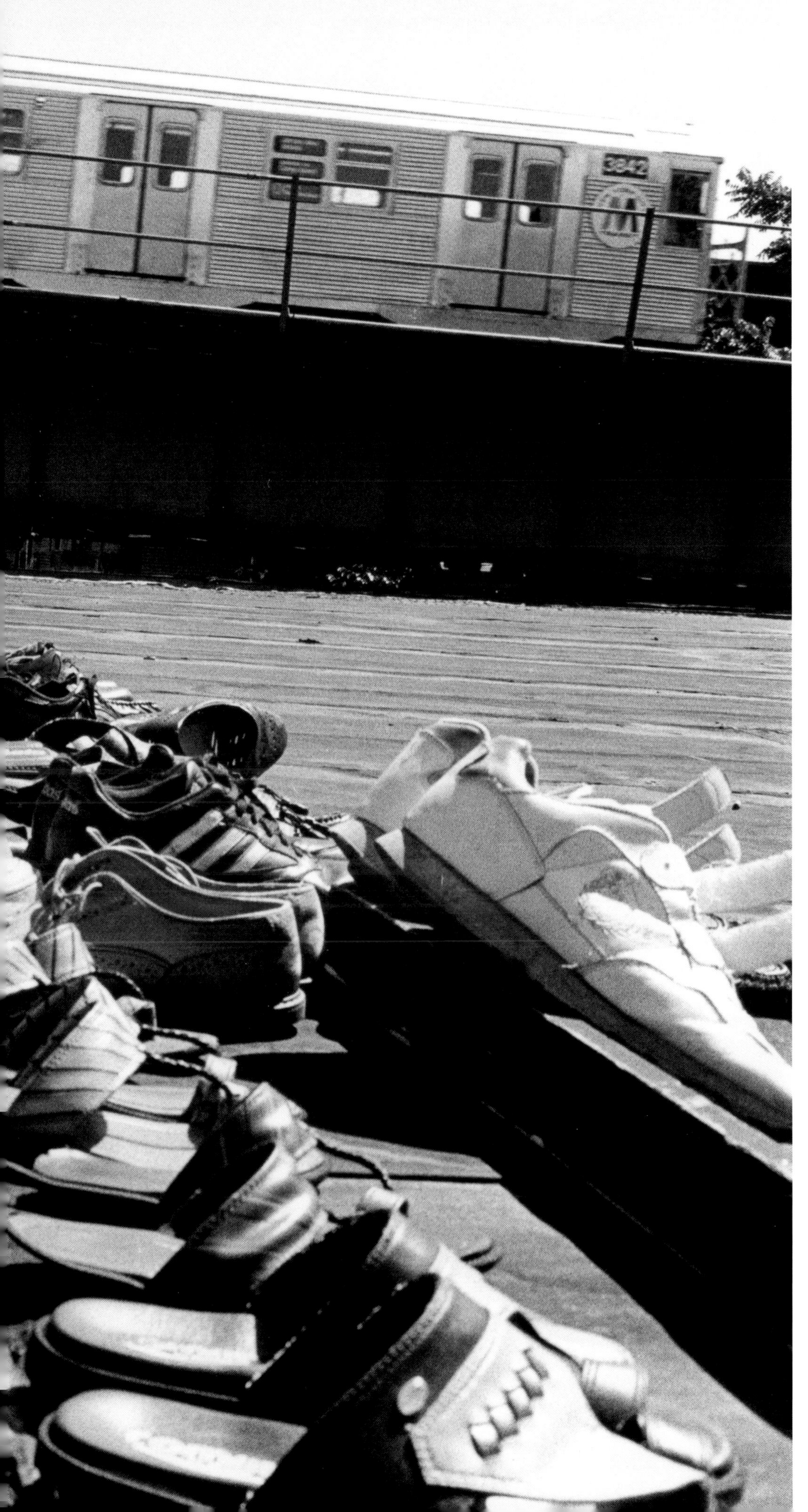

Gawsiah Jame Masjid, Queens

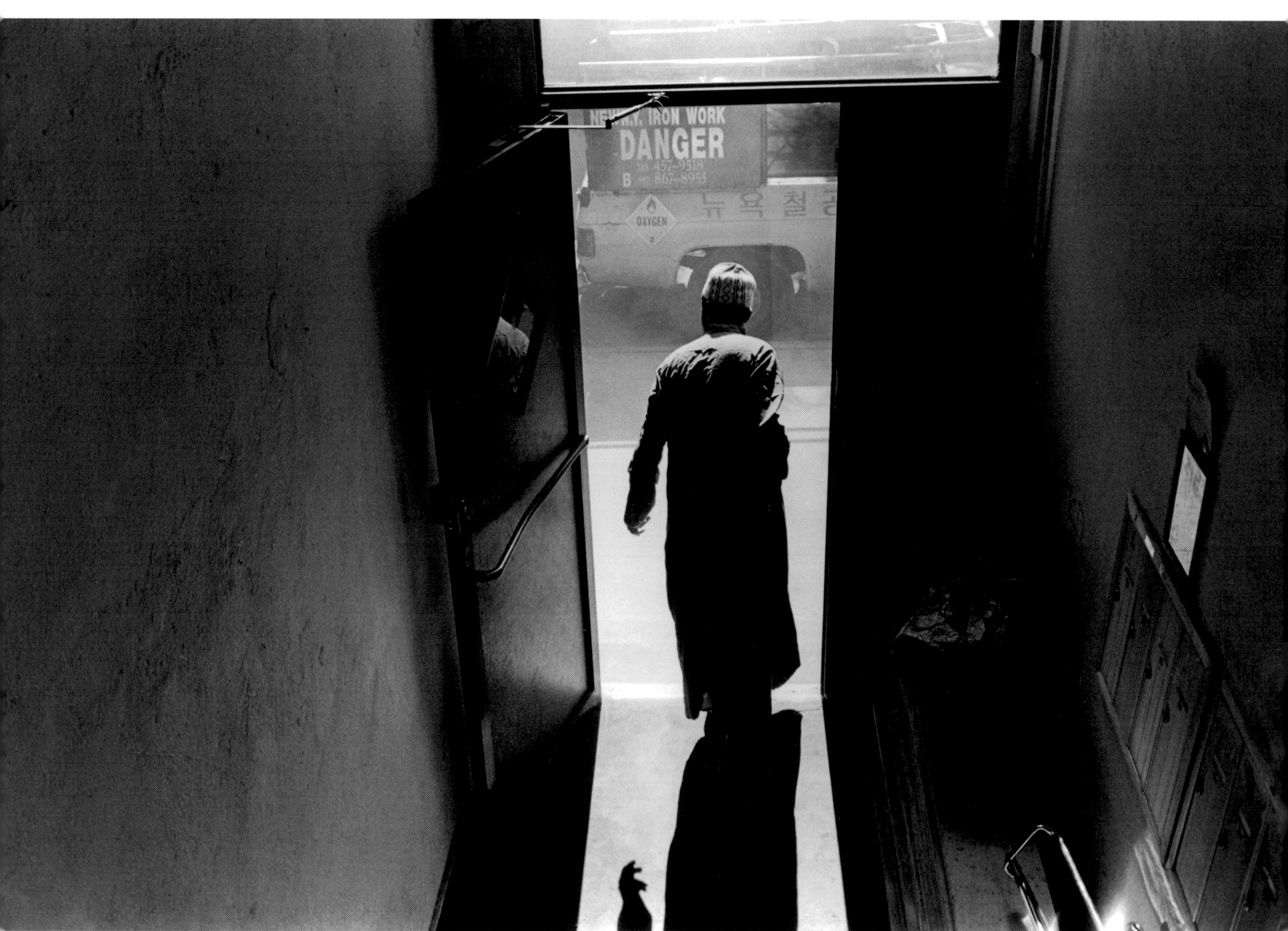

Madina Masjid, Manhattan

"WE SEEM LIKE STRANGERS..."

"In Bayside, kids would throw rocks at the windows. They wrote graffiti against Islam. We would clean it. They would repeat it. Finally we tried to write the name of the mosque so that people might not notice. But even that was destroyed. I would get quite upset, but the other community members were understanding. They said 'This is only a building. And we are new in their own country; their own neighborhood. We are in somebody else's neighborhood and we seem like strangers.'" [Nisar Zuri, Masjid Sayyed Jamal 'Udin]

On February 26, 1993, a New York City that could not yet imagine the events of September 11, 2001 seemed collectively frozen in a stricken gaze at a hole in its most mammoth monument. A car bomb had been planted in the basement garage of the World Trade Center in a then unprecedented terrorist attack: six people were killed, and more than 1000 were injured. Twenty-two defendants were brought to trial, distinguished in the press and in official reports as "Muslim Fundamentalist Conspirators." The event loosed the first inkling of a vulnerability to terrorism on American soil, and the lean, prosaic landmark chosen for the attack soon resonated with projected symbolic meaning. We learned for the first time that the World Trade Center was more meaningful as an object—more powerful and, at the same time, more ambivalent in its meanings—to those outside American culture than within. The towers had been chosen as much for their visual recognition as for their function, which is surely how the tallest buildings in New York were attacked as symbols of America's casual assumption of its global economic, political, and cultural hegemony.

In both written and televised media, photos of shredded concrete were crowned with headlines that read "Muslim Terrorist," as if the religion held the key to the unspeakable act. The constant fraternizing of those two words created the sense that they were bound, like secret synonyms, leaving a kind of easy, familiar ideological detritus behind for the city to feed upon.[1] In the two years that followed, open attacks on American Muslims and their mosques surged. After the Oklahoma City bombing on April 19, 1995, for which the extremist Timothy McVeigh was later convicted and executed, 222 attacks against Muslims were recorded, including death threats, arson, and shots fired at mosques.[2]

The license with which Muslims could still be publicly encapsulated into a violent, reductive other, and the glee with which the popular media harnessed recumbent public fears nestled in that fictive image, was staggering in the years following the 1993 World Trade Center bombing. And the fears evoked by these dangerous stereotypes were quickly exploited by the entertainment industry, in such films as *True Lies, Executive Decision,* and *The Siege.*[3]

The middle of the last decade of the 20th century may emerge, however, as a significant transitional moment in the American perception of Islam within its borders. Already by 1995, President Clinton warned against violent stereotypes associating Muslims and terrorism, declaring, "that

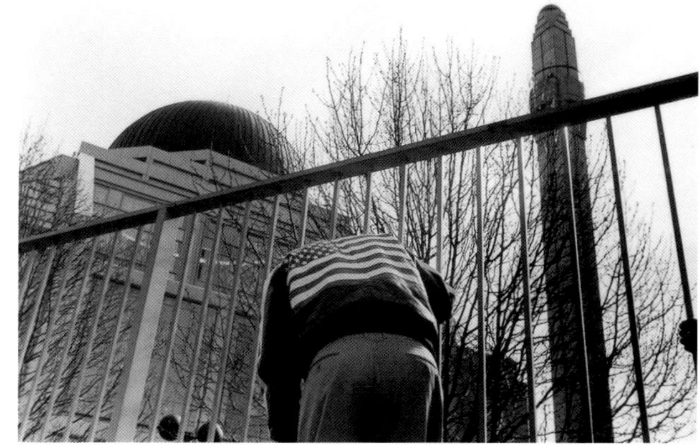

Islamic Cultural Center, Manhattan

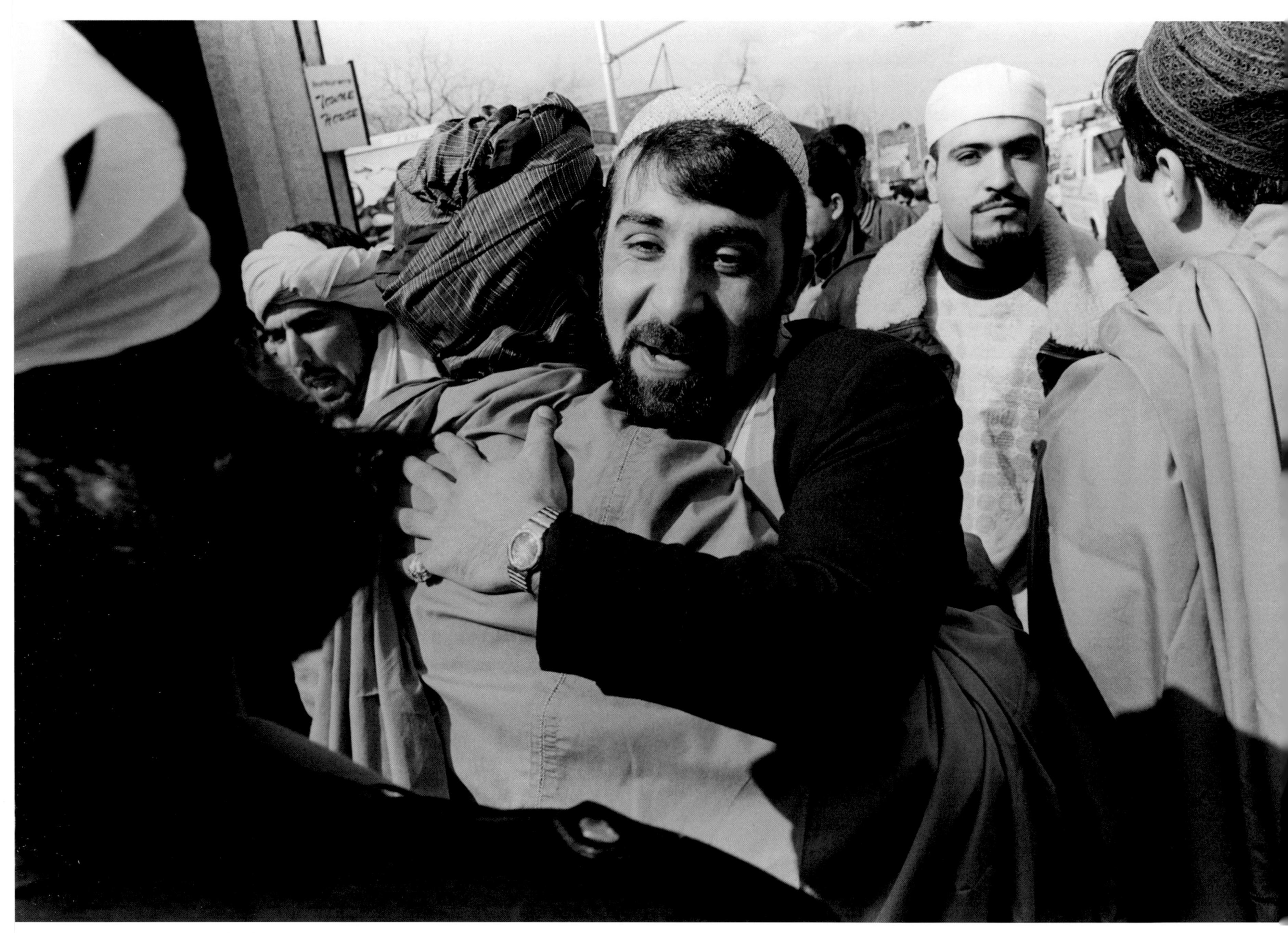

After Eid Prayers, Flushing, Queens

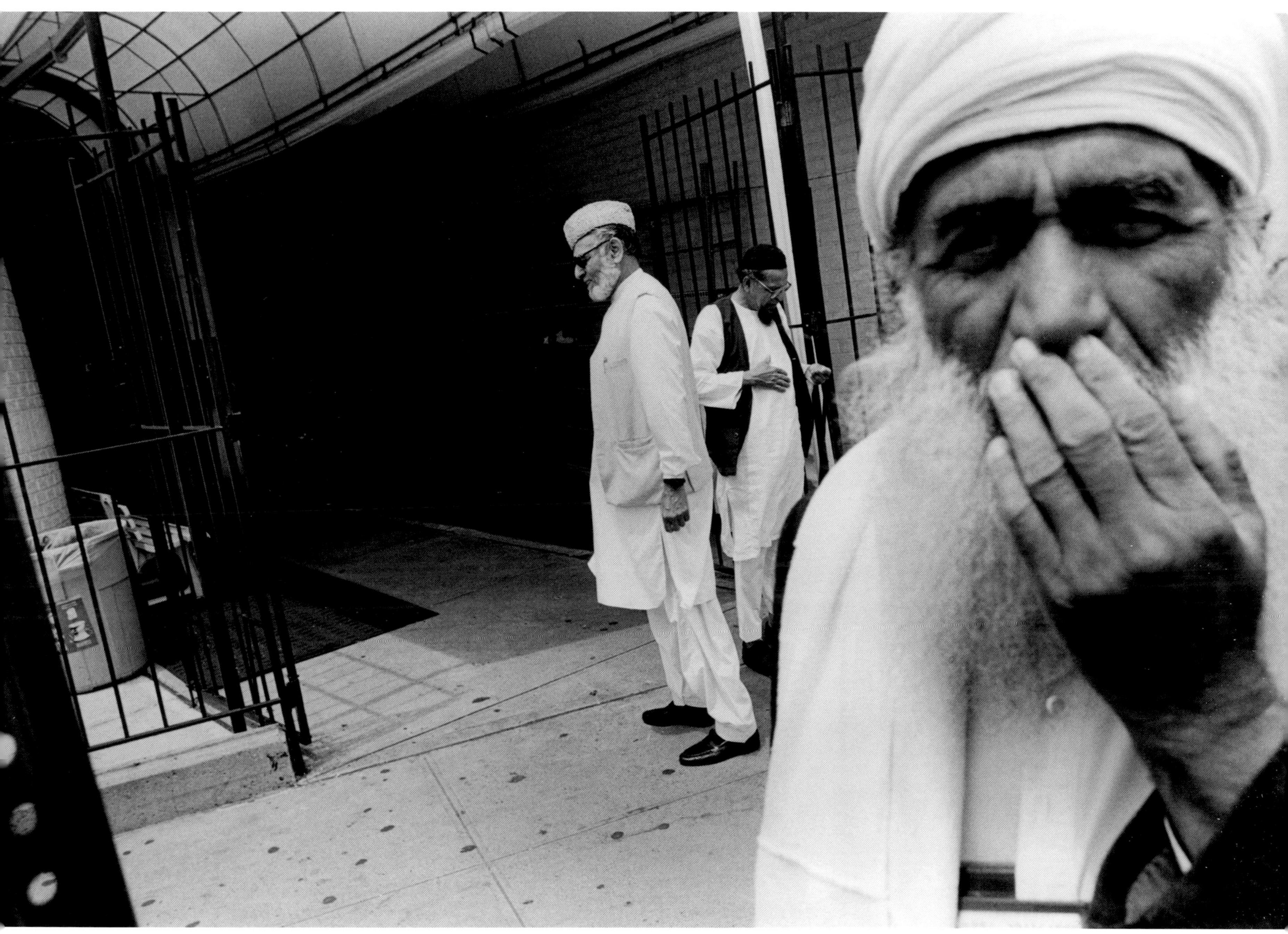

Masjid Alfalah, Queens

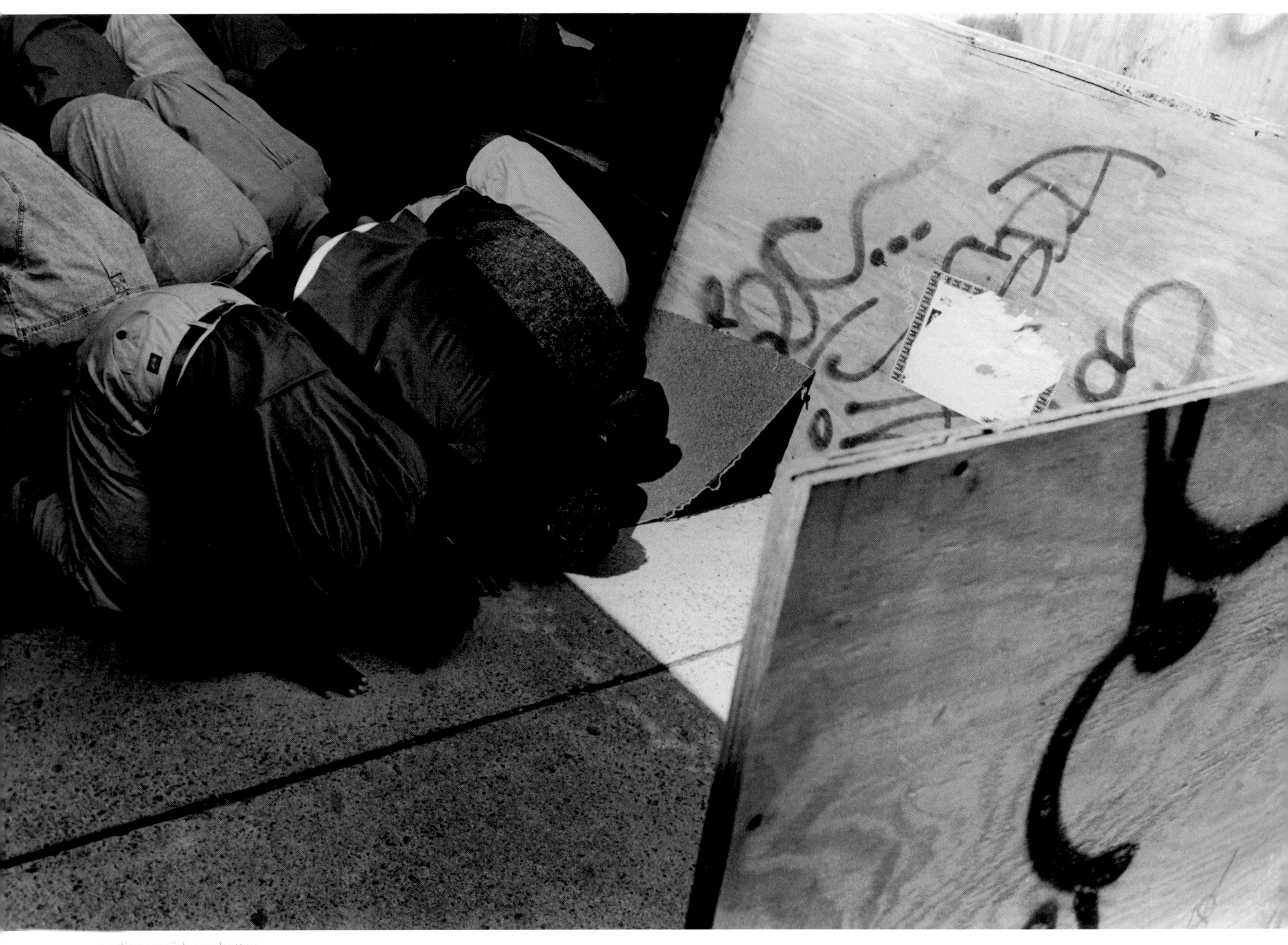

Madina Masjid, Manhattan

TO BUILD A MOSQUE

"we all worked incredibly hard to make this mosque happen. we worked extra jobs; everyone in the community sacrificed. But it was not really a sacrifice, because the mosque brings everything to us. Not the place, but the mosque. Everyone knows that the mosque is not a building." [Muhammed Said, Masjid Al Ber]

"The most beautiful mosques are recognized by the way they care for their communities. A mosque ought to be a community center; it ought to be the place where people are helped to find jobs, or care, or homes. sometimes when I look at the grandest mosque buildings, I wonder if an elaborate building does not mean that someone, somewhere is being neglected." [Aisha Al-Adawiya, Schomburg Center for Research in Black Culture]

BUILDING COMMUNITIES

There are over 100 mosques in the five boroughs of New York City, of which no more than half a dozen can be said to have been designed as mosques from the outset.[12] The rest are storefront buildings, lofts, stores, warehouses, or private homes that have been converted to mosques to serve communities that are the result of the impressive diaspora of the past two decades from dozens of Islamic countries to the United States, and an active American community that observes orthodox Islam as a religion and a way of life.[13] The buildings range in cost and scale from the multi-million dollar Islamic Cultural Center in Manhattan, to tiny prayer halls carved out of basements and garages in all five boroughs. They embrace a breathtaking ethnic, social, and economic diversity.

Only in a discussion limited entirely to architecture would masjid, or mosque, be understood as a building. A mosque is composed of an Islamic community, the ummah, and the functions that nurture and support it. In *Aljumuah*, a monthly journal published by the Islamic Revival Association U.S.A., the role of the masjid is defined in terms of thirteen functions, only one of which involves providing a place for prayer. Among others figure the teaching of religious and worldly affairs, the acquisition of knowledge and education of community members, the housing of poor Muslims, the collection and distribution of charity, the holding of consultative meetings (Shura councils), and most importantly, the building of community.

These values are born out in the mosques of New York, where it is not unusual to find a quite rudimentary prayer hall, accompanied by an elaborate and effective primary school. In fact, fourteen of New York's mosques incorporate accredited private schools and five of these offer secondary education. Mosque schools not only educate Muslims of divergent ethnic and national groups, but children of other religions as well, creating wider links within the community.

It is not surprising, then, that the presence of a new mosque in a run-down neighborhood is now recognized as a positive step in both the physical and social restoration of communities. Speaking of

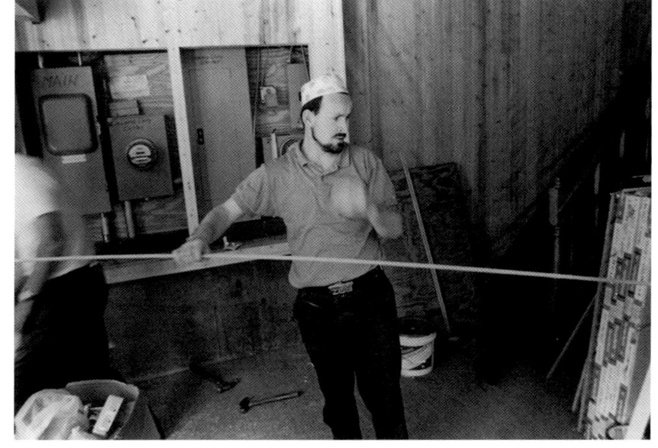

Ali Pasha Mosque, Queens

Fatih Cami in Brooklyn, Lt. Vincent Fragapane, Community Affairs Officer of the New York Police Department's 66th Precinct in Sunset Park, commented that "since the congregation renovated the building and began to function, the entire neighborhood has profited. New businesses have appeared, and the whole strip is safer and more alive." Within various New York neighborhoods, devout Muslims are finding they share common values with groups like Borough Park's Orthodox Jews. "This is a place where children learn the right things: no kissing in the streets, no drugs or alcohol, everybody well behaved," said Abdul Majeed Tabusam, a grocer on Utrecht Avenue.[14]

Muslim communities have also taken the initiative, in the past decade, to establish wider relationships within the larger community. Khutbahs, or Friday sermons, often contain encouragement to participate in local government: "Write to your State Representative," an Imam at the Islamic Congress declared, "we have the address for you right here."[15] The Alianza Islamica, among other groups, offers sensitivity training concerning Islam to New York police officers. And the Islamic Cultural Center now features a revolving message in red letters at its gate, which relates the basic principals of Islamic worship to the vast non-Muslim community of Manhattan's Upper East Side.

Indeed, the notion of a mosque as a site for the creation of community is intensified in New York, where Muslims are dispersed geographically and socially across the city fabric. In this manner, Islam in New York today mimics early Islam, the period when the concept of the mosque was formed. In the 7th century, the mosque was the means by which Muslims, in the initial expansion of the faith, found identity in largely non-Muslim contexts. The mosque became the site in which the community could experience itself as a collective and practice Islam together both as a faith and a way of life.

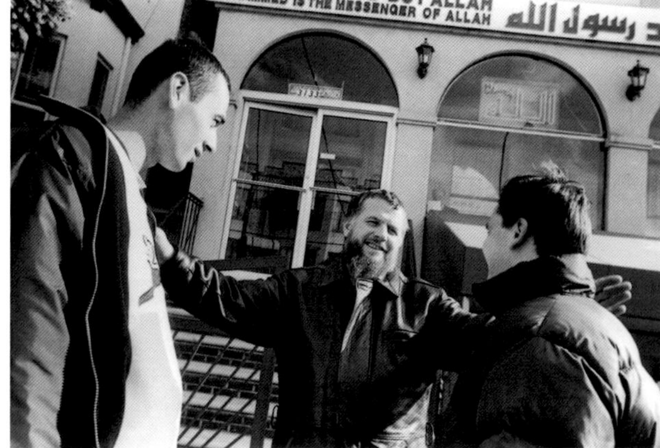

Ali Pasha Mosque, Queens

How this experience is still transforming the practice of Islam today can be seen at the Albanian Islamic Cultural Center in Staten Island. This lively cohesive community constructed a spacious mosque in 1994, making significant sacrifices to create "not just a place for prayer, but a community center, where there is a school, a library, and a room for weddings and celebrations." The community is now financing the reconstruction of two mosques destroyed in Kosovo, but they are concerned with "more than the building," says Imam Dhul Kareign. Their concern is also to transplant the notion of the community center from New York back to Kosovo, where much was lost during the socialist years. They are "building mosques with space for a school and other functions," Imam Ferid Bedrolli points out. "In this way," he says, "it will be a real center for the community in Kosovo, as we have here."

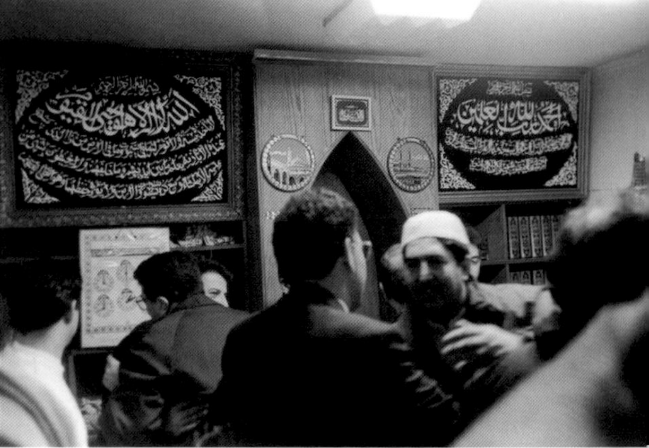
Hazrat-i-abu Bakr, Queens

Prayer is part of the mosque's function of forming and upholding the concept of community. For in Islam, the mosque is the sight of communal prayer, meant in part to allow the community to feel its breadth and unity. Prayer occurs five times a day. It can take place in a mosque, but also in virtually any other place that is clean. It is to this practice that we owe the awesome sight of hundreds of Muslims at prayer one September morning a year ago on Madison Avenue, as they prepared for the Muslim Day Parade, or the hushed spectacle of overflow crowds on their knees, in Flushing Meadow Park or on 3rd Avenue, during prayer on the feast of Id. One can pray at home, or at work, or in another institution, if need be. But there is a particular mandate for the community to assemble in a mosque on Friday for midday prayer, called Juma, when the Imam will lead prayer and give a sermon. In New York, a place where Islamic identity and the feeling of commonly held religious concerns for Muslims is diffused, submerged in the workplace and on the street, the experience of communal prayer and the sense of community it brings can become enormously important.

MAKING SPACE

The construction of a mosque building is, however, a separate issue from the formation of a community. The architectural enterprise of a mosque is accomplished by a lay group, sometimes called the Shura, a council of congregation members responsible for the financing and virtually all practical and organizational concerns surrounding the mosque and its decoration. Clergy are, on the whole, expected to isolate themselves from such material issues, although their participation varies with each community. Since according to many, the purchase, maintenance, and upkeep of the building must be financed without payment of any interest, the founding of a mosque can represent enormous community effort and sacrifice.[16]

Most of the mosques introduced in these pages were renovations of existing buildings, in which primary formal decisions were determined by a lay council working together with contractors. In a number of cases, the contractors themselves were congregants, and in-kind donations to the mosque's construction constituted a significant proportion of the construction budget[17]. In the few cases in which an architect was employed for design, they speak of active and persistent participation of the community in every step. "I had in mind more abstract windows and modernist values, but the gentlemen of the board were quite firm that they wanted windows that recalled the Ottoman style of Albania, so those are the windows we have today," smiles architect Brent Porter, who admires the dedication and involvement of his clients at the Albanian Islamic Cultural Center. "The design grew from the community's ideas," Imam Sherzad of Masjid Hazrat-i-abu Bakr declared proudly. The architect "helped us accomplish this."

The long history of the construction of the Islamic Cultural Center in 1991 in Manhattan is legendary for its complexity, and included Iranian-American architect Ali Dadras before the final selection of Michael McCarthy of the prestigious New York firm Skidmore, Owings & Merrill. As a building, the Cultural Center is the most opulent of New York's mosques, unique for having been financed, not only by its community, but by a consortium of Islamic governments represented in the United Nations, for whom it was meant to be symbolic—a landmark for Islam in New York. And yet the design process was extraordinary for "its inclusiveness," recalls Mustafa Abadan, a partner at Skidmore, Owings & Merrill, who was project architect at the time of the mosque's

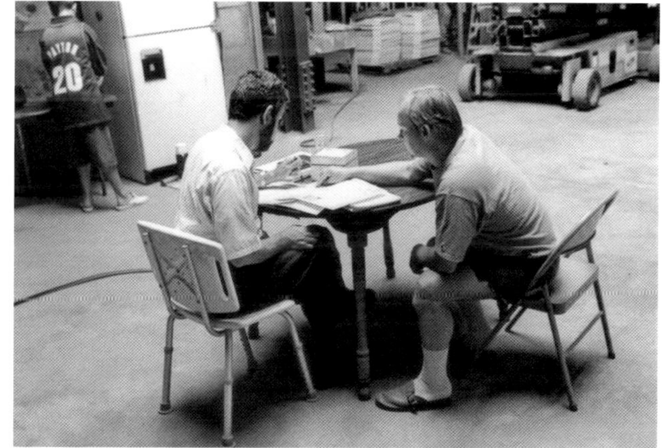

Mosque Representative and Project Manager at Masjid Hazrat-i-abu Bakr, Queens

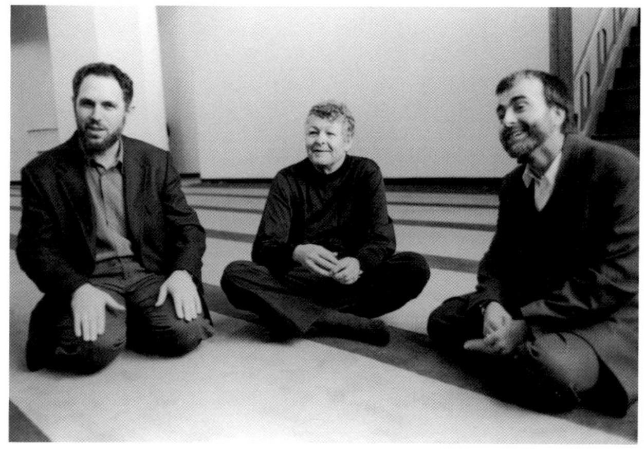

Architect and Imams at the Albanian Islamic Cultural Center, Staten Island

construction. "There were diplomats, U.N. and trade commission representatives, community members from all walks of life, and a board of scholars and architects. There developed a schism between those who wanted to import architectural forms, and those who wanted instead to explore what a worship space in Islam means. There was constant negotiation, and in the end, compromises were made by all of us." The firm found itself working in the end with some forms to which it had initially been opposed.

But such opulent, architect-designed mosques are exceptions in New York. Masjid Alfalah, by contrast, was designed by a construction engineer, William Park, whose drawings were signed subsequently by a registered architect, an arrangement that is more typical of the foundations chronicled here.[18] And it is a formula which, together with community financing, and in some cases contracting, provides for a high degree of community involvement in all aspects of design—but not the kind of unified, fetishized design concept typical of architect-designed projects in New York City. Indeed, in most of the buildings pictured in these pages, the use of architects was kept to the minimum legal intervention, and a spirit of practicality reigned; there was even, in many of the renovations we charted, a kind of cool contempt regarding any discussion of visual planning or architectural form. And this ambivalent attitude toward the sanctity of design can be extended to the democratic participation of the community as a whole: as we shall see, to block or alter a decorative or even architectural addition offered by a donor in order to maintain the visual integrity of a mosque design is generally frowned upon, for such an act would give the material aesthetics of the mosque precedence over its function and meaning.

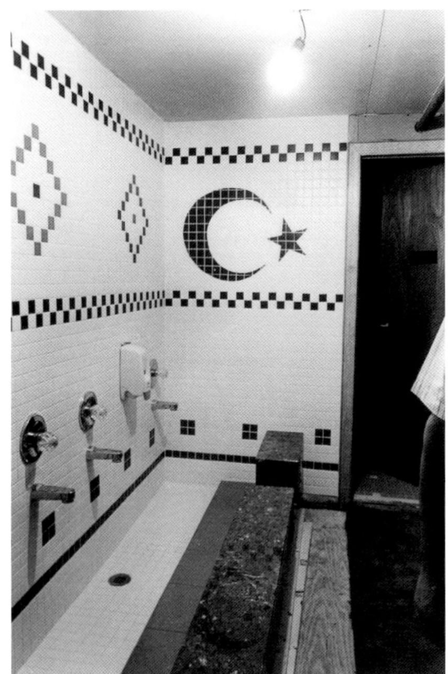
Ali Pasha Mosque, Queens

Because of the issues surrounding the making of community and the purposeful remoteness of the institution's confessional functions from architectural typology, new mosque communities in New York can create spaces whose architectural expression is enormously discrete and restricted. Some are experienced almost exclusively as interiors—as unadorned, protected spaces. These can carry very subtle markers on their street facades, or at times signage that seems to blend purposefully into a commercial neighborhood. Primarily places for prayer at the outset, these austere spaces illustrate the extent to which experience is privileged over expression in the early foundation of a mosque in New York City.

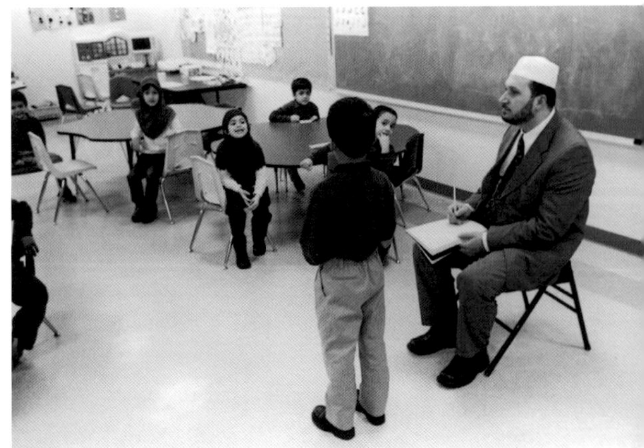
Albanian Islamic Cultural Center, Staten Island

In fact, the architectural requirements for a mosque are few, and include no symbolic forms. Minarets, which we tend to associate with the site where the Muezzin makes the Adhan, or call to prayer, are common in new-built mosques, where they serve more often simply as markers of exterior identity. Indeed, the original minarets of Islam probably served a similar function,[19] but minarets are in no way necessary for a mosque, and far from a requirement. Other monumental forms such as domes and arches can carry particular cultural meanings, even nostalgic or projected meanings in New York, but they carry no essential or universal association with Islam, and have no intrinsic association with the function of a mosque.

Among the few essential architectural components of a mosque, a place for ritual ablutions must be provided, and these can range anywhere from a small, pre-existing sink in the corner of a hall to elaborate tiled fountains, such as the one built at Fatih Cami in Brooklyn. Any congregation in New York City must, however, confront three architectural concerns common to all ethnic and linguistic groups that seek to establish a mosque: (1) the separation of sexes during prayer; (2) the restriction of images of animate beings within the mosque; and (3) the establishment of the qibla (the orientation of prayer in the direction of the Kaaba in Mecca). Significantly, none of these requirements touch on the physical appearance or form of the mosque as a building, and only the restriction of images effects ornamentation in any real way. These strictures pertain rather to function, while the appearance and presentation of the structure remains completely estranged from the sacred center: the acts of prayer that occur within.

SEPARATION OF SEXES

The formal means of separating men from women here takes on particular importance in New York City, because it is a social and religious custom so imperiled by the images and practice of every day life here. On crowded days at the mosque held in New York's Indonesian Consulate, men and women pray in a hall that is split by a partition drawn perpendicular to the qibla, placing them equidistant to it, side by side. At Fatih Cami in Brooklyn, a movable screen near the back of the prayer hall can expand and contract with the number of men or women attending. The Islamic Cultural Center in Manhattan and the Albanian Islamic Cultural Center in Staten Island were designed with elaborate tribunes and balconies to accommodate women separately, and in a large number of storefront mosques a separate room or an entire floor is dedicated to women. These separate floors are most often equipped with a PA system—or in the case of the Ali Pasha Mosque, closed circuit TV—to insure that those separated from the main prayer hall are able to hear the khutbah, or sermon, delivered during Juma, or Friday prayer.

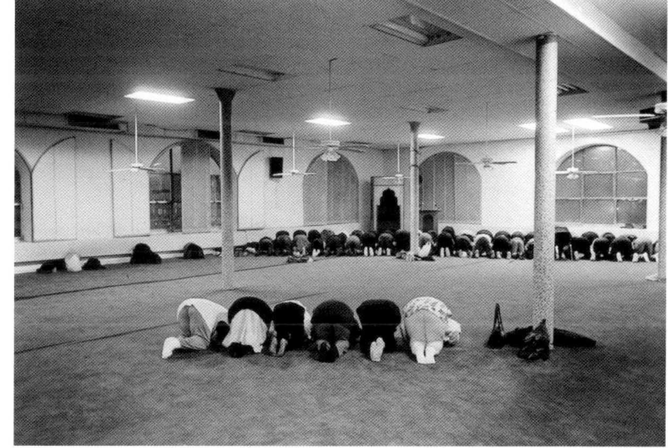

Masjid Malcolm Shabazz, Manhattan

Technology—closed circuit TV, or loudspeaker systems—can become the means by which separation in the constricted, pre-built spaces of New York's commercial and residential buildings can be made more workable; but that same technology also permits a separation which is at times more complete, and more rigidly codified into the architectural structure, than it is in many Islamic countries. For nearly every primarily immigrant congregation we spoke with during this study, the separation of the sexes had a heightened meaning in an unbridled, secular New York; the separation was, at times, defined architecturally in a more restrictive way than in an immigrant's Islamic home country.

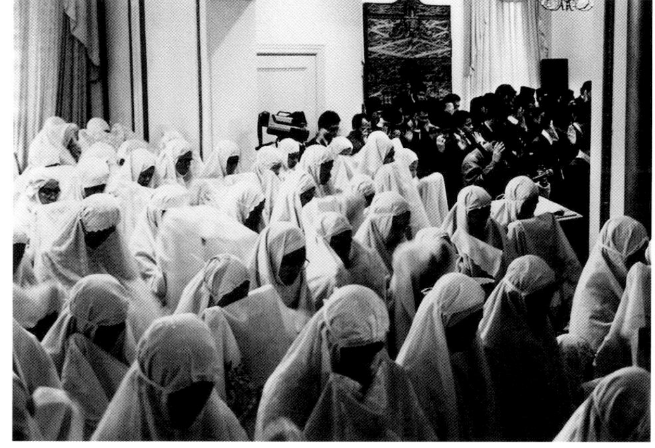

Indonesian Consulate, Manhattan. Photo by Reina Loeis

Though the accommodation of women in a separate floor or room is most often the result of the exigencies of space, the architectural provision made for the separation of sexes is can be culturally determined. At Gawsiah Jame Masjid, a tiny mosque in Astoria, Queens, there were no women present for prayer one Friday. "The women prefer to pray at home," one congregant told me.

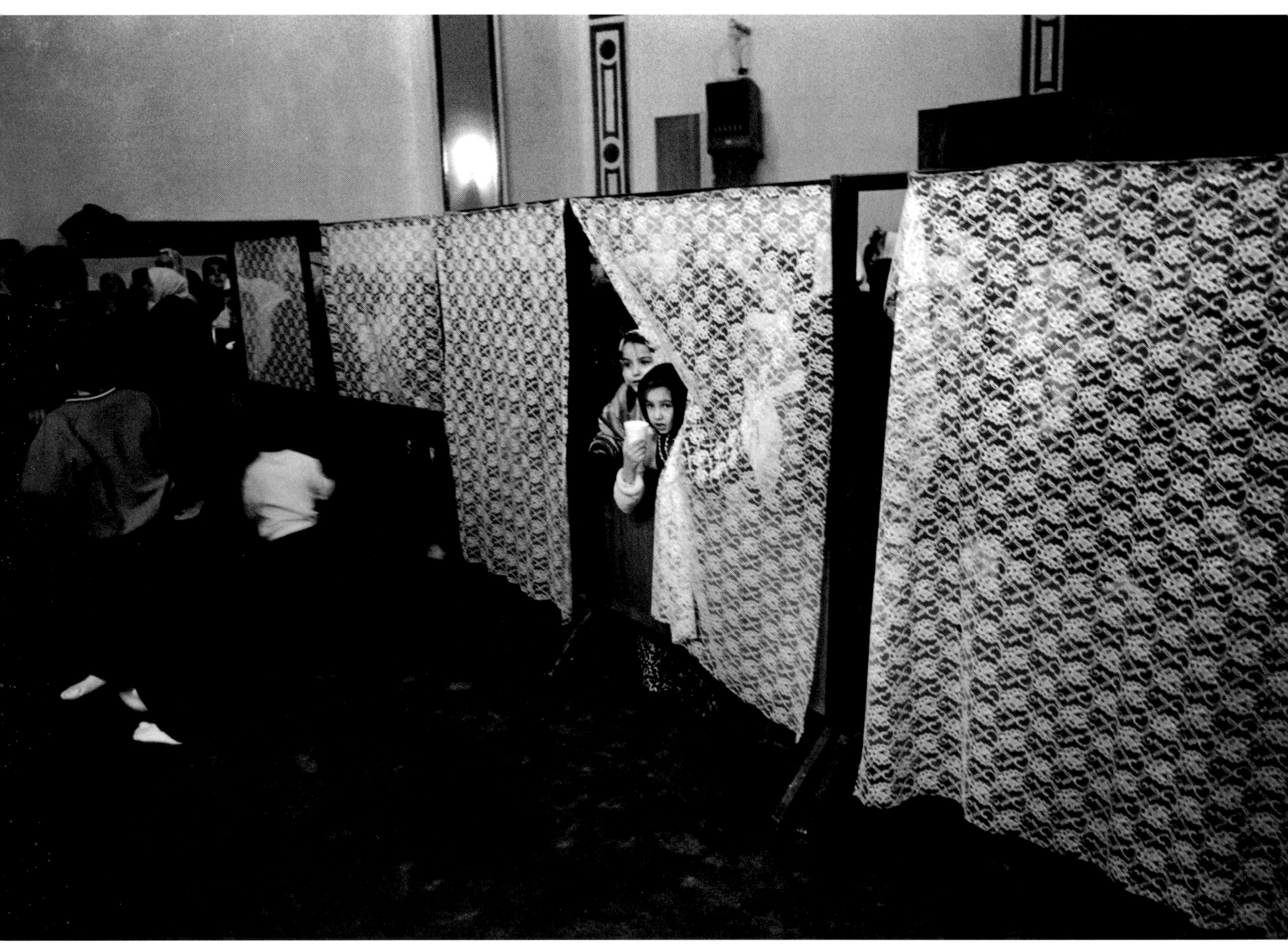

Fatih Cami, Brooklyn

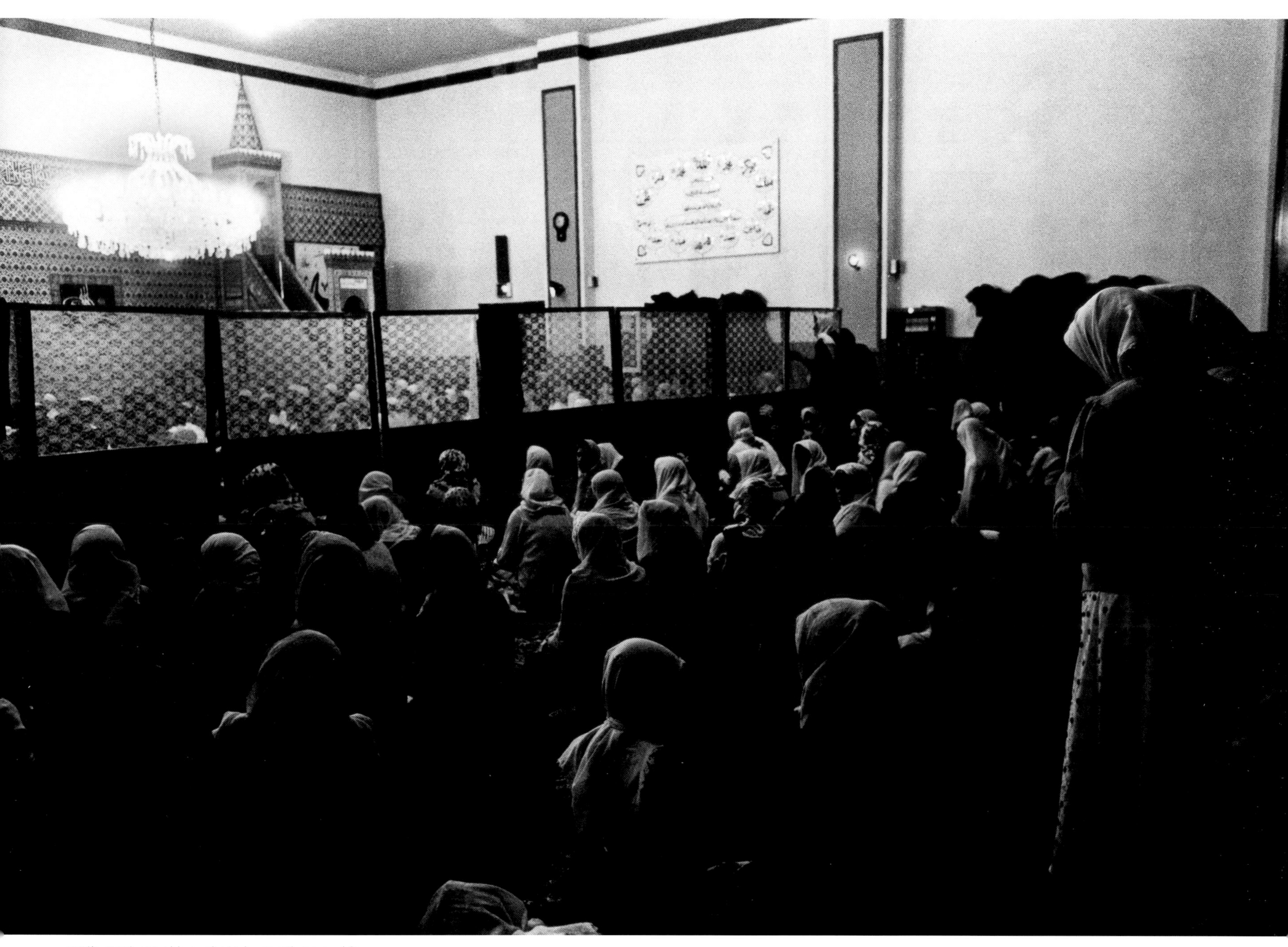

Fatih Cami, Brooklyn. photo by Jerrilynn Dodds

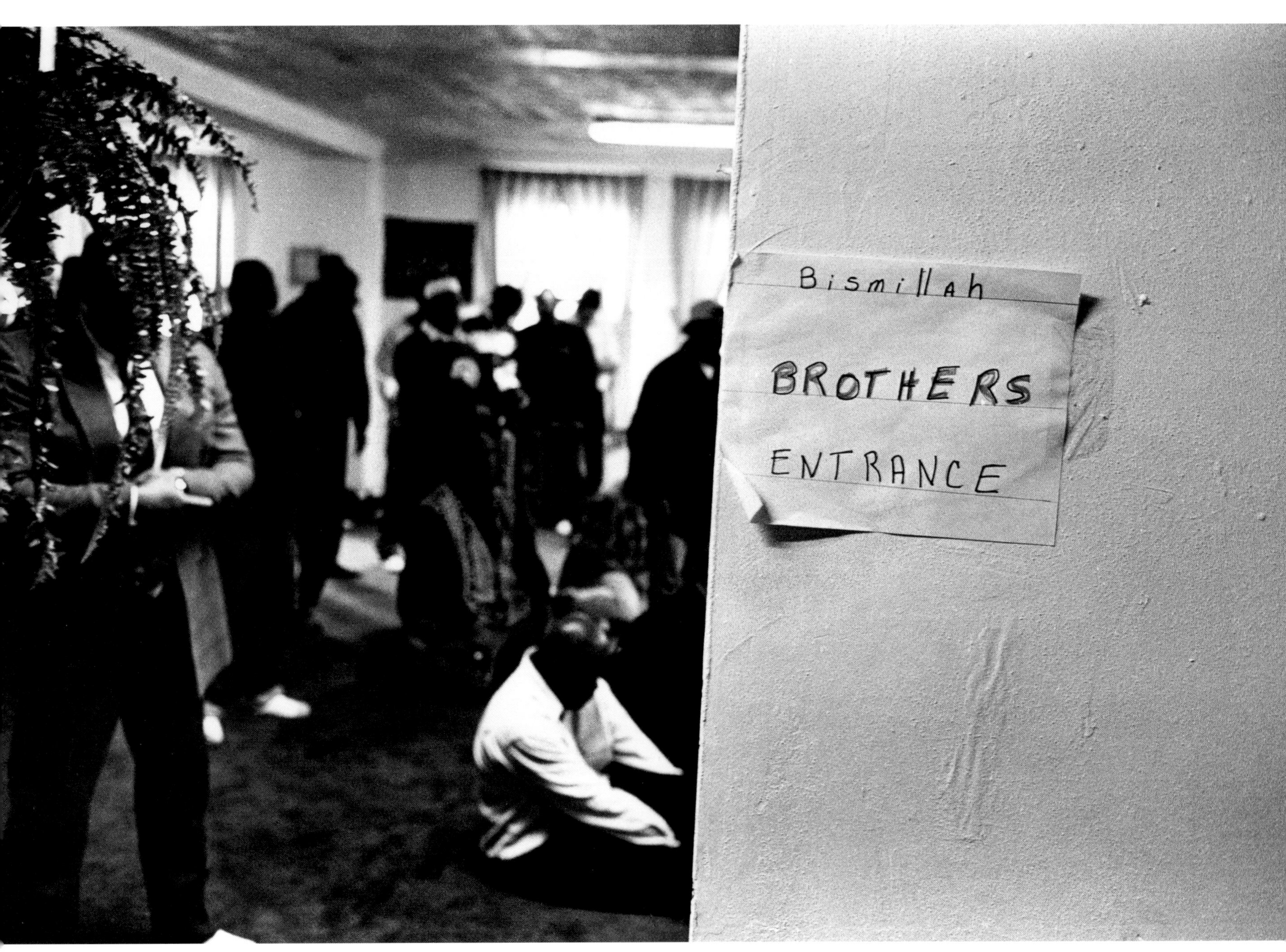

Masjid Taqwa Wa-Jihad, Bronx

"We do not yet have the space to provide for them properly, so we feel they are safer at home. Anyway, in Islam men are required to attend mosque, while women are not." On the other side of the spectrum, at Masjid Malcolm Shabazz, a long-standing African American community with a growing immigrant minority in Harlem, women pray in the same open prayer hall as men, together but separate, at a distance behind them. This is the provision used for separation in a number of Islamic countries, but is less usual in New York City. Here, it reflects "the strong and active participation of the sisters in our masjid community," Imam Izak El Pasha commented; and it echoes, as well, American cultural expectations of women's participation in religious institutions.

The subtle intersection of available space, economics, and changing cultural values can be seen in a vibrant mosque like Fatih Cami in Sunset Park, Brooklyn. Entering from the women's door during Ramadan, there is a lively international crowd of women, including throngs of second and third generation teenage girls, many of Turkish decent. Though they are separated from the front of the prayer hall by a fabric screen, its translucence and provisional, movable nature allows a sense of participation in the service beyond it; there is a tremendous sense of community in the room. When asked what she thought about the separation of girls and boys during prayer, one seventeen year old in Doc Martins, a headscarf, and a man's Oxford shirt rolled her eyes: "It isn't a big deal," she said. "If we were in the same row as the boys we would be checking each other out all the time. This way, it keeps our minds on God."[20]

The cultural choice to place women behind men in open prayer halls (rather than in front) and in tribunes is, it seems, rarely challenged, and is regarded as a practical necessity founded in propriety: "This does not reflect an inferior status for women, but is an issue of modesty," Imam Osman of the Islamic Cultural Center explained. "I assure you this is not a question of hierarchy or dominance," reflects Aisha Al Adawiya of the Schomburg Center in Harlem. "We simply should not be regarded from behind while at prayer." The less hierarchical alternative, offered on crowded days at the mosque of the Indonesian Consulate—discrete groups of women and men, separated by a partition perpendicular to the qibla, so that each is equidistant from it—does not seem to have been considered by the other congregations.

As communities become more internationalized, however, a dialogue has developed around the participation of women in the mosque. Cultural attitudes toward this participation, which have at times been linked to Islam, are separated from religious doctrine through interchange between Muslims who hold divergent cultural expectations. When the crowd at a Brooklyn mosque filled to overflow for prayers on a Friday during Ramadan, an African American woman, hands on hips, faced off a mosque functionary from an immigrant community: "I'm an American and a Muslim; you can't tell me there is only room left for men to pray." In this case, there was a religious mandate that overrode her claim of political rights as a religious entitlement: male members of an Islamic community are required to join prayer at Friday prayer, while females are not, and so

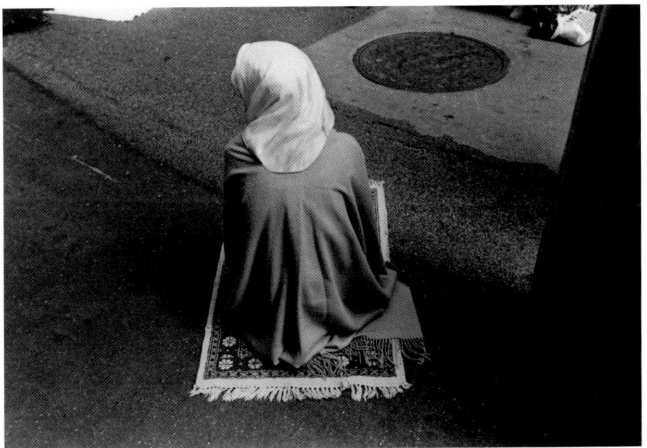

Muslim Day Parade, Manhattan

provision must be made for the admission of males when space is limited. But this kind of questioning, which sorts through cultural, political, and doctrinal concerns, is slowly transforming socially conservative immigrant communities. A Bangladeshi congregant at the Islamic Mission of America remarked that women did not attend the mosque in her neighborhood, but that she had begun to join a friend from work who prayed in the Mission's Astoria mosque. "My husband at first objected," she admitted, "but these people, too, are Muslims. So sometimes I come here from work."

"Though cultural traditions vary, there is nothing in Islam itself that suggests women ought to be shut away in separate rooms; what is required is simply separation of the sexes," Ms. Adawiya reminded me. "Part of what happens in a mosque ought to be the education of all American Muslims about these and other issues."[21]

IMAGES

The second requirement for a mosque is the restriction of images. Any mosque must exclude representations of animate beings, which in Islam can only be conceived and created by God. It is a stricture firmly adhered to in New York mosques, but in a number of divergent ways. In a few new mosques, geometric patterning that grows from traditional Islamic design is adapted to contemporary architectural language and materials. At Masjid Hazrat-i-abu Bakr, for instance, expanding geometric patterns are etched into the glass of balustrades and partitions. Significantly, in a mosque with a primarily Afghan congregation, these are motifs that might be more properly described as pan-Islamic, and they veer away from the use of ornament to make a specific regional or cultural reference, a point to which we shall return presently.

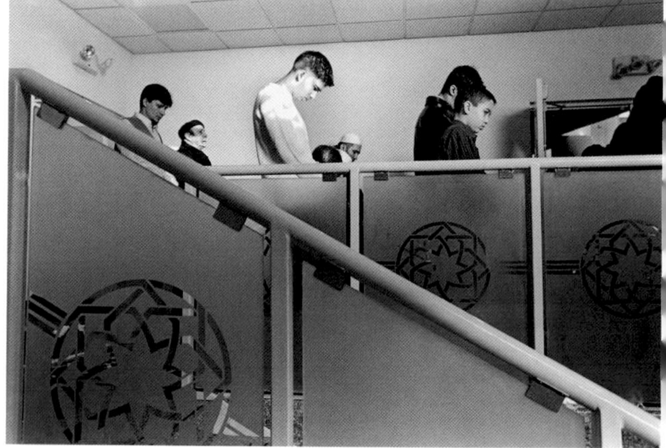

Masjid Hazrat-i-abu Bakr, Queens

In the Islamic Cultural Center, architect Michael McCarthy devised a Mihrab composed of planes of tinted glass, which recalls Muqarnas, the three-dimensional abstract ornament often called "stalactite" decoration. Muqarnas, historically , can be seen as a response to the need for a sculpted ornamentation that is three-dimensional, but one which is intellectually and spatially complex, in keeping with the developments of the aniconic ornament of traditional Islam. The planar illusion conceived by Mr. McCarthy and his associates answers this development with a modernist take which is both consistent with tradition and true to the materials and values of a mosque designed for a modernist landscape. And like some of the most profound Islamic ornament, it is multilayered and meditative.

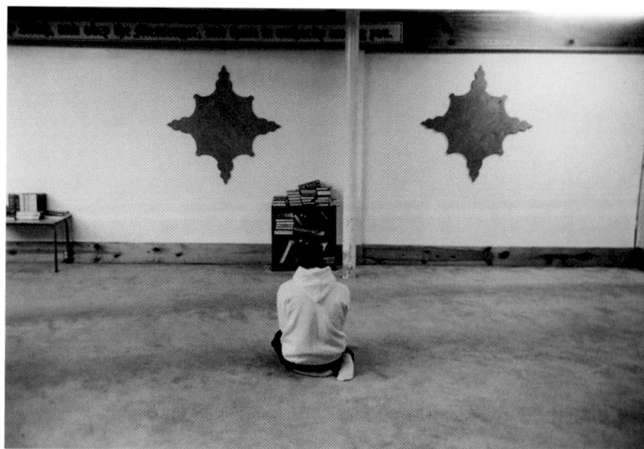

Masjid At-Taqwa, Brooklyn

However, the overwhelming majority of the ornamental schemes found in the mosques of New York are addressed with such subtlety and reticence that it is difficult to find any decorative thread in such austere spaces. In many mosques, a calendar of color photos of Mecca and Medina is the only adornment. Nevertheless, the diversity of ornamental ideas that result from community engendered projects—diversity of concept, material, and form—is astounding, and has the effect of quickly breaking down a single reductive image of New York's Muslim communities. It is not uncommon for a brownstone to receive a fanciful wrought iron gate with an abstract pattern or a half moon; bold geometric forms, recalling African design, adorn the qibla at Masjid At-Taqwa in Brooklyn; 60s modernist mosaics cover the columns on the prayer hall at Masjid Malcolm Shabazz in a random abstract pattern; traditional Iznik tile work was imported at Fatih Cami, and friezes of painted arches and domes sprout from the residential facades of Masjid Baitul Mukarram, Masjidul Aman, the prayer hall of Masjid Taqwa wa-Jihad, and any number of other reused buildings. At Al-Farouq Masjid, such a frieze of silhouetted domes is picked out with contact paper along the bottom of the prayer hall windows.

On the surface, the restriction of images would seem a difficult kind of abstention in New York, a city whose public spaces vibrate with images and narratives. But the creation of spaces in which there is no narrative in which to project oneself, no figure with whom to identify emotionally, privileges the private, meditative acts performed in the mosque over its surroundings.

THE QIBLA

The third requirement for a mosque building, the establishment of the qibla, has significant visual potential in New York, for orientation towards Mecca must always push against the grid, defying the city's relentlessly Cartesian fabric. The qibla can be marked by the rotation of the entire building in the direction of Mecca, as in the case of the Islamic Cultural Center in Manhattan or the Masjid Alfalah in Corona, Queens. The rotation disengages each of these mosques from the urban grid, giving each an object-like autonomy. This device is not unique to New York or the urban west; throughout the Islamic world, rotation becomes a means by which the mosque—a place where you leave the cares of your life to reconnect with God—takes on the image of a place loosed from the normal bonds of urban routine.

And yet, overt defiance of the grid is not exploited as a public, exterior gesture as often as one might imagine in New York's mosques: at the Albanian Islamic Cultural Center, architect Brent Porter cut a diagonal wall through a box-shaped building to create an interior qibla unexpressed on the building's exterior. In the more usual case of renovated space, however, orientation towards the qibla is accomplished through the rotation of the congregation itself within an existing building. At Fatih Cami, which is located in a refurbished theater, orientation towards Mecca required that the congregation face away from the theater's stage. The Mihrab—a niche that can be used to indicate the qibla wall—is located at the back of the theater structure, and, on crowded days, women congregants participate in prayer from the position of the old stage, which now mutely anchors the back of the prayer hall. In the majority of New York's mosques, lines of masking tape indicate the proper alignment of worshippers at the moment of prayer. This can be seen at Masjid Daoud on State Street in Brooklyn (New York's earliest surviving mosque), at Masjidul Aman in Ozone Park, Masjid Al-Abidin in Richmond Hills, at Masjid Taqwa wa-Jihad and at Islamic Sunnatul Jam'ah in the Bronx, and in countless other reused spaces.

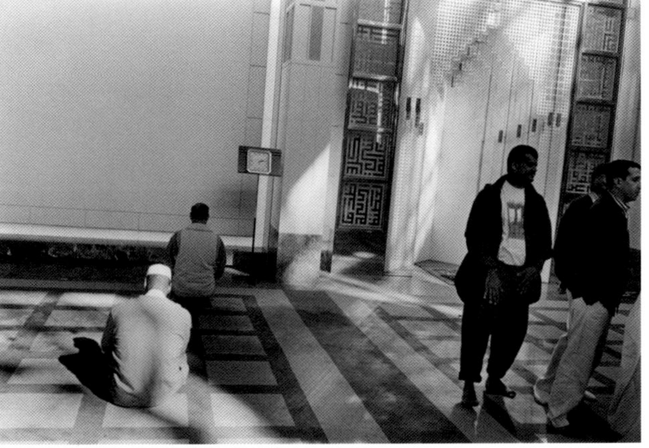

Islamic cultural center, Manhattan

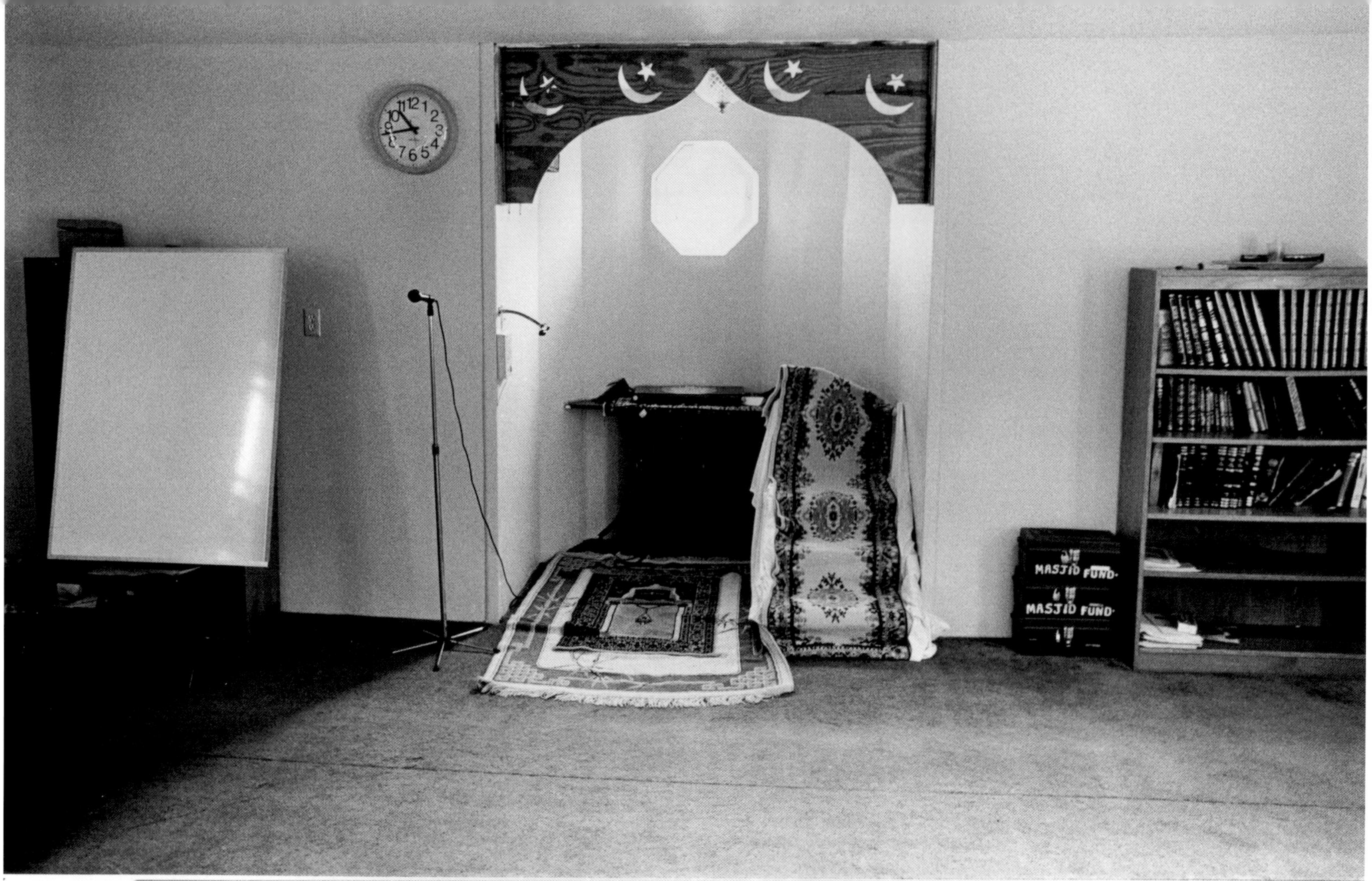
MASJID FUND
MASJID FUND

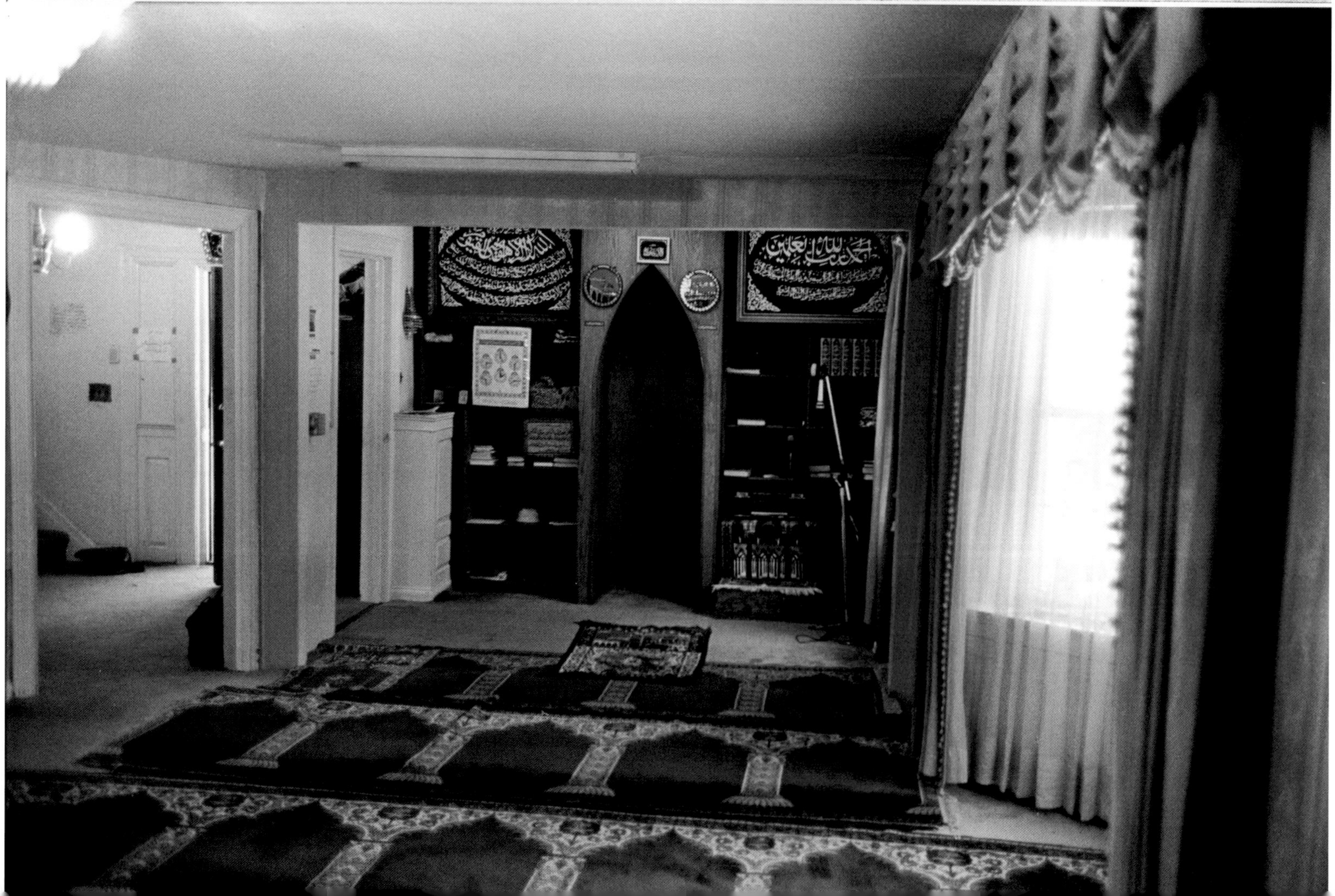

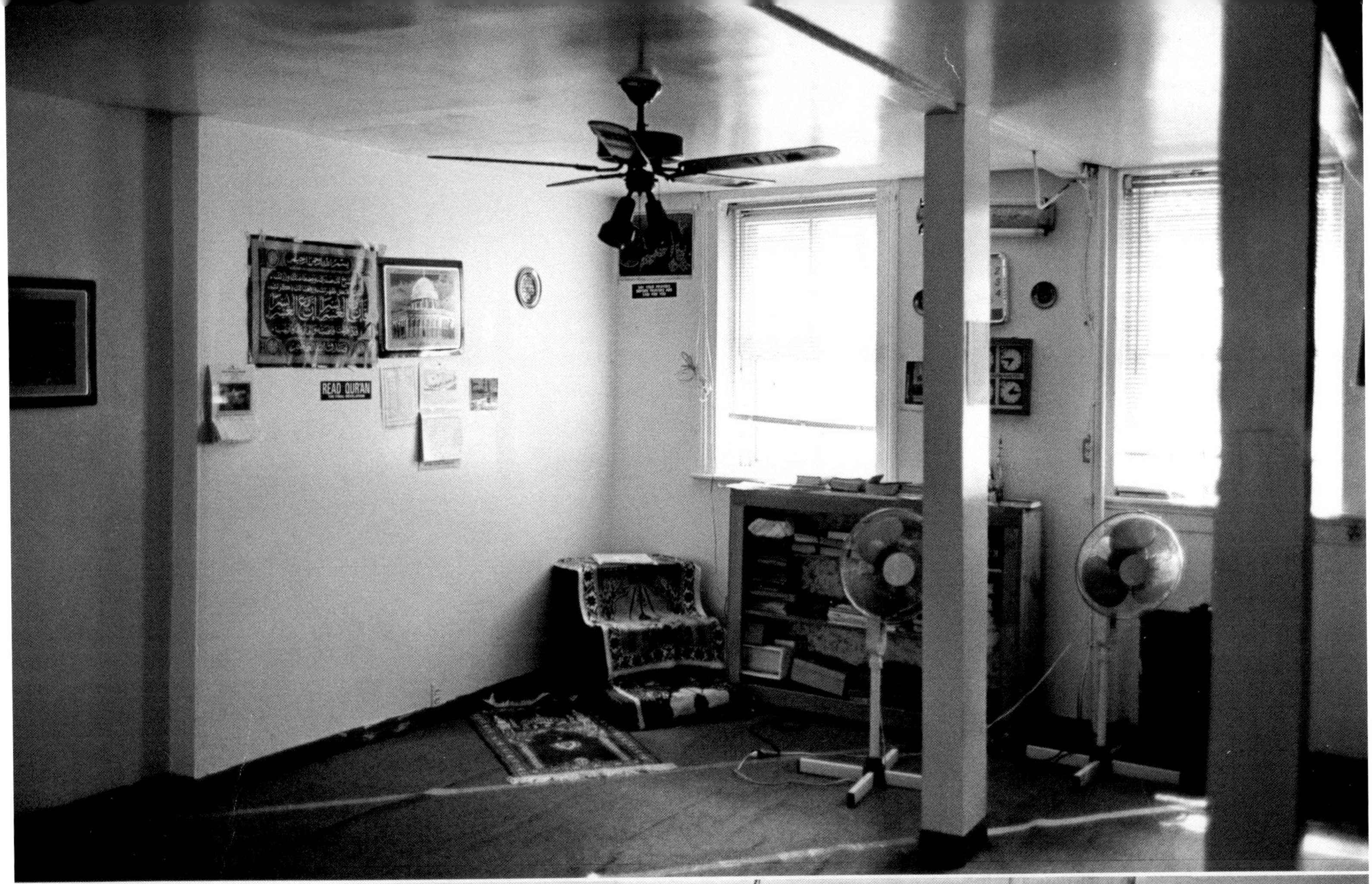

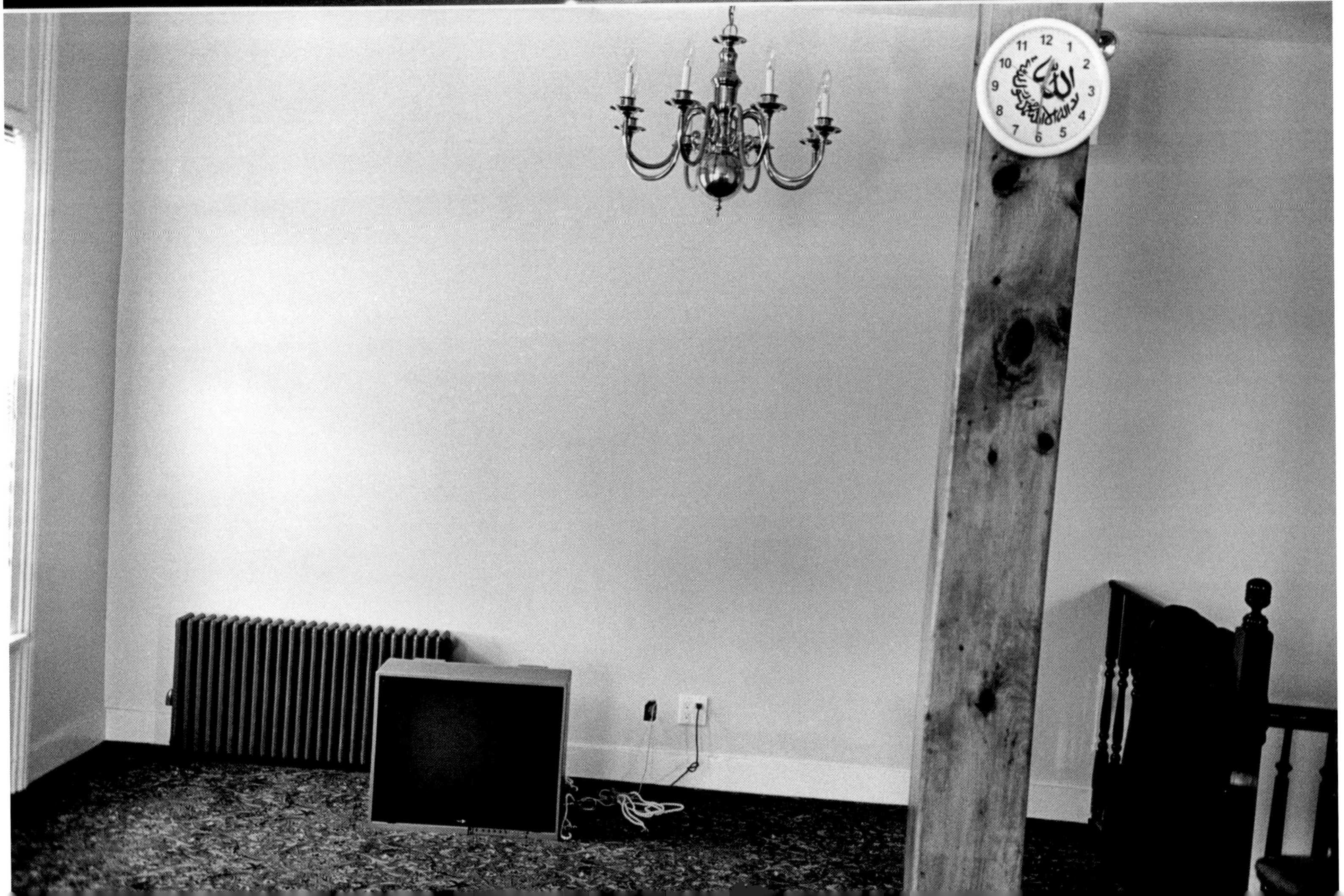

The Qibla

Al-Abidin
Abu Bakar

Shah Jalal
Ali Pasha

The qibla is common to all mosques in the world, and is meant, in part, to reorient worshippers, dislodge them from a familiar, worldly context to better mind the dictates of prayer and the wider community of Islam. Diaspora congregants, however, can at times give it an additional meaning, one fueled perhaps by the desire to see the transcendence of Islamic faith over daily life recognized in this dense, secular city. "We do not pray to Atlantic Avenue," a congregant at Al-Farouq Masjid once told me, "we pray to Mecca." Or, as a taxi driver from Bangladesh pronounced proudly, "At the Masjid, Third Avenue comes to its knees before God."

CHANGING COMMUNITIES

There is no central administration that oversees the mosques of New York; no hierarchy among mosques, no central advisory or governing council. The community of a particular mosque can be in no way restricted, though congregations in New York City tend to reflect neighborhood demographics and the languages in which the Khutbah, or Friday sermon, is given. Increasingly, however, mosques that began to serve a local, linguistically determined community are being internationalized by the greater community they serve. In the late 1990s, researcher Louis Abdellatif Cristillo found "the composition of many congregations began to reflect the ethnic diversity of the neighborhood rather than the nationality or ethnicity of the core founding body." He finds a significant push towards "a more universal Islamic identity" rather than a specific, ethnic one.

In the first years after the 1993 World Trade Center bombings, however, a number of the communities studied in this project were isolated or embattled, and uncomprehending or suspicious of our interest in some of the less presupposing building spaces. In some of the newer communities, there was an understandable reticence to inquiries from the outside, concerns that were often voiced in terms of religious ideology. Many of the congregations approached in this study had experienced harassment and vandalism of some sort in their histories. At Masjid Alfalah, the new mosque was set on fire in 1984 "by unknown parties at a time of political tension."[22] Many others had become particularly insular after the media campaigns following the 1993 attacks. For Al-Farouq Masjid, a large and established congregation on Atlantic Avenue, the secret insertion of a covert government agent into the mosque community as part of the investigation of the bombings had propelled some prominent community members into a firmly polarized position. After a number of unanswered calls and failed appointments with council members, one congregant asked me bitterly, "Why do you come to us? Why must you write about this mosque? Why don't you go and write about a church or a synagogue instead?" Other members suggested we might be CIA agents in disguise[23]

These more restrained stances, which range from reticence in the face of the unknown to active resistance to outside forces, are more typical in new, first foundations, but in times of political pressure they could also be found in firmly established mosques, like Al-Farouq Masjid. What kind of dialogue does such an embattled stance create between a mosque and its urban context?

Historians and sociologists within New York have charted the settlement histories of various new religious minorities—early German protestants, Catholics, and Jews in particular—histories that usually begin with a modest initial place of prayer established in a storefront or reused architectural space. As with storefront mosques in New York, severe economic restrictions suggest that all of these spaces be makeshift and even bare at the outset. However, the austerity born of this initial exigency is embraced within diaspora Islam with a particular ideological fervor, creating meanings that cling to New York mosques even as social, economic, and political pressures ease.

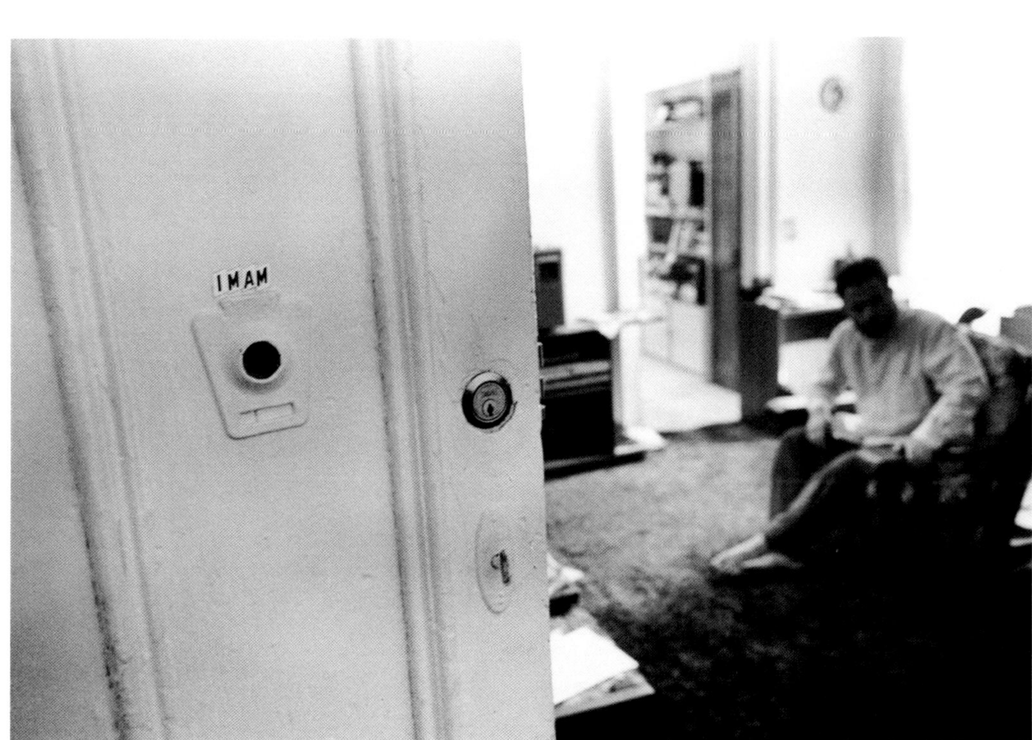

Ali Pasha Mosque, Queens

Fatih cami

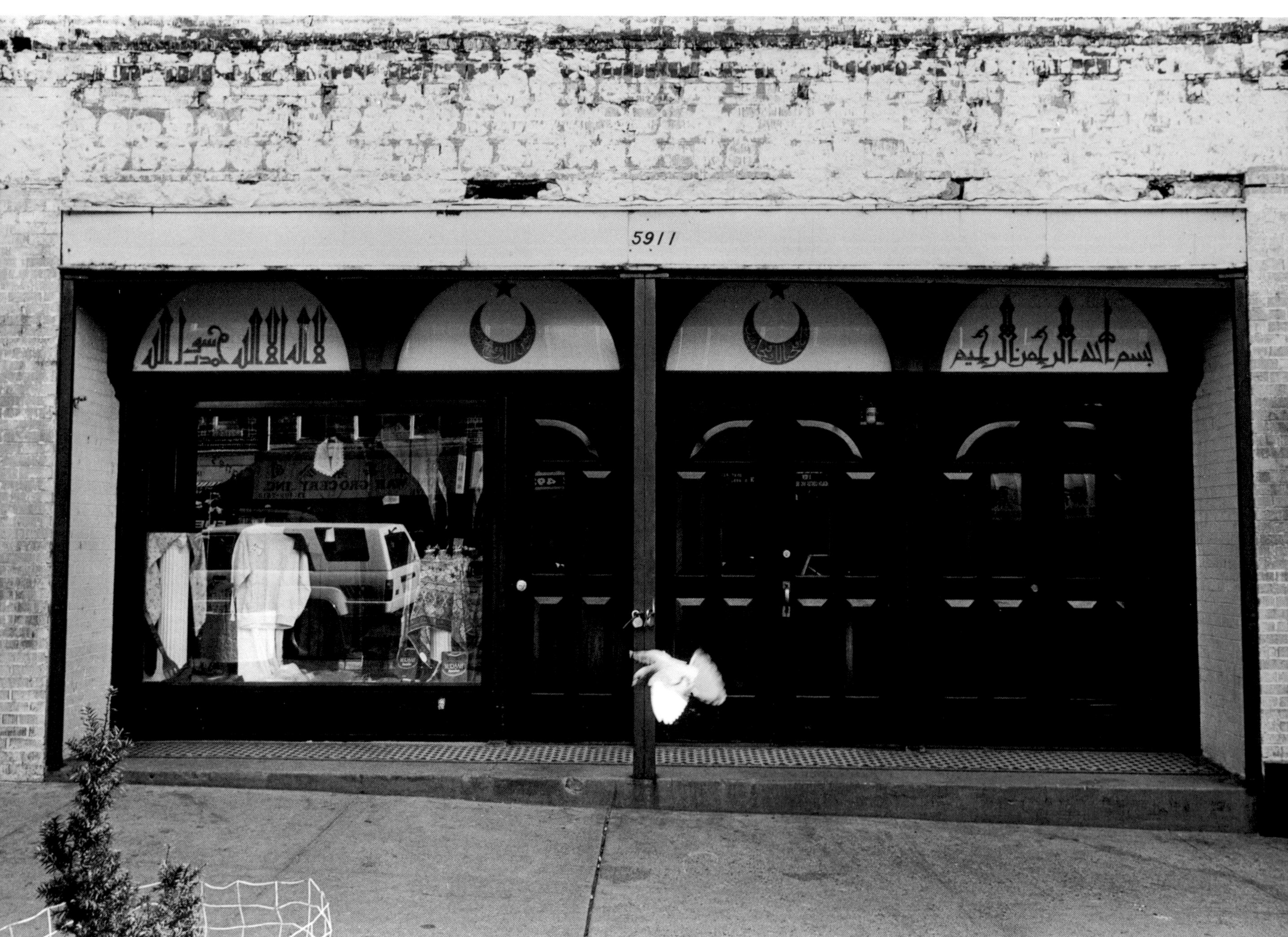

Fatih cami, Brooklyn

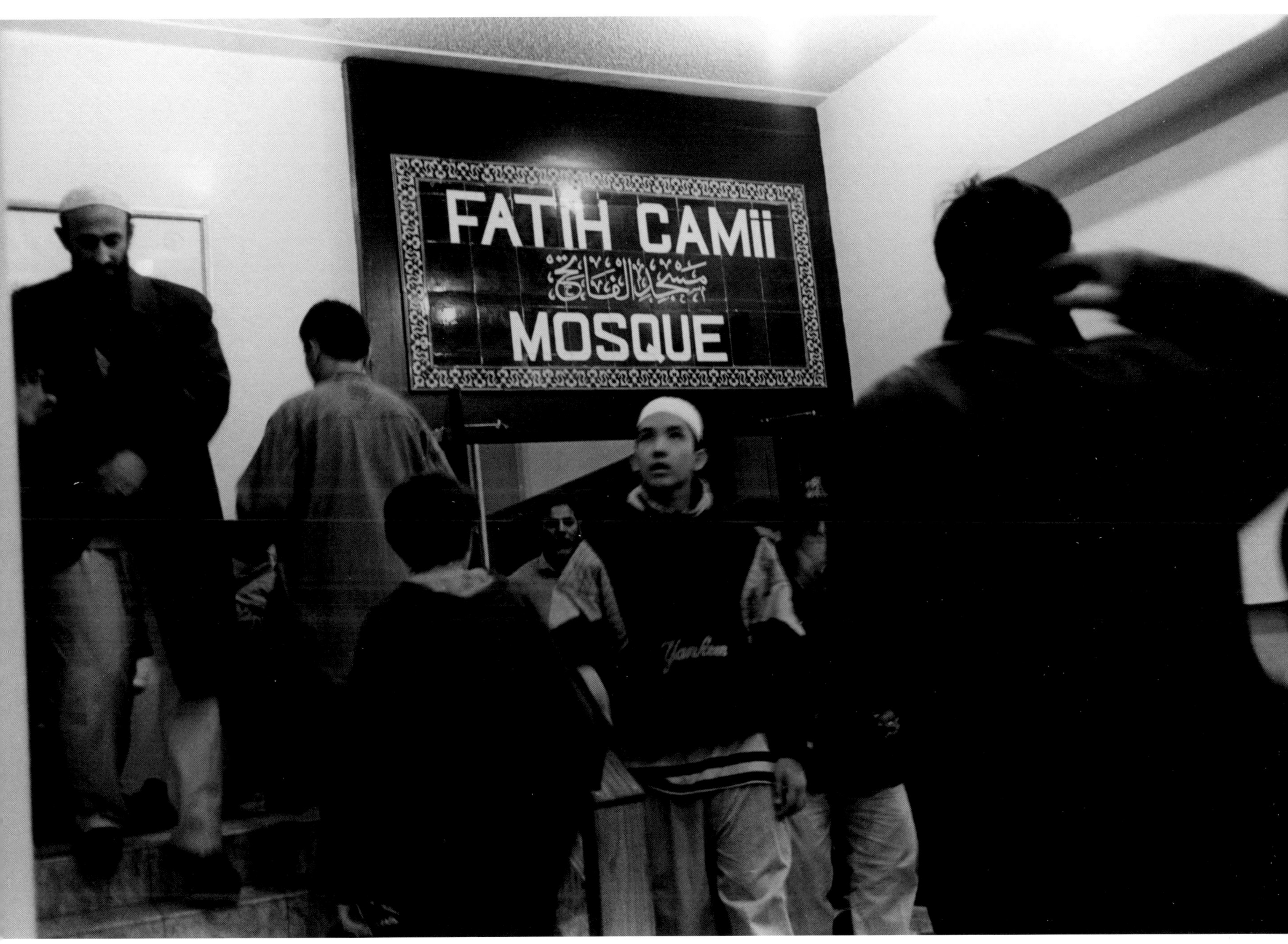

Fatih cami, Brooklyn

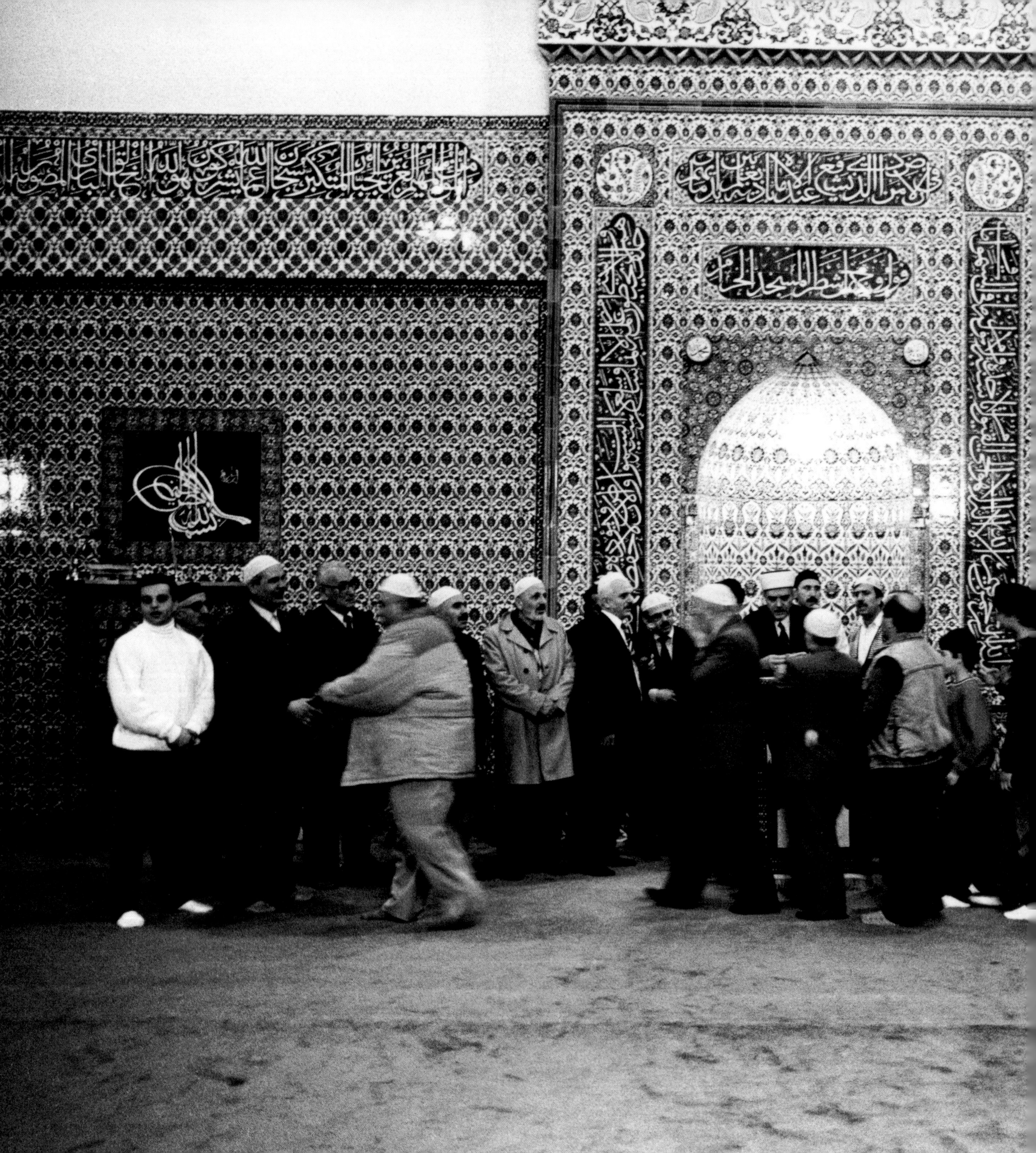

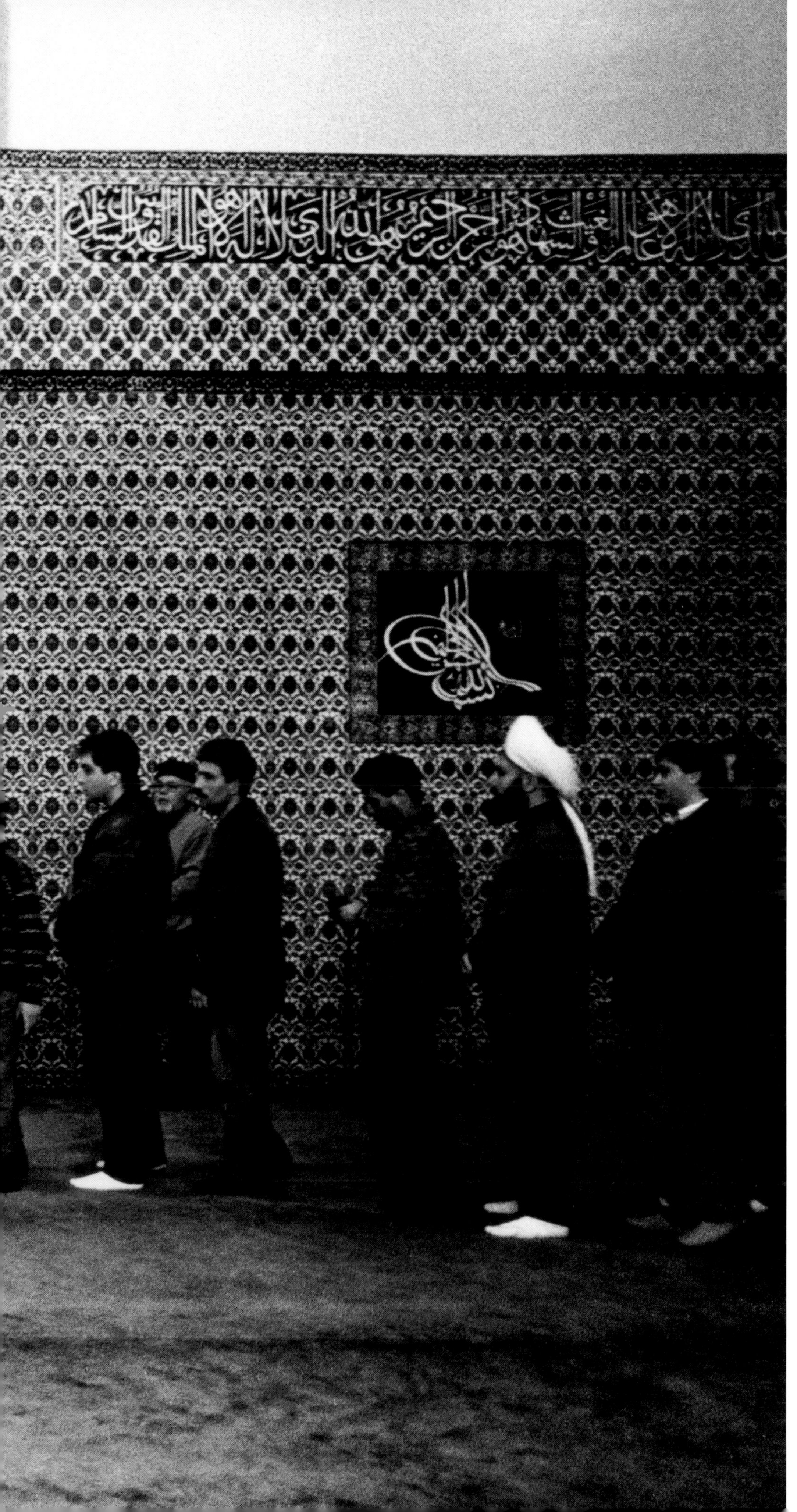

Fatih Cami, Brooklyn

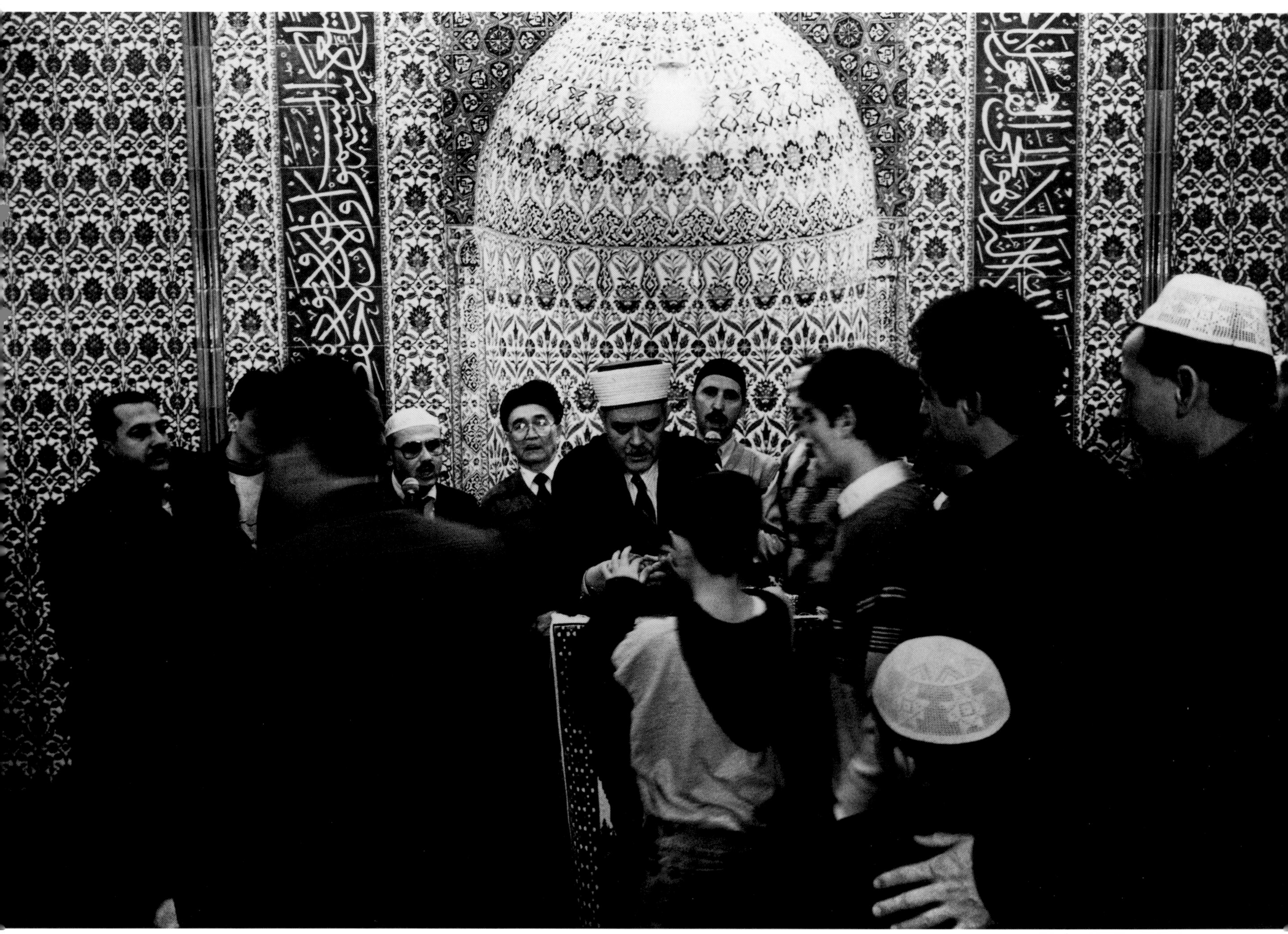

Fatih Cami, Brooklyn

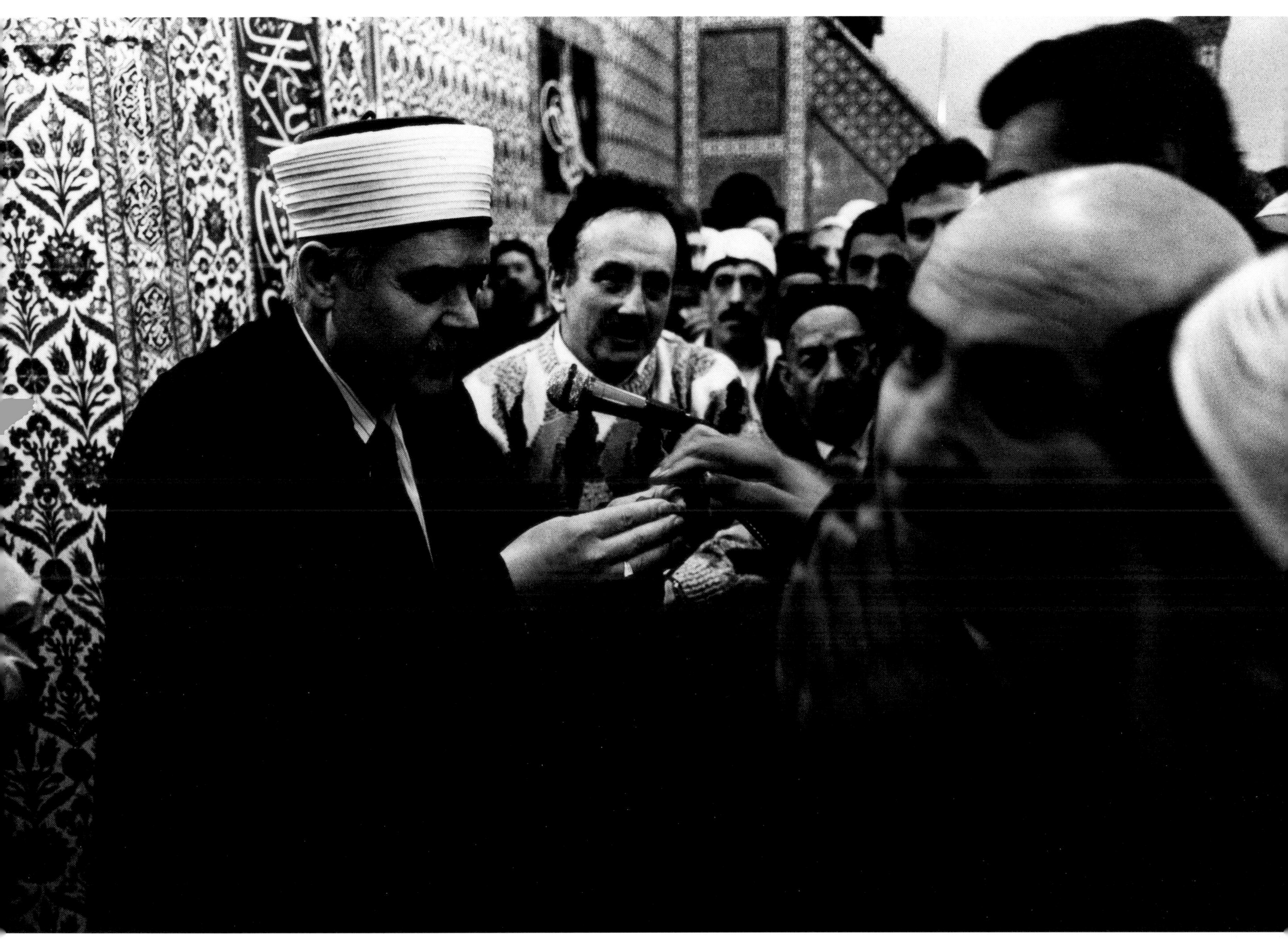

Fatih Cami, Brooklyn

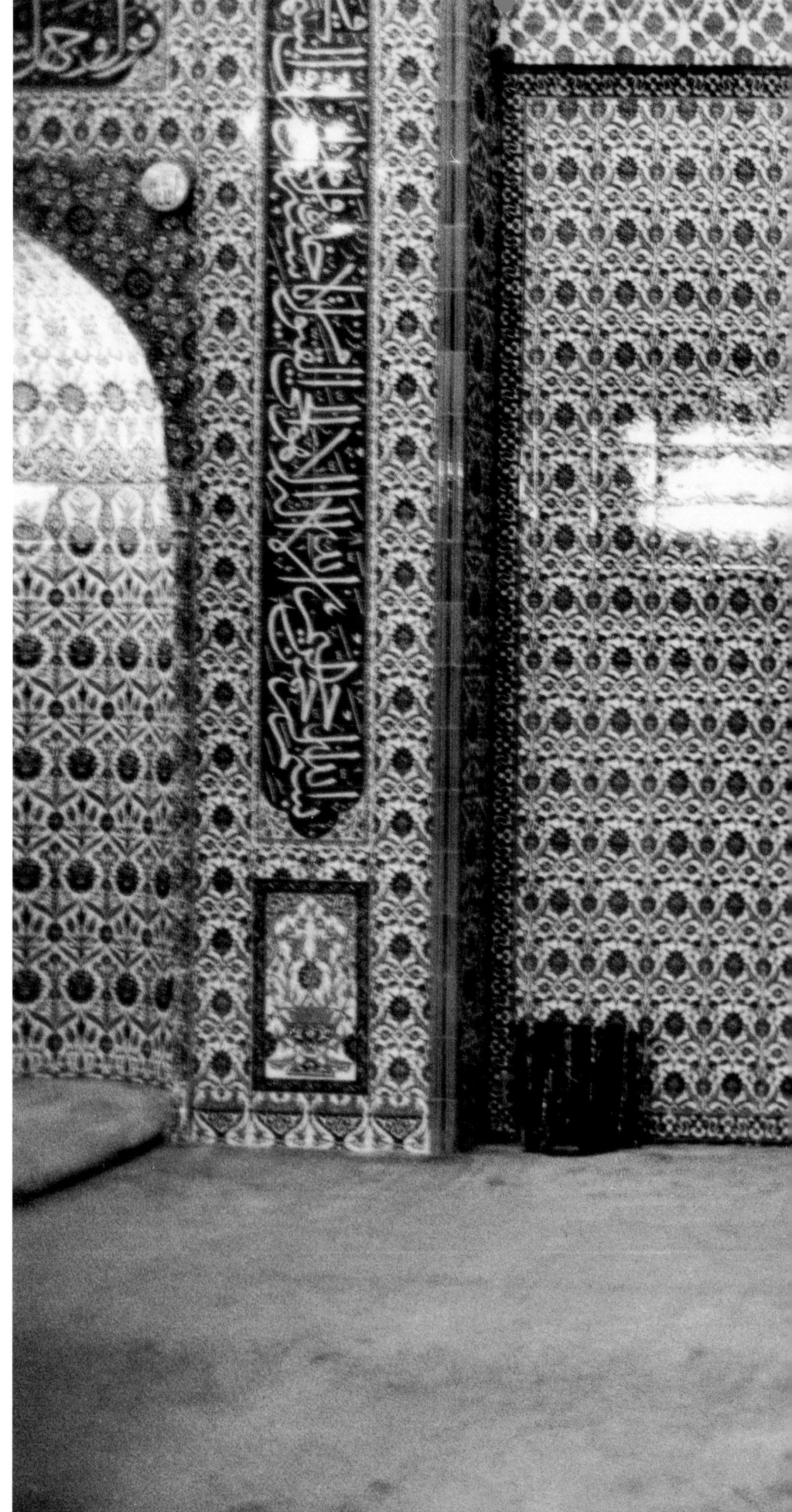

Fatih cami, Brooklyn

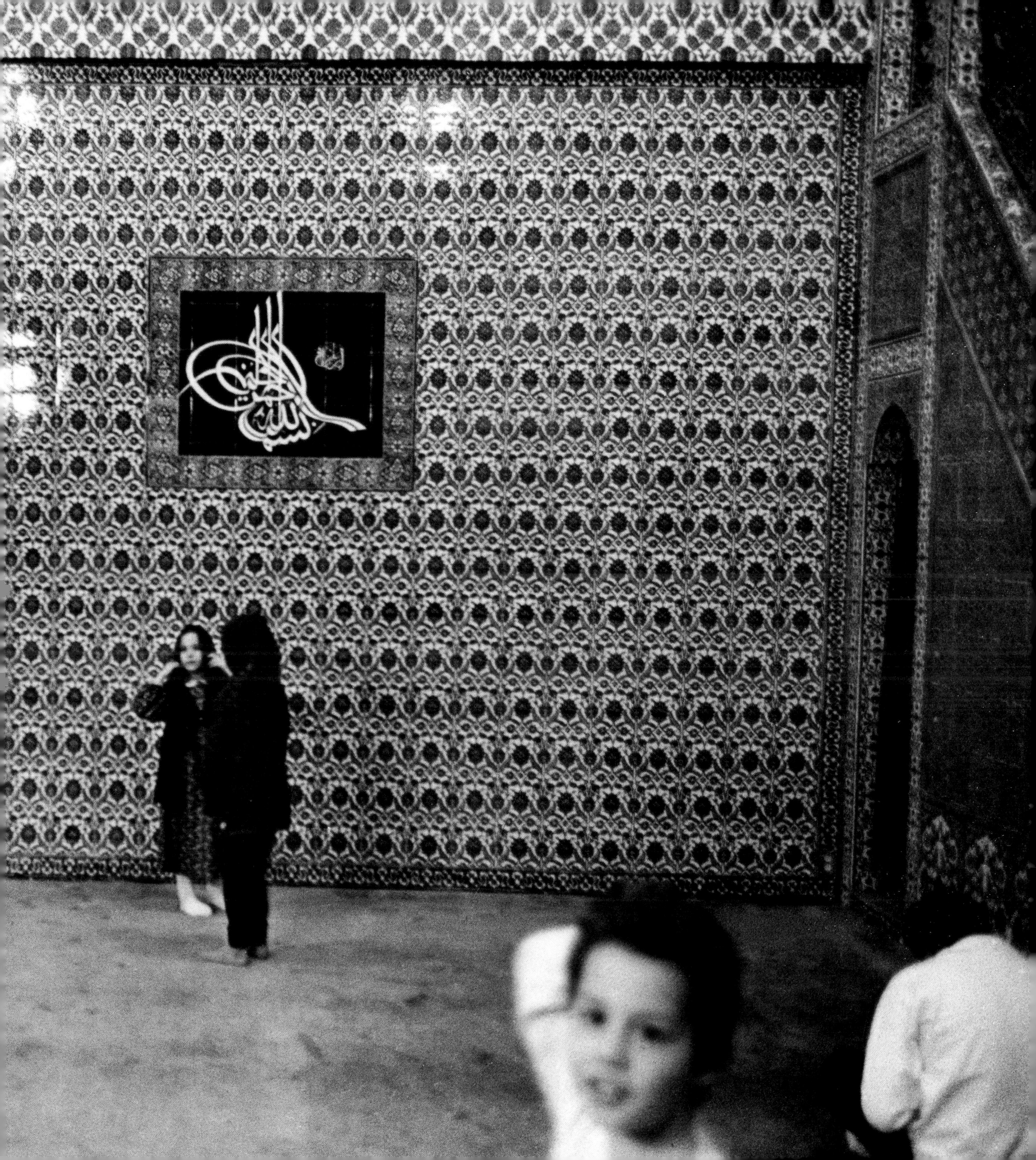

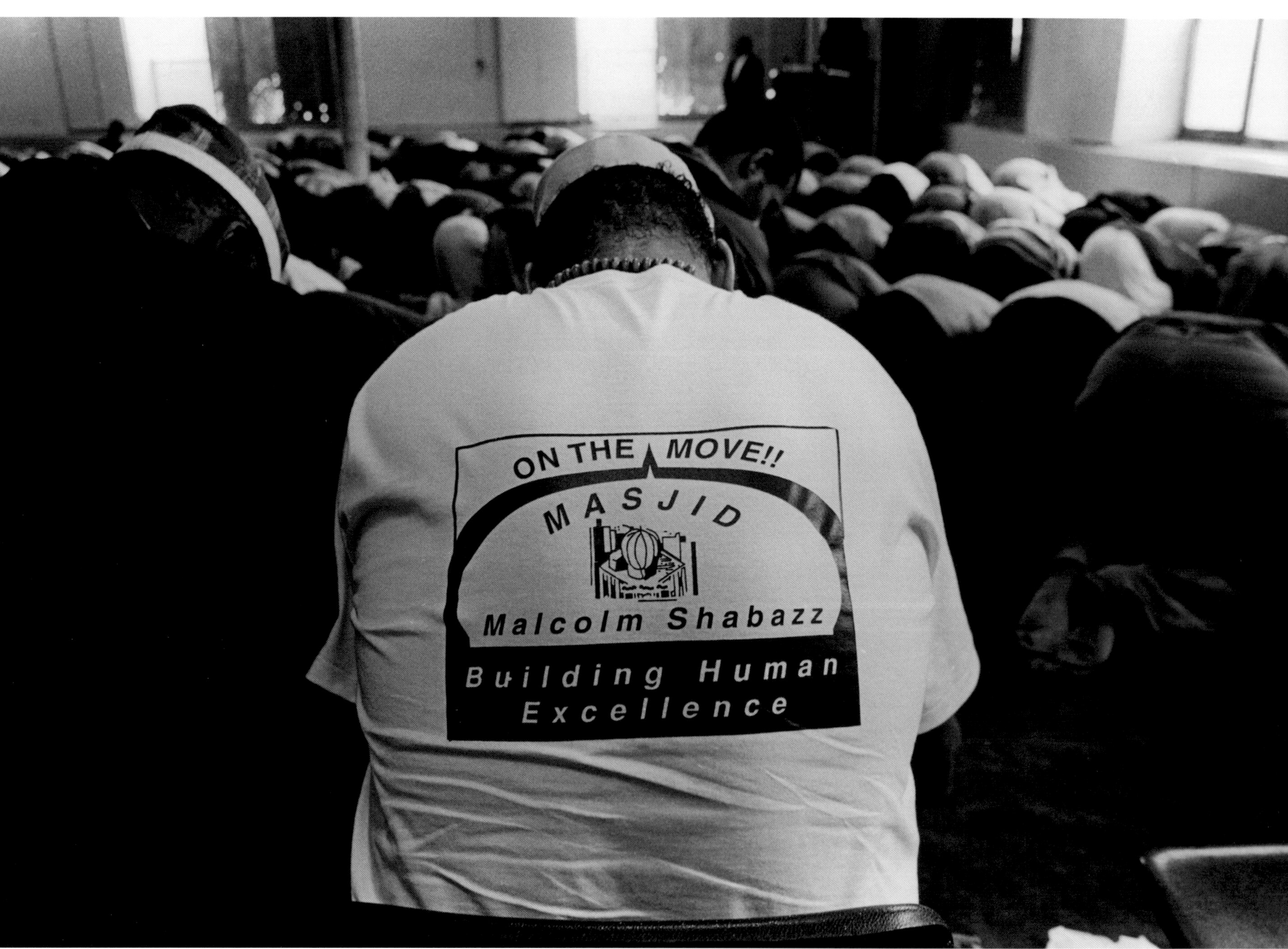

Masjid Malcolm Shabazz, Manhattan

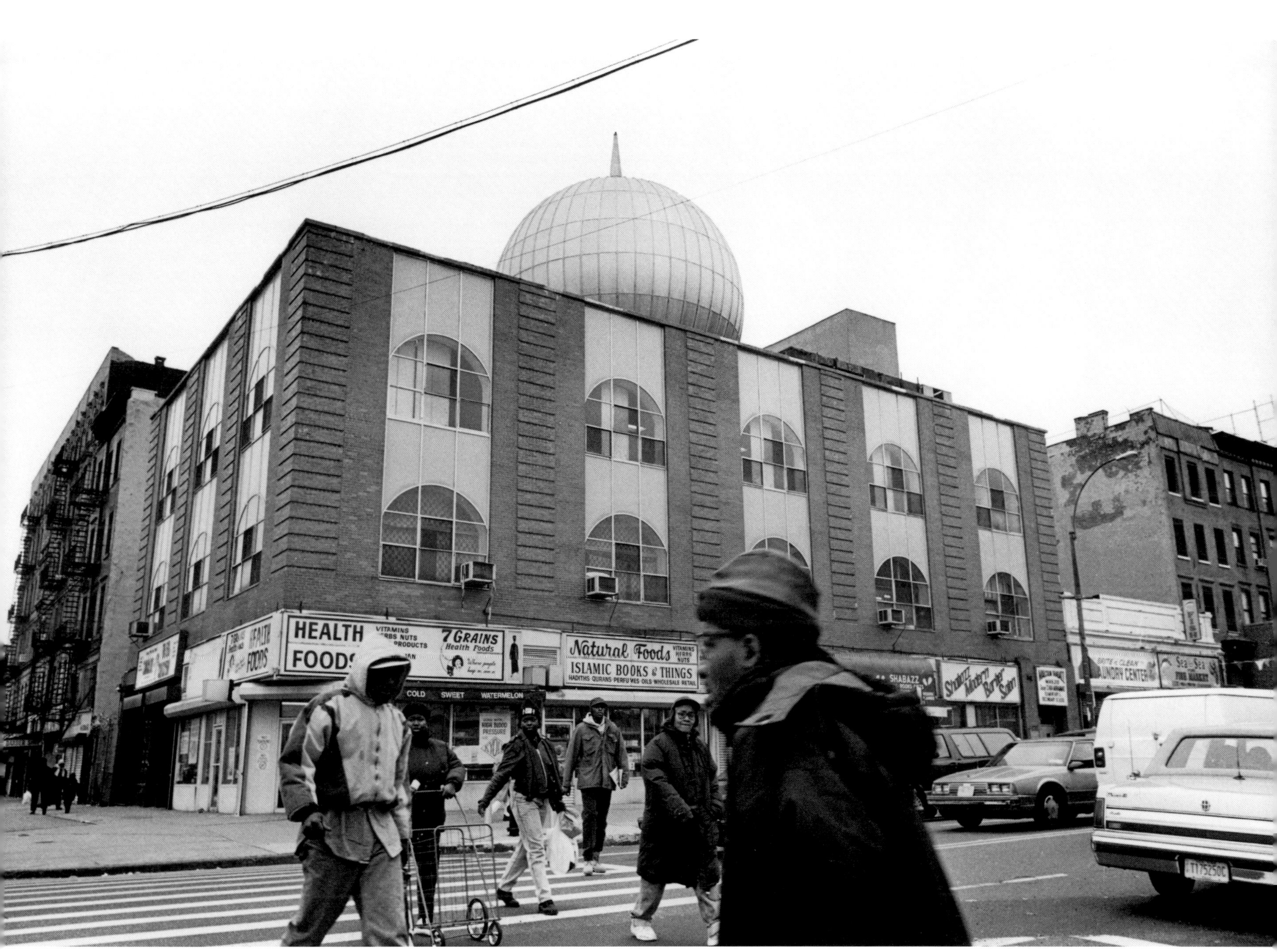

Masjid Malcolm Shabazz, Manhattan

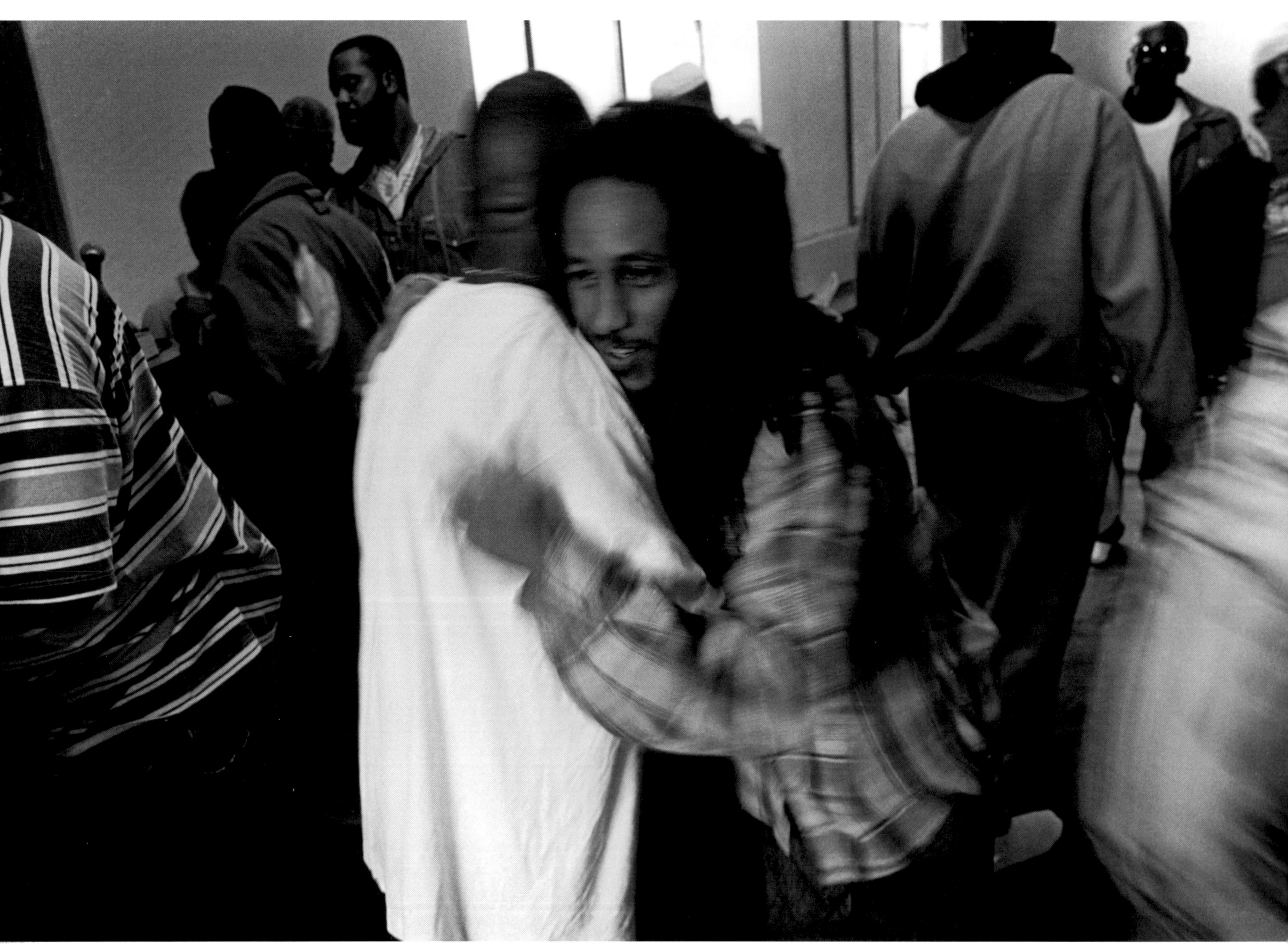

Masjid Malcolm Shabazz, Manhattan

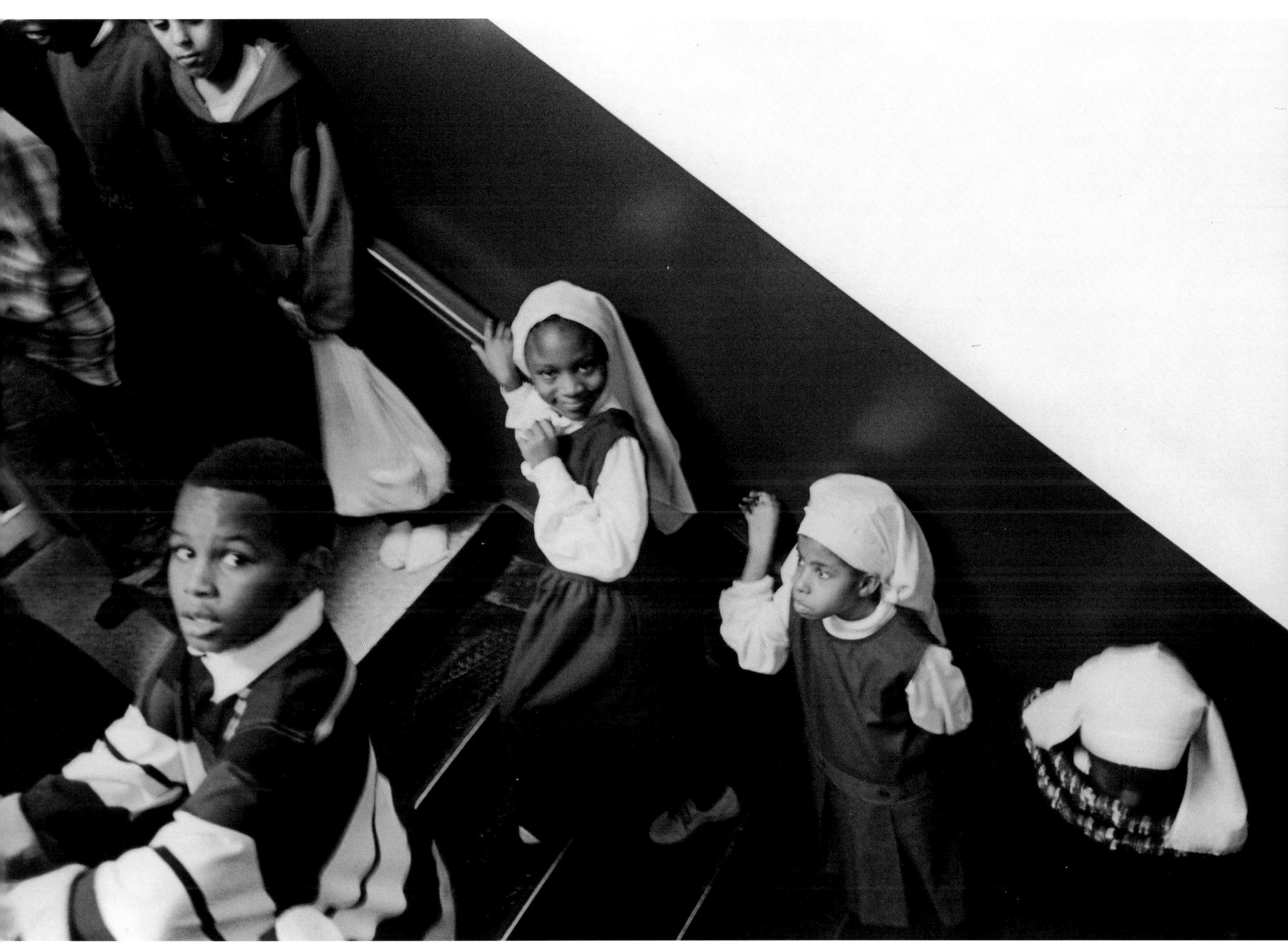

Masjid Malcolm Shabazz, Manhattan

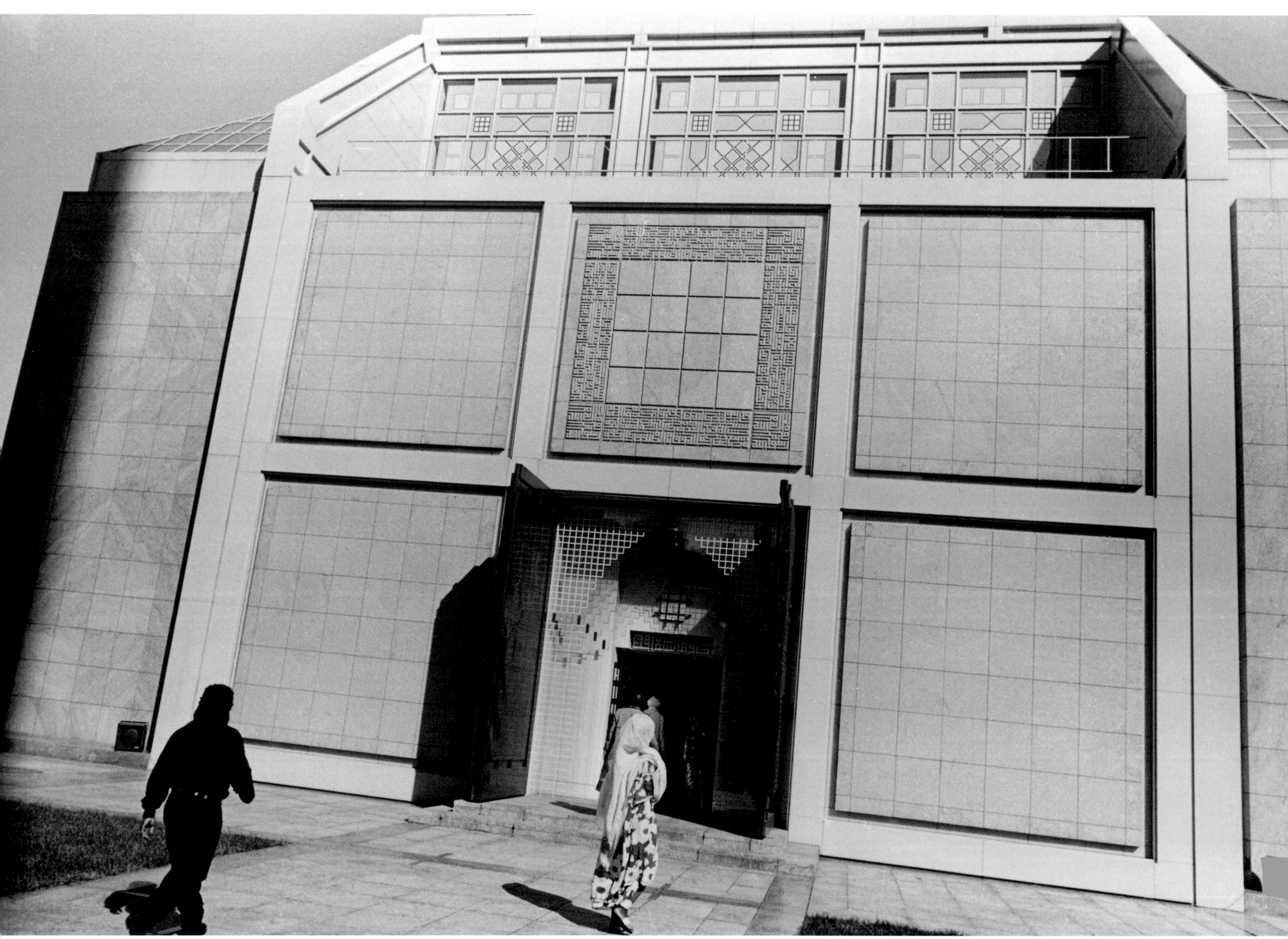

Islamic cultural center, Manhattan

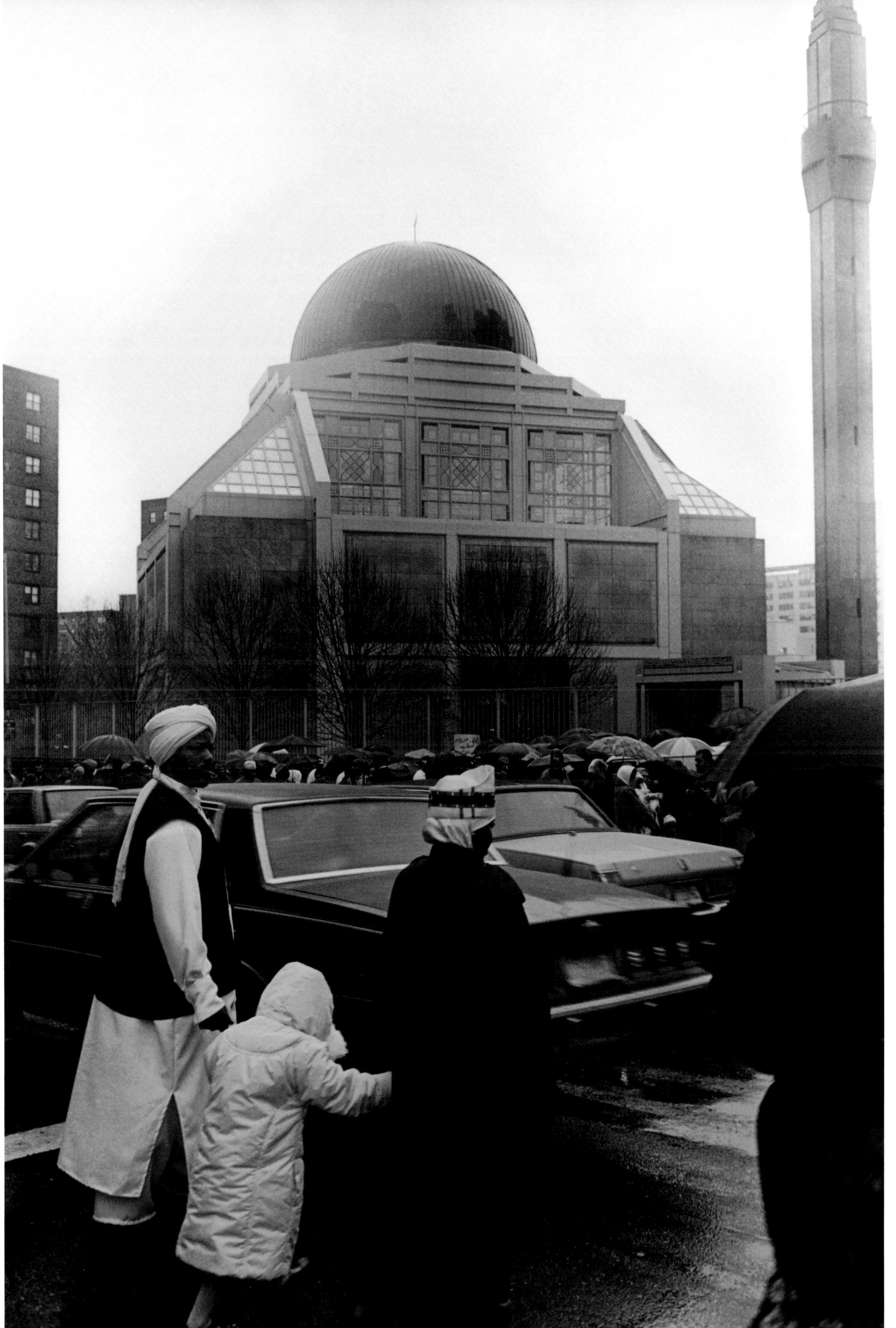

Islamic cultural center, Manhattan

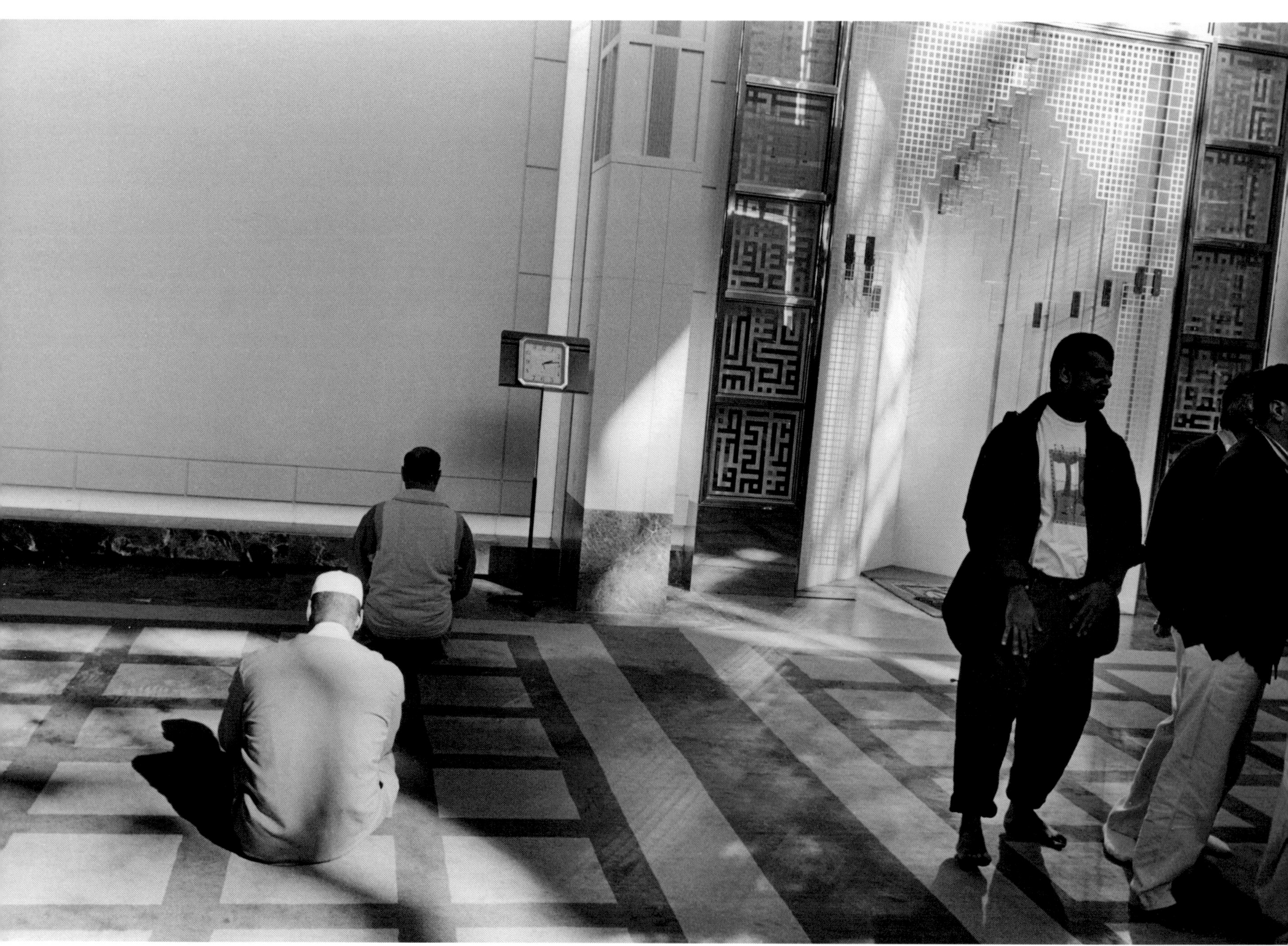

Islamic cultural center, Manhattan

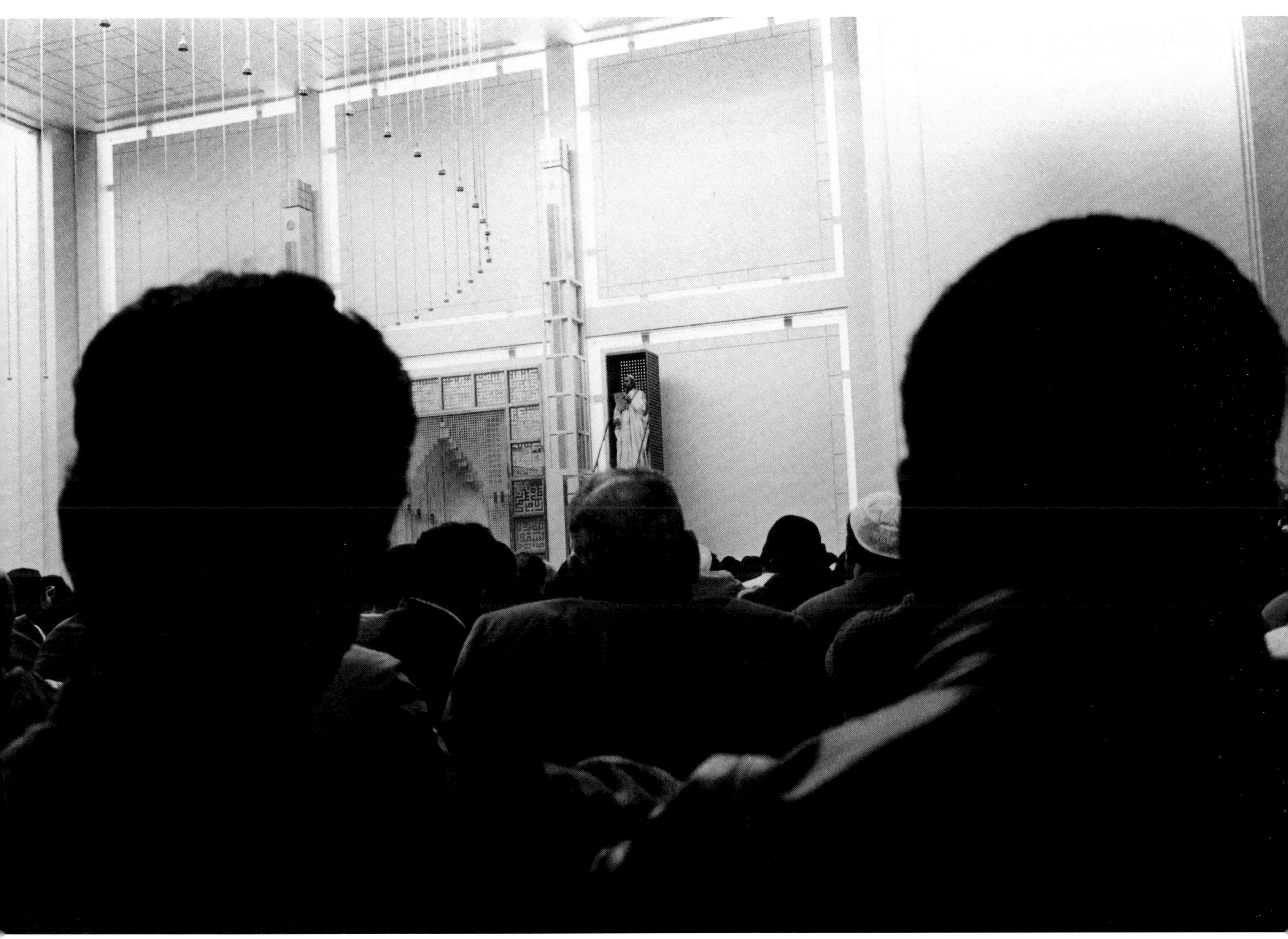

Islamic cultural center, Manhattan

Al-Farouq Masjid

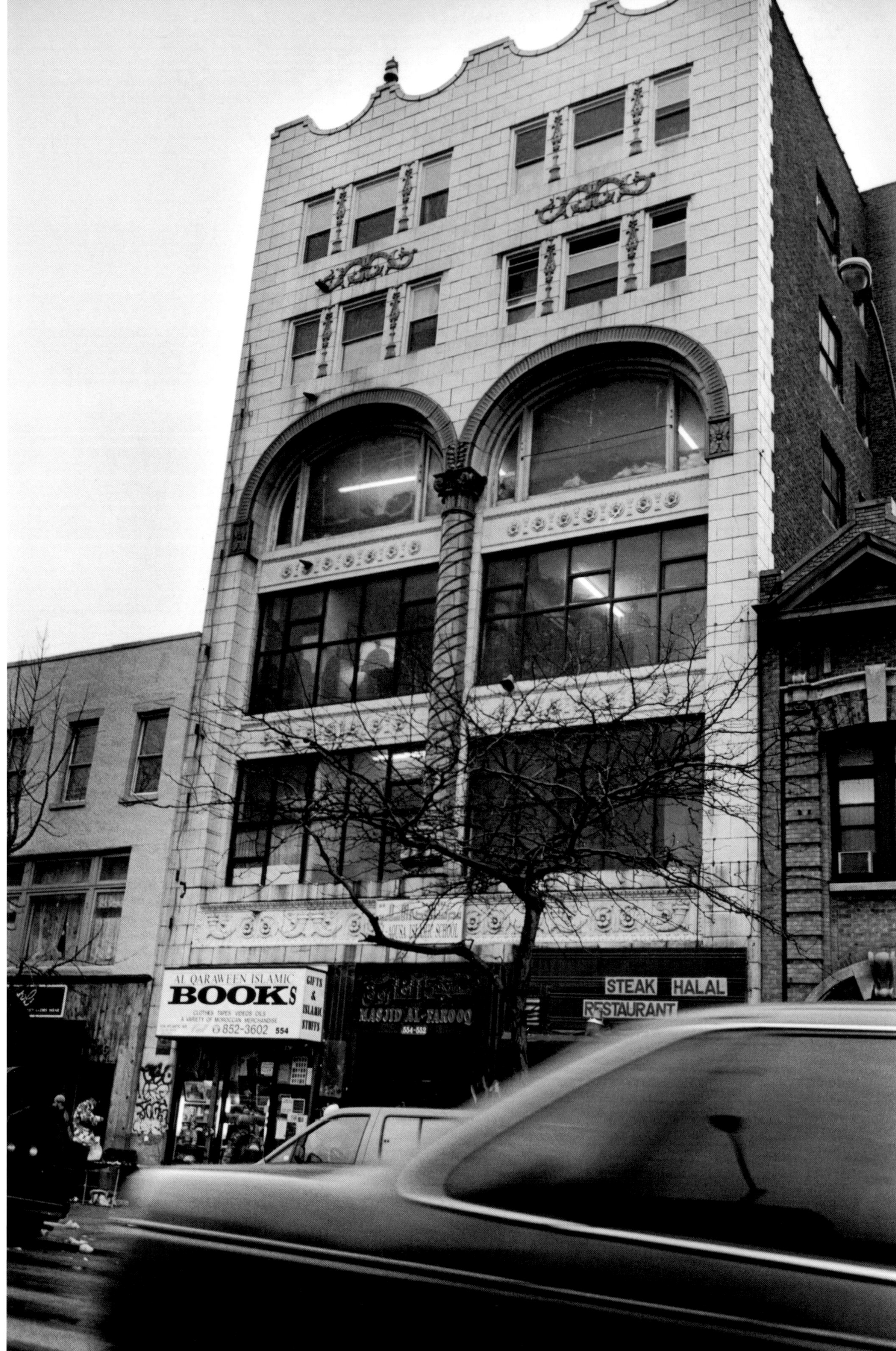

Al-Farouq Masjid, Brooklyn

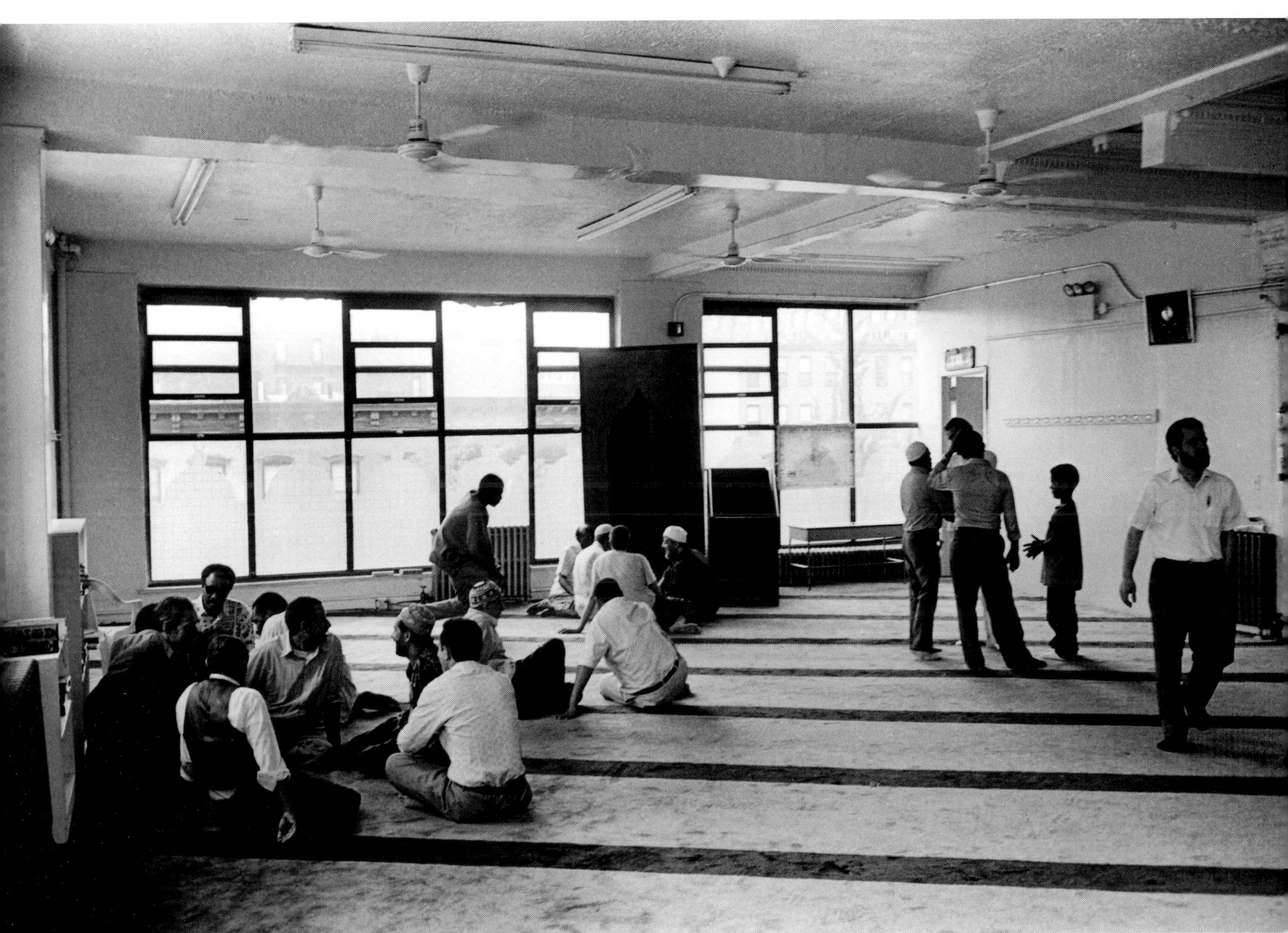

Al-Farouq Masjid, Brooklyn

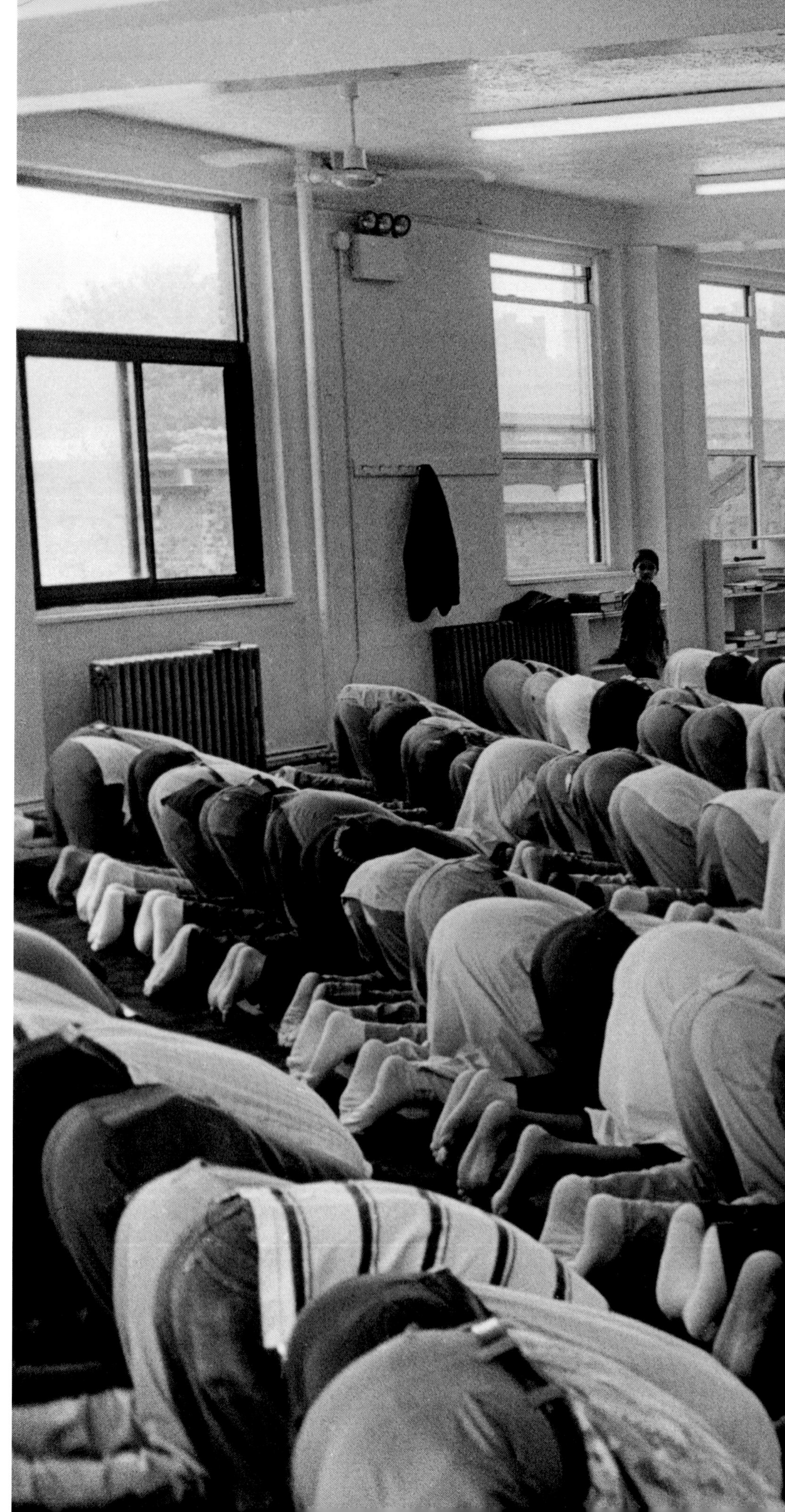

Al-Farouq Masjid, Brooklyn

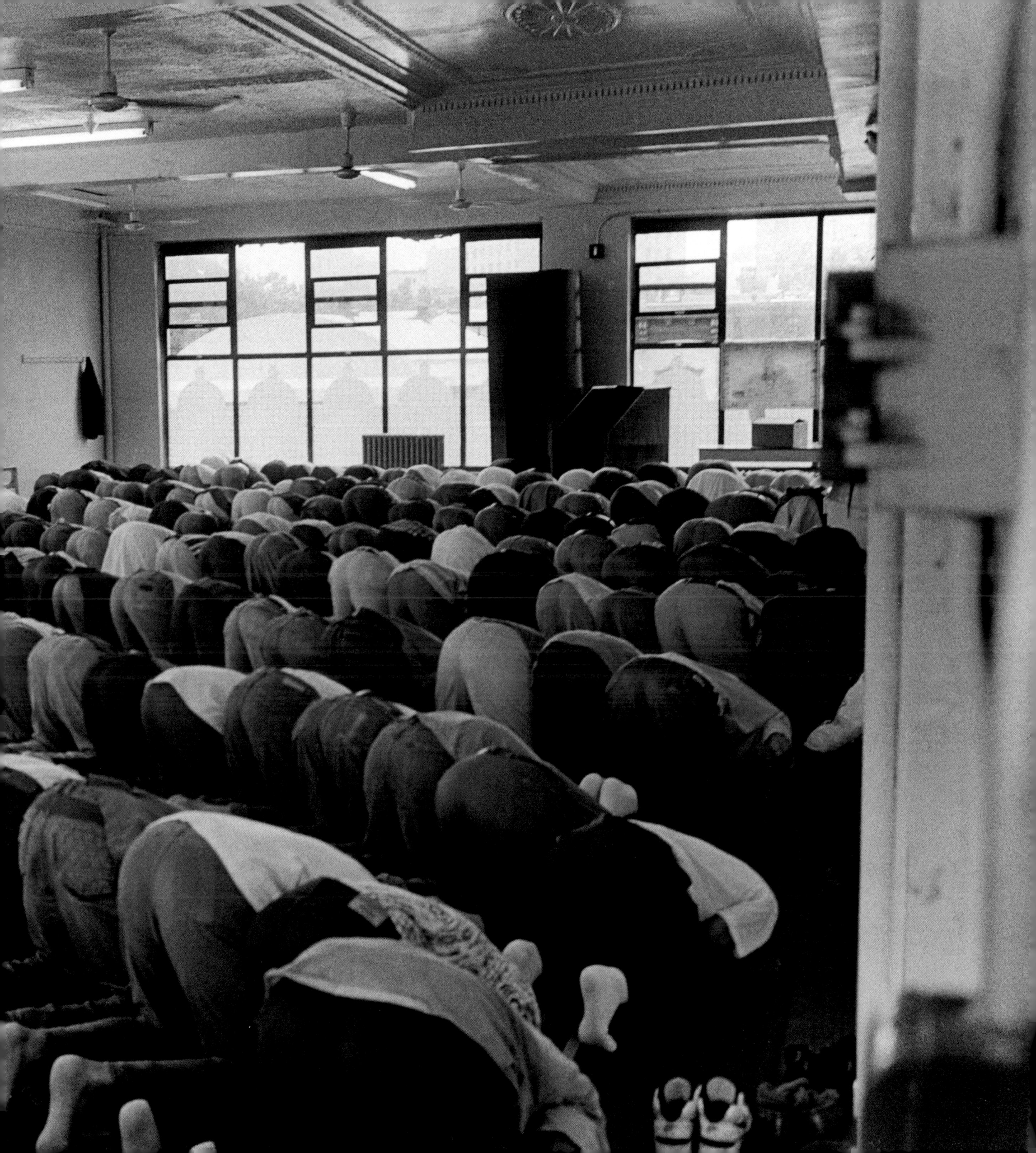

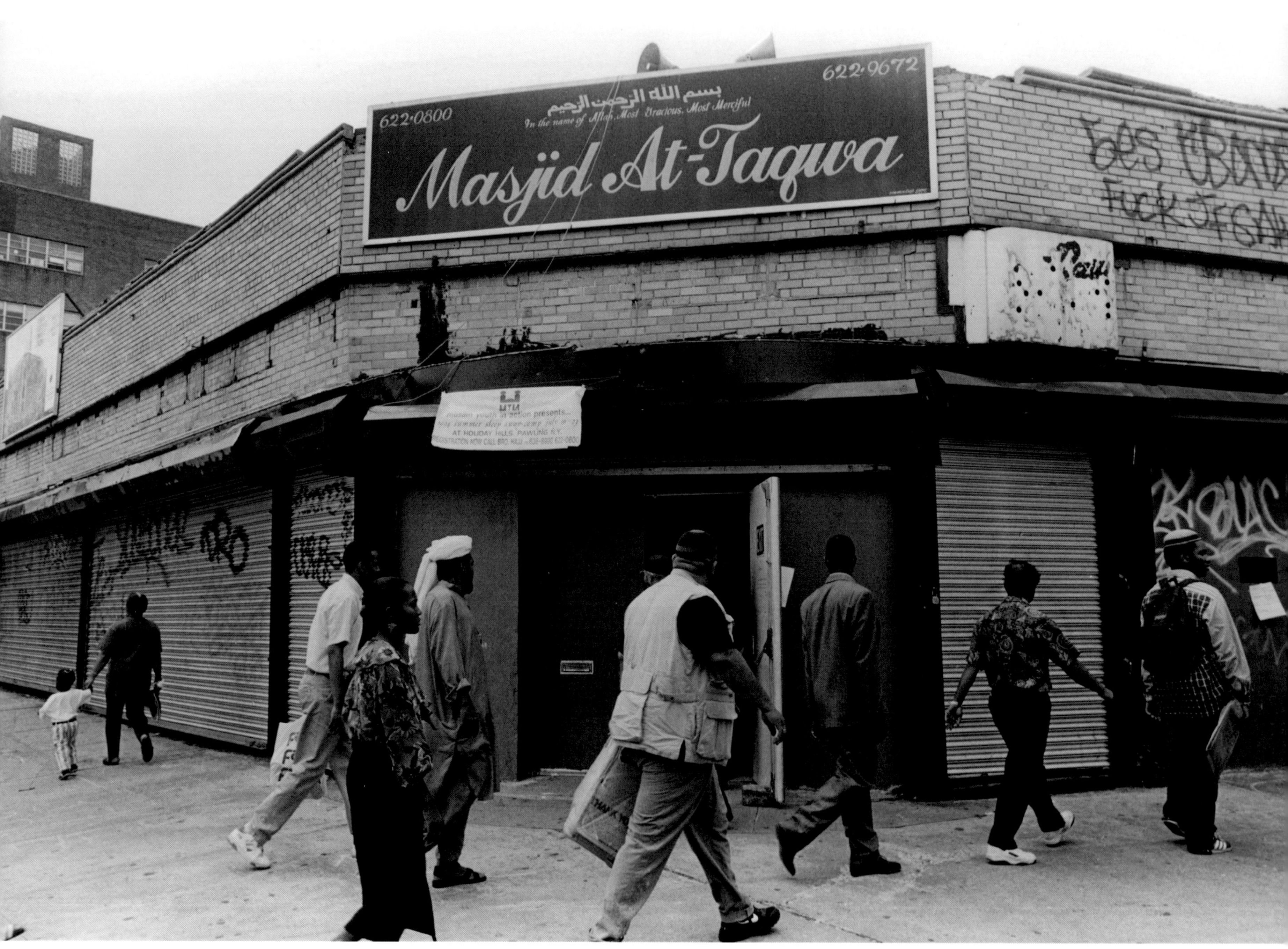

Masjid At-Taqwa, Brooklyn

ARCHITECTURE HAS NO MEANING

"After this, after 'Allah Akbar,' there is no thought other than prayer, no view or gaze aside from the activities of prayer. There is only complete concentration. You are far from the cares and demands of your life. Architecture is the least of the things you have forgotten." [Imam Muhibbur Rahman, Masjidul Aman, 1994]

"You have watched us pray here so many times. How is it you are not tempted to become a Muslim? Is it the building which distracts you?" [A congregant at the Islamic Cultural Center to the author, 1996]

"Of course, the architecture of this mosque has no meaning," Imam Osman of the Islamic Cultural Center of New York once told me, quite deliberately. "In prayer all external concerns must vanish." This statement, which I have heard a dozen times from Imams, congregants, and Shura council members in mosques in New York City, lies at the heart of any study of mosque architecture in the recent Muslim diaspora. The separation of the act of worship from the material creation of the mosque might be taken for granted in Isfahan or Rabat, but it is a fact that needs to be reasserted especially in New York. And that dichotomy needs to be emphasized in particular to non-Muslim New Yorkers, who tend to fetishize architecture and canonize architects, and who live in a place where cultural authority has laid claim to countless abandoned spiritual territories.

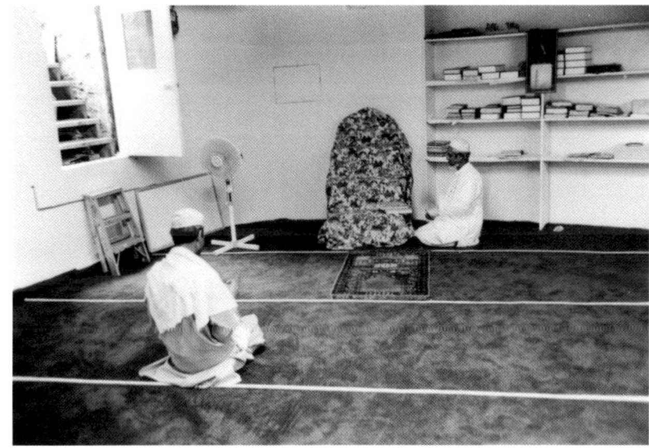

As-Safa Islamic Center, Brooklyn

This separation of architecture's cultural content from its spiritual and community functions is essential to any mosque, regardless of the financial conditions of its congregation, or the willingness of the community to embark on a monumental enterprise when creating a new mosque building. No matter how assimilated or financially sound the community, no matter how grand the architectural gesture, the forms and materials that spring from aesthetic considerations around the building—its decoration, its signage, its profile in the cityscape—are considered separately from the mosque's principal functions. They are completely independent of prayer, and the community services and spaces that are embraced within the mosque building. For in Islam, prayer implies that all consciousness is focused on God; one submits completely to God. It is an act out of time; it is not considered possible that any physical surrounding might hasten or encourage this spiritual engagement, as can be the case in certain Christian approaches toward buildings. Images and symbols, like the presence of the opposite sex, are distractions.

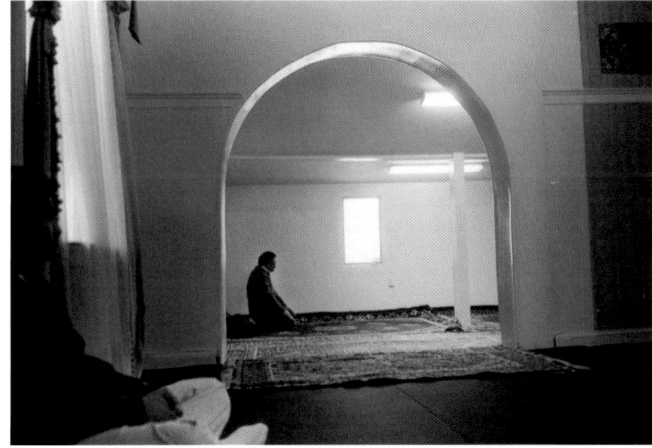

Hazrat-i-abu Bakr, Queens

This attitude extends to the furnishing of the mosque. Detachment from aesthetic considerations often runs parallel to the practice of accepting ad hoc pious donations. In a number of cases, the lay council of a New York mosque was quick to point out that a distinctive element in the mosque building or interior was the choice of a donor, and did not have any particular meaning for the mosque as a whole. The dome of Masjid Al-Abidin, and the tiles of Fatih Cami—architectural elements that provide these mosques with their strongest statements of visual identity—were attributed to the desire of a patron by mosque officials. To have acquired these design elements by specific plan was considered unseemly.

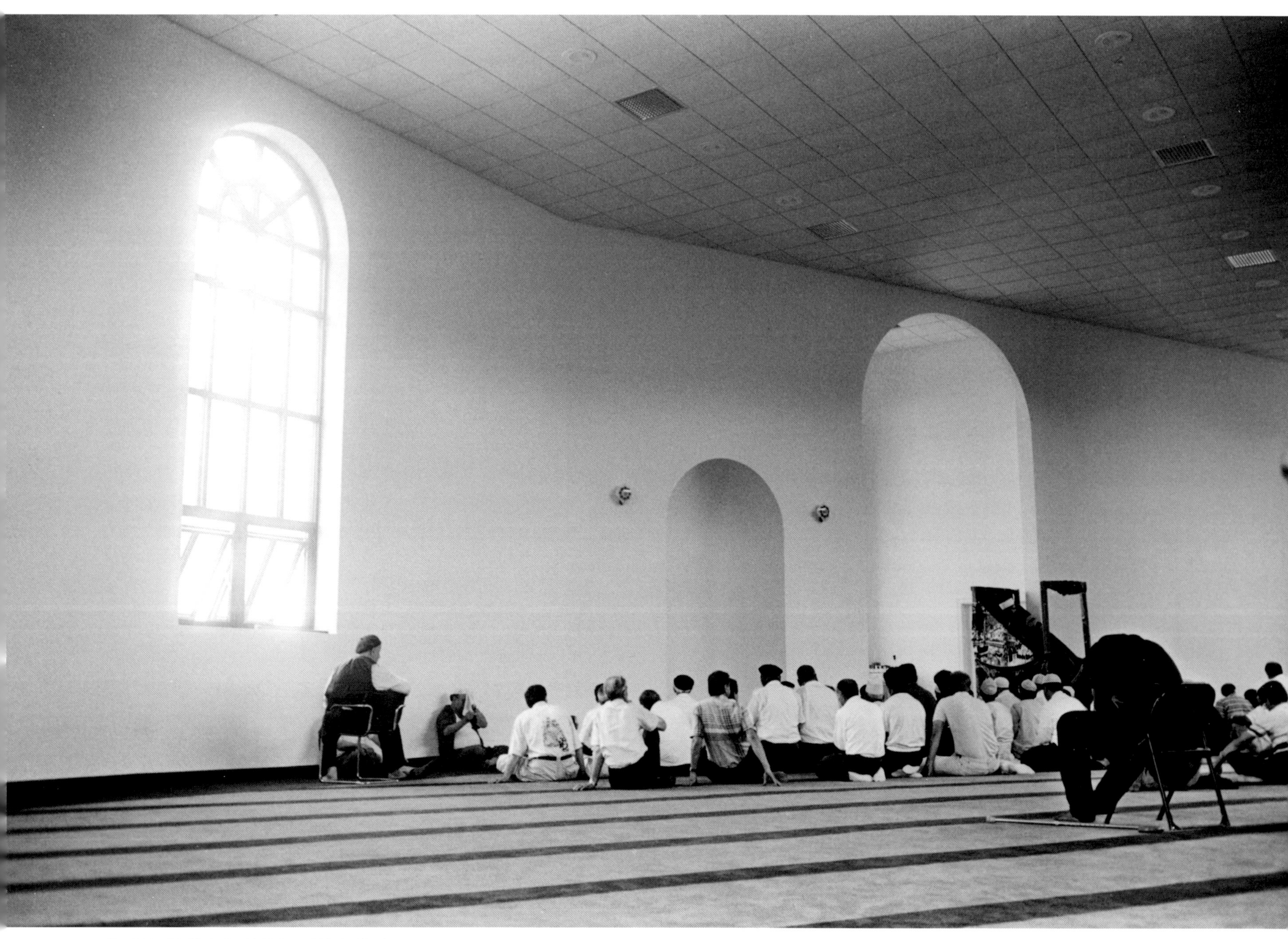

Albanian Islamic cultural center, Staten Island

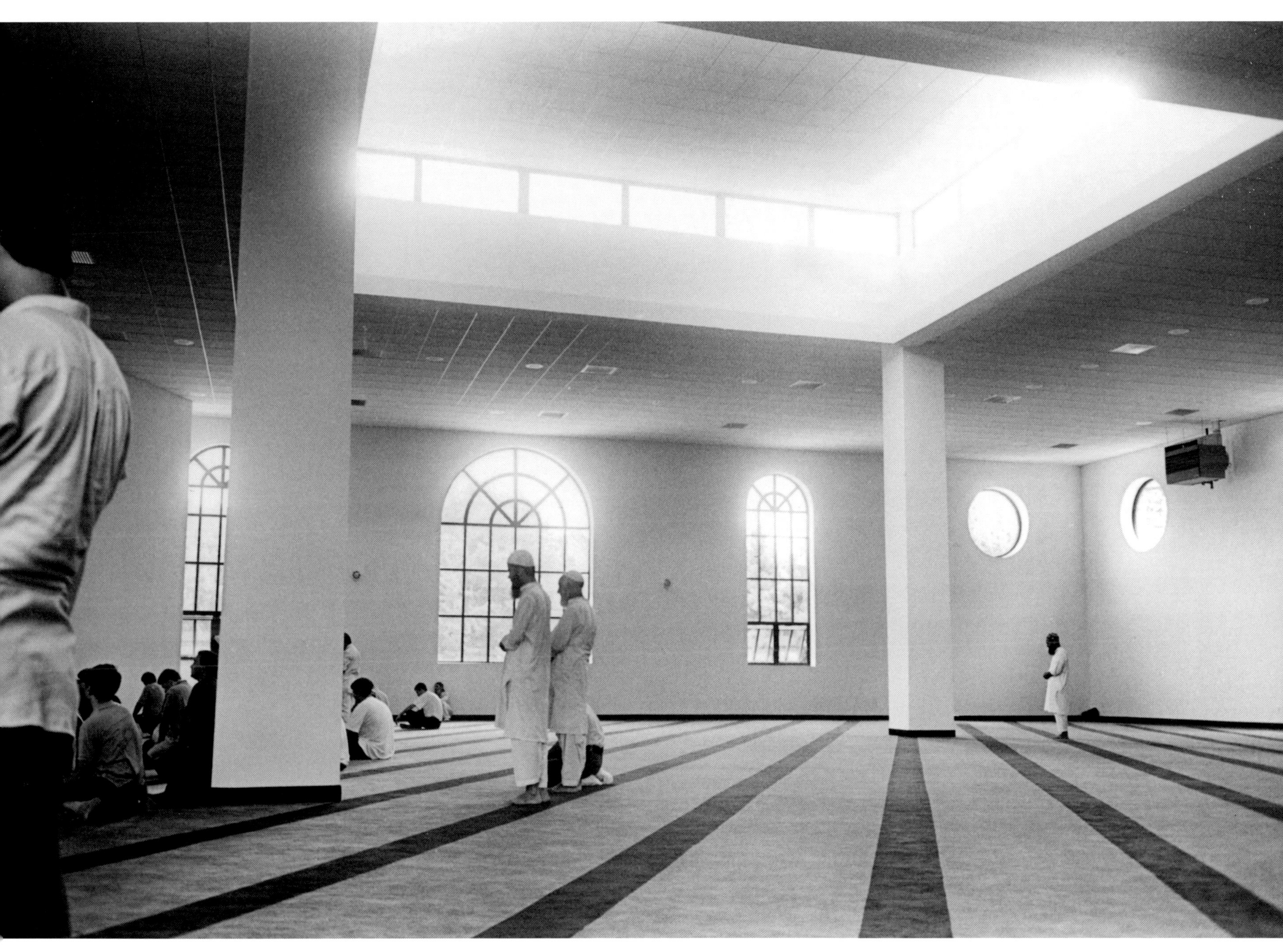

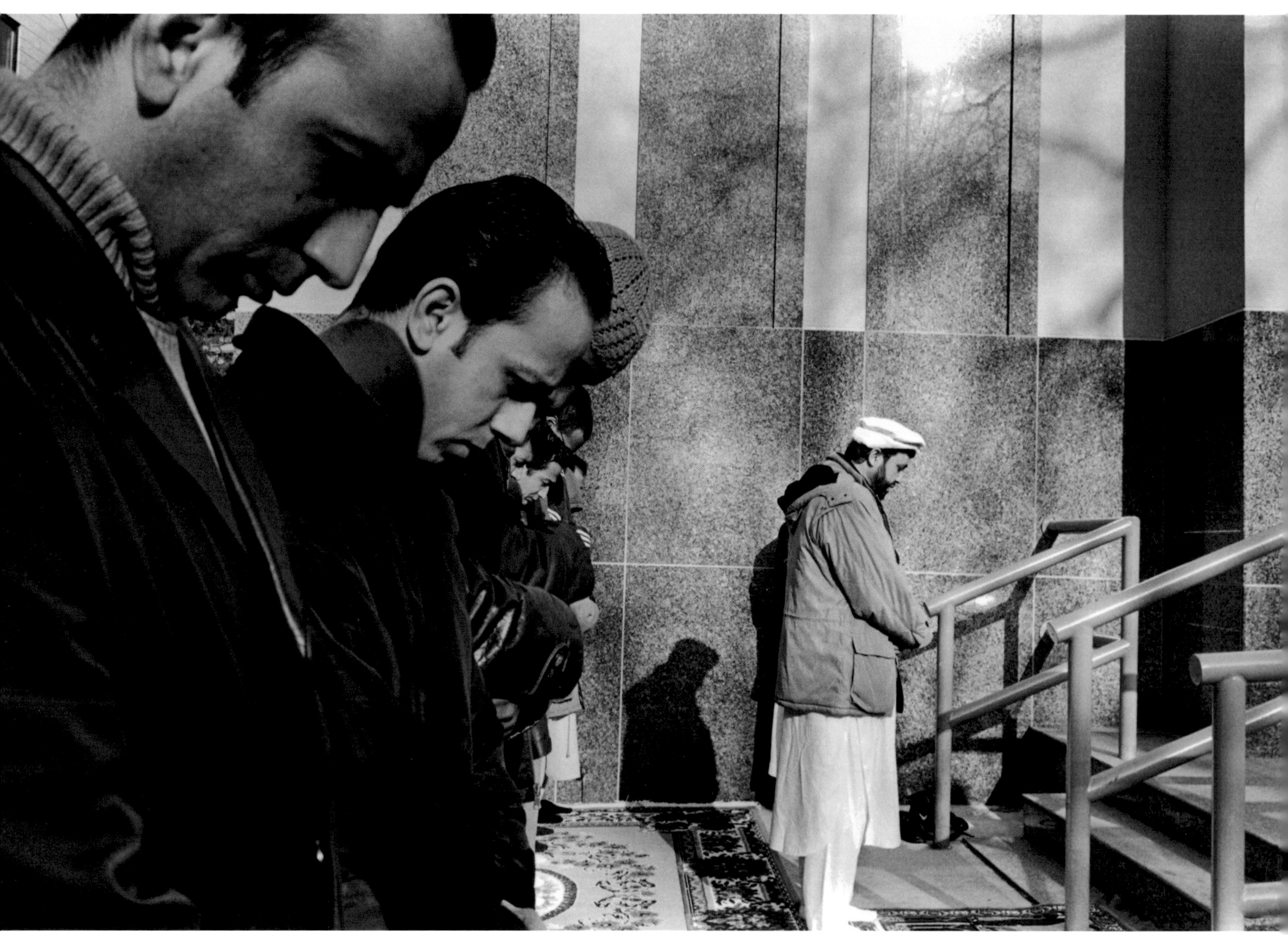

Masjid Hazrat-i-abu Bakr, Queens

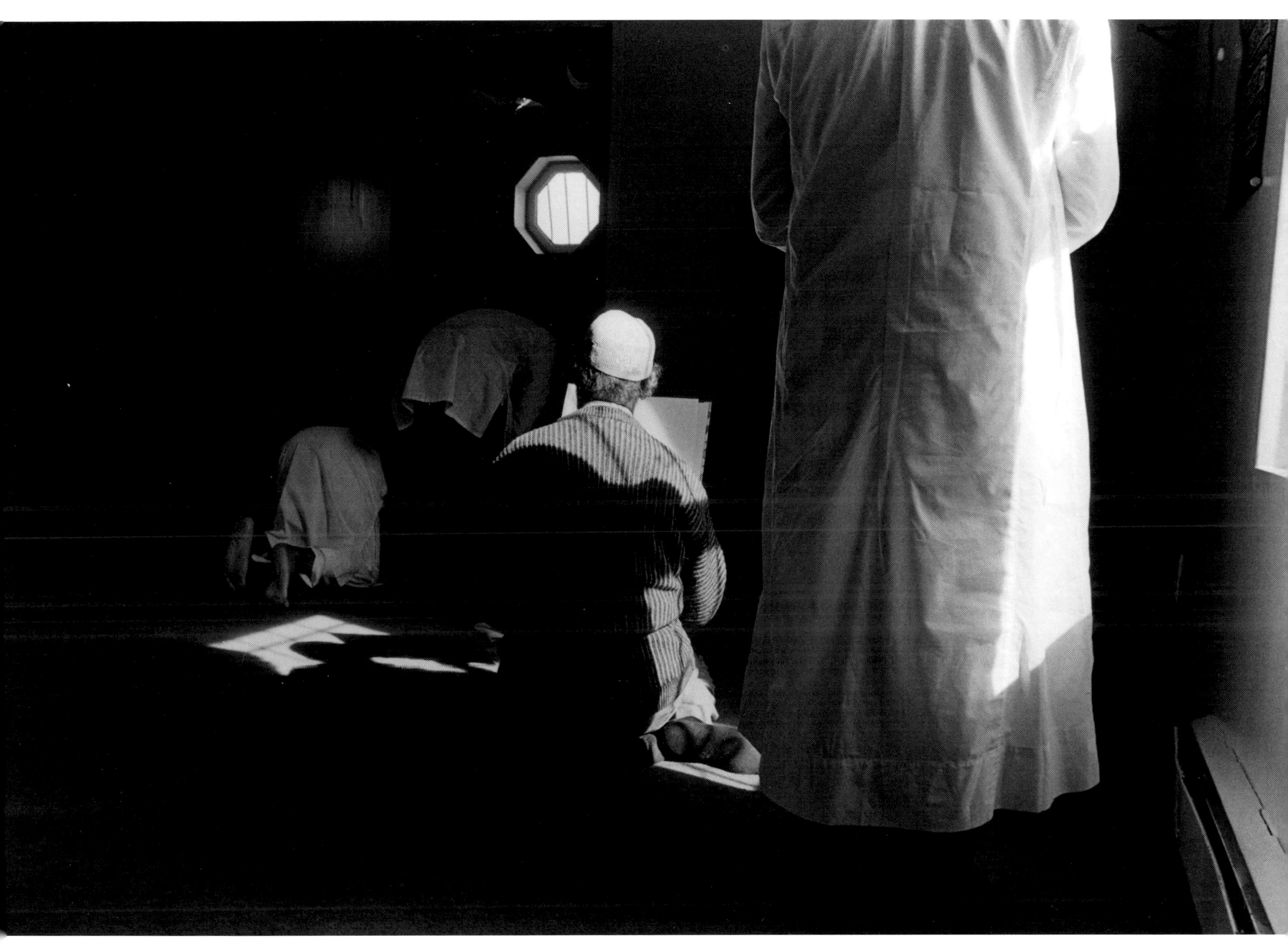

Masjid Al-Abidin, Queens

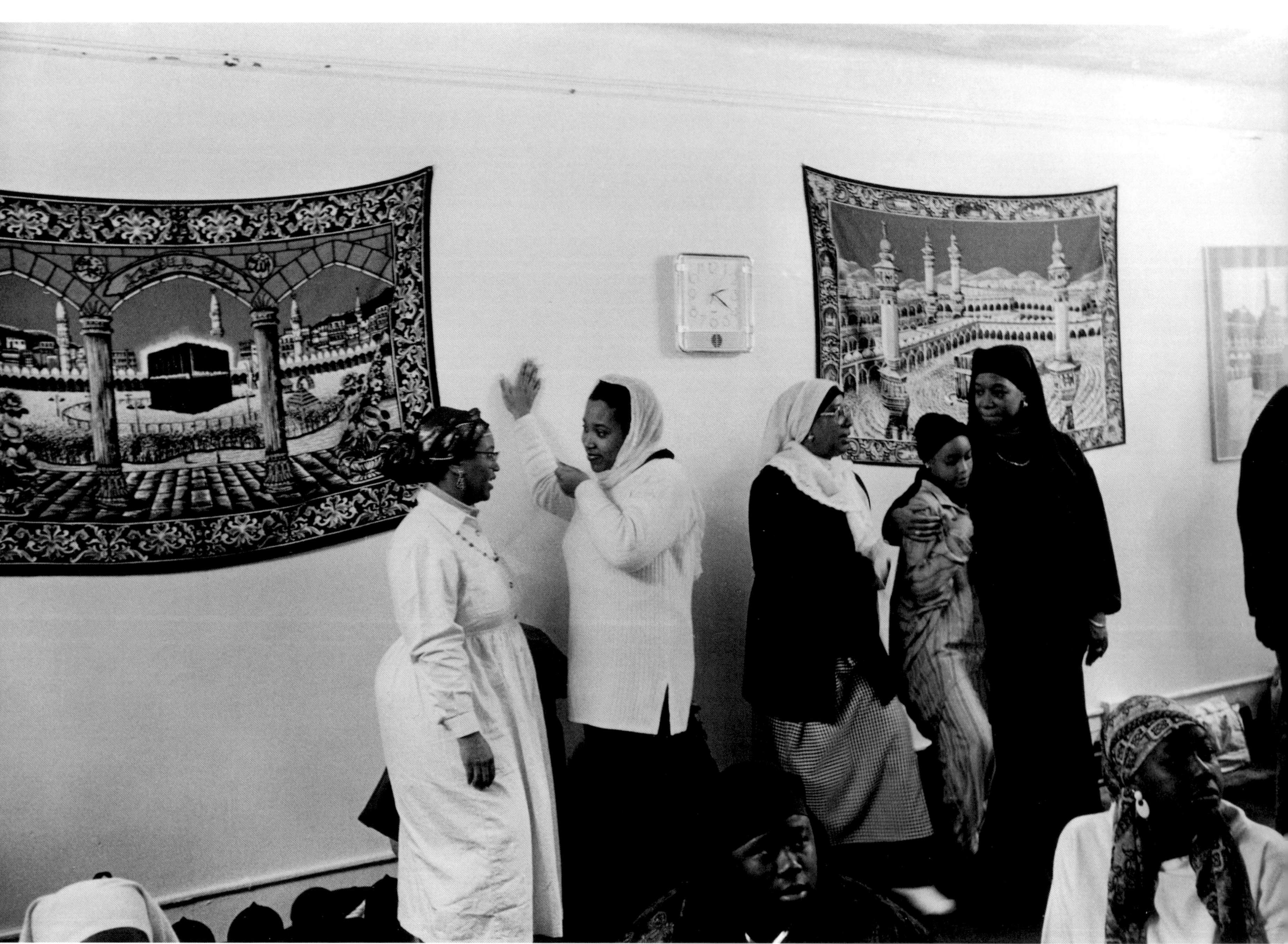

Masjid At-Taqwa wa Jihad, Bronx. Photo by Jerrilynn Dodds

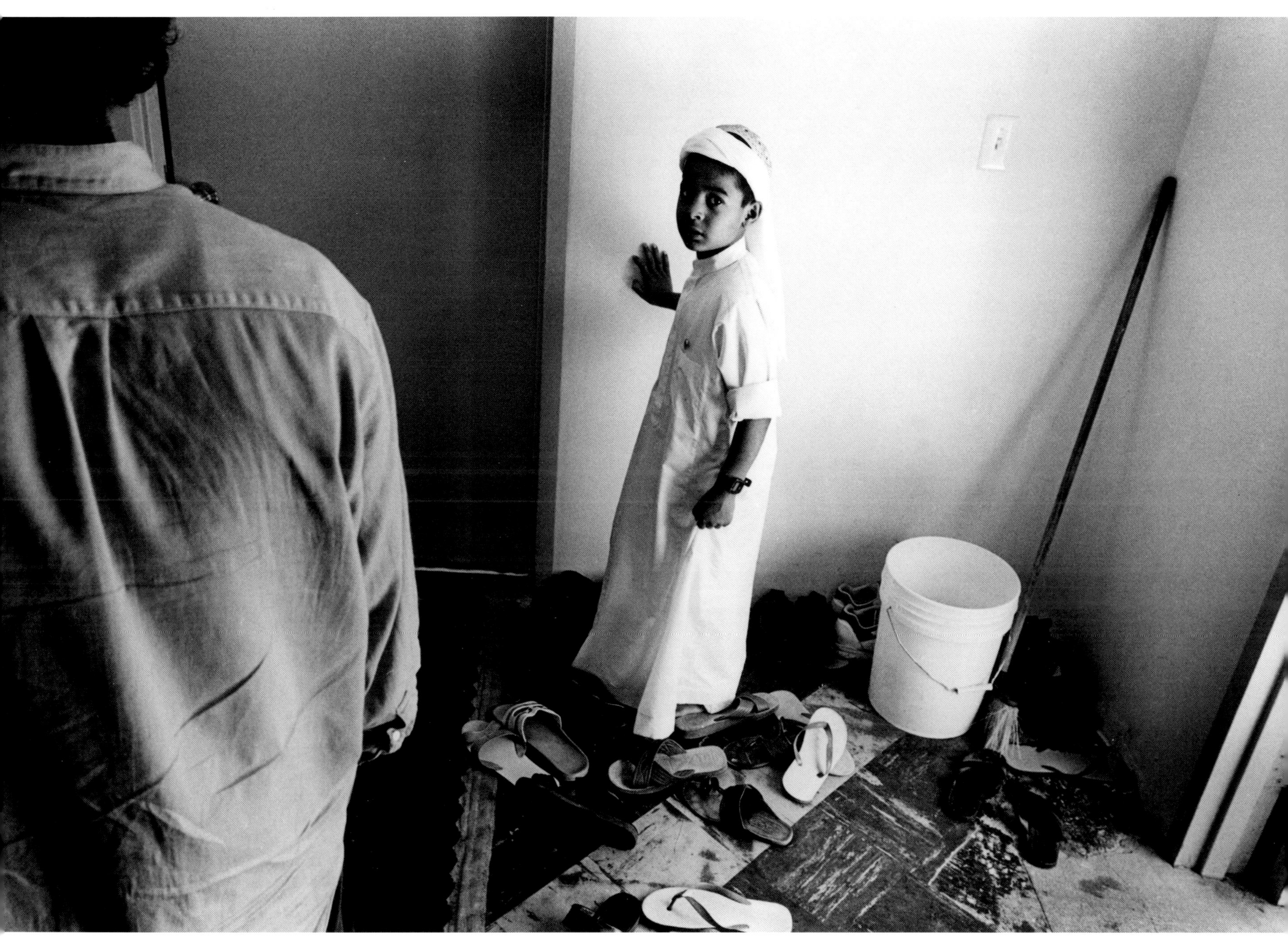

Madina Masjid, Manhattan

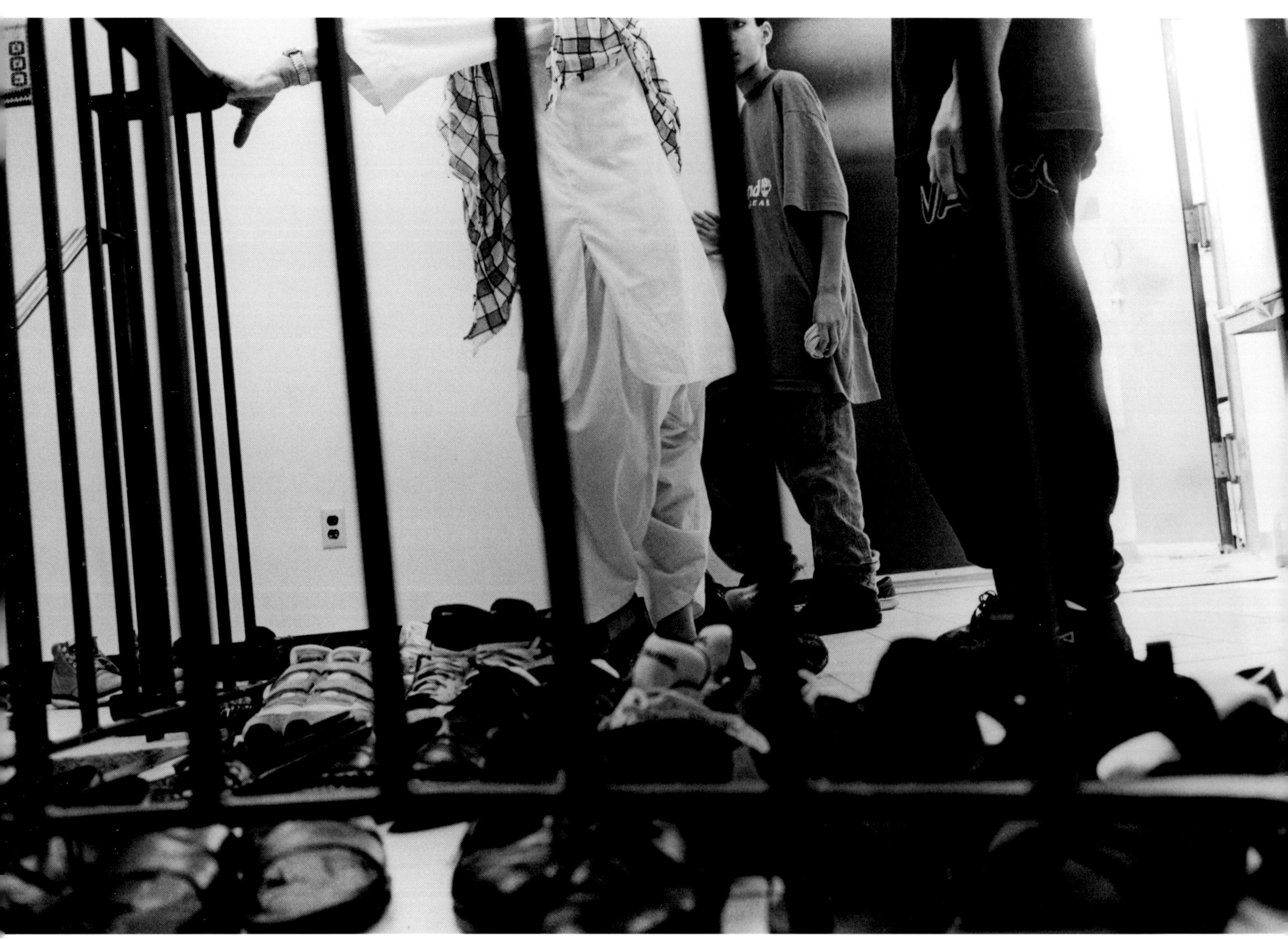

Masjid Al Noor, Staten Island

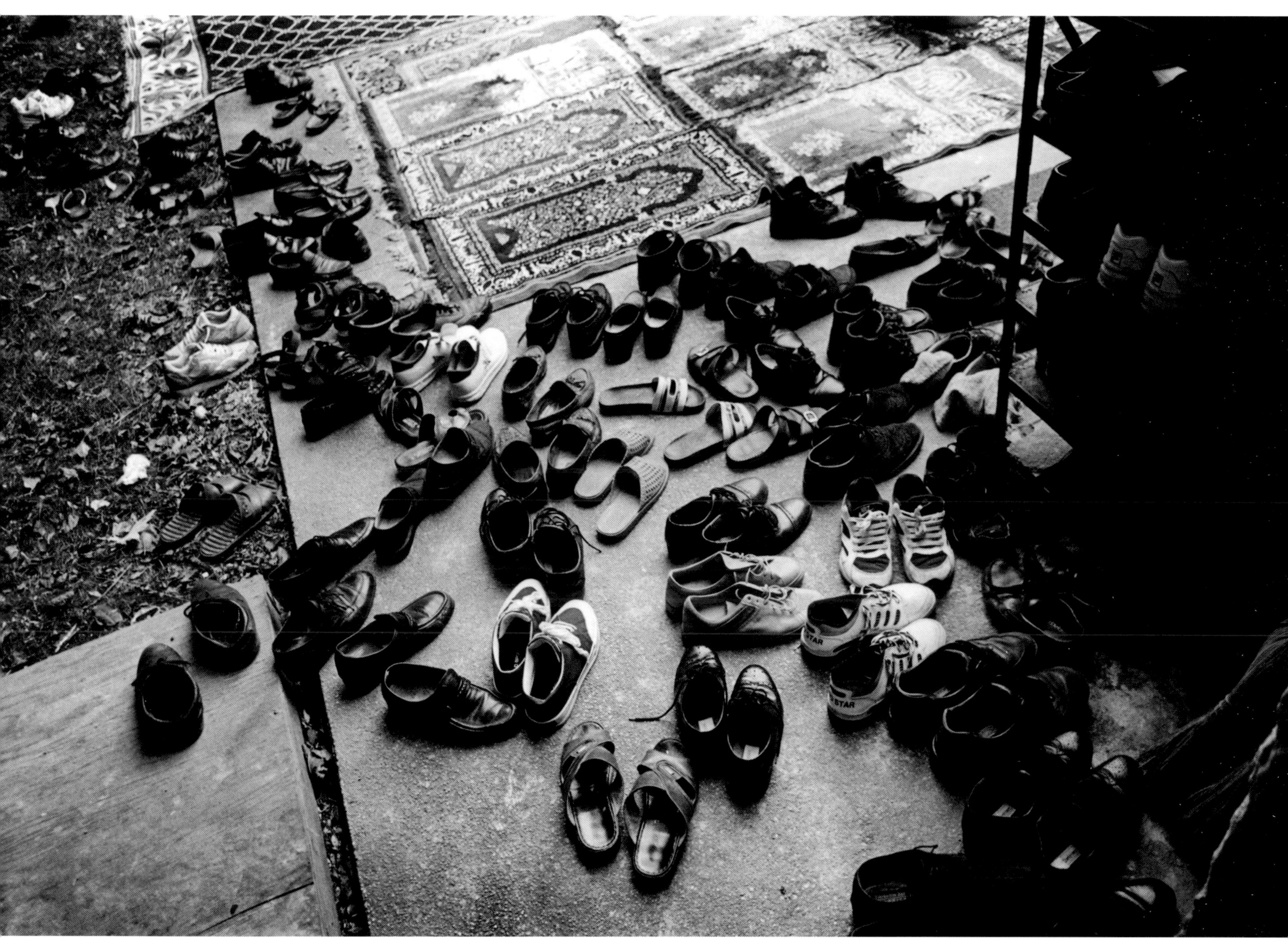

Masjid Hazrat-i-abu Bakr, Queens

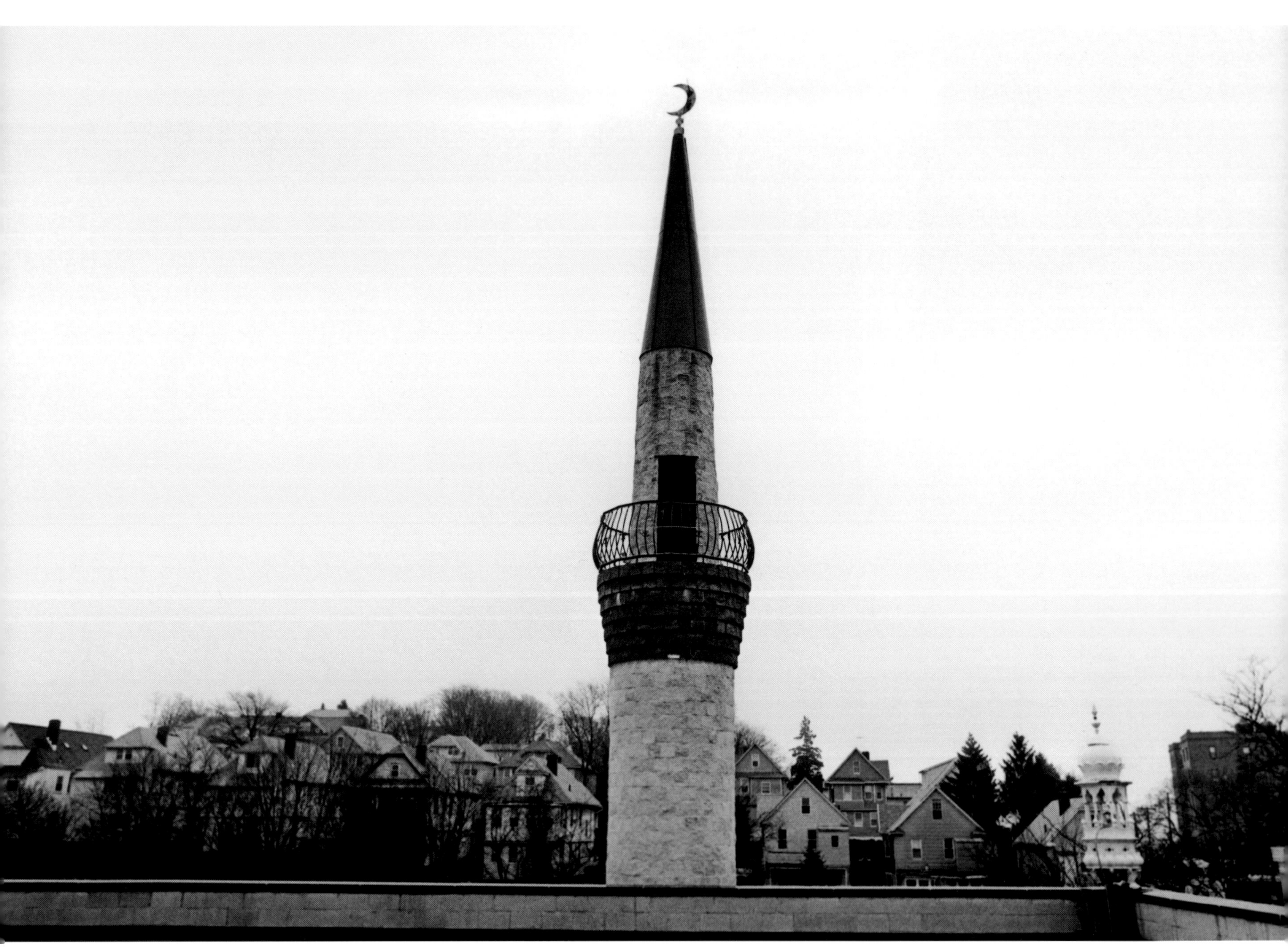

Albanian Islamic cultural center, staten Island

TRADITION

"You should not call this a Turkish mosque. Many of us are from Turkey, but this is not a Turkish mosque. It belongs to the whole neighborhood; there are Americans and Pakistanis and Africans. It is for all Muslims." [Imam Hilmi Akdag, Fatih Cami]

The use of visual forms that evoke a particular ethnic or national group or an identifiable historical tradition is somewhat rare among the mosques of New York, and it is not evident as a conscious position in any of the new-built mosques.[28] At Masjid Hazrat–i–abu Bakr, for instance, a new building completed in 1999 by a predominantly Afghan community in Queens replaced their most recent mosque, a yellow split level home on the same site. The new structure's substantial blocky base mounts to an intensely blue dome over which a net of white lines swirls provocatively. This contemporary riff on architectural tradition from northeastern lands of Islam—Iran, Afghanistan, Soviet Central Asia, and Pakistan in particular—is, like Hazrat-i-abu Bakr's interior ornamentation, too generic to evoke a particular national or historical identity. It is, in fact, purposefully general. "You know, we are Americans," Nisar Zuri explains, "we came here to escape religious persecution under the Russians. We see the United States as a religious place. It is true we care about Afghanistan. We all have family there, and many of us were born there. But now we are here. We are not going back. We are not looking to reproducing Afghanistan here."

Three communities in particular, however, do embrace historical tradition, but the motive is not, as one might expect, embattlement or resistance to American cultural assimilation. The adoption of traditional form for each has a different, and more specific, motivation.

The United American Muslim Association, which administrates Fatih Cami, faced a need in the early 1980s to find a space large enough to hold their entire community during prayer, a number that could grow from 400 during Juma to over a thousand during the month of Ramadan. In 1981, they purchased a building in Sunset Park, Brooklyn which had previously served as a theater, then a church. At the time of its purchase, it was in ruins: the roof was in the process of collapsing, and the window frames and doors all had to be replaced. The transformation, which was a significant one, is represented by the Imam as a prosaic act remote from the mosque itself. He prefers to define the mosque in terms of its weekend school for children, its dormitory for visiting students from Turkey, rooms for ceremonies and celebrations, its night school for adults, and its office which publishes a religious and cultural magazine.

From Fatih Cami's neat, ample lobby one passes, today, beneath a tiled sign into a voluminous space beneath a shallow stucco dome. This is the prayer hall, a gathering place that had once been the auditorium of the old converted theater, its seats and screen long removed, but its plaster dome-shaped ceiling surviving. Susan Slyomovics has observed how the reorientation of the original theater building becomes a kind of repossession of its American Orientalist decoration. Those

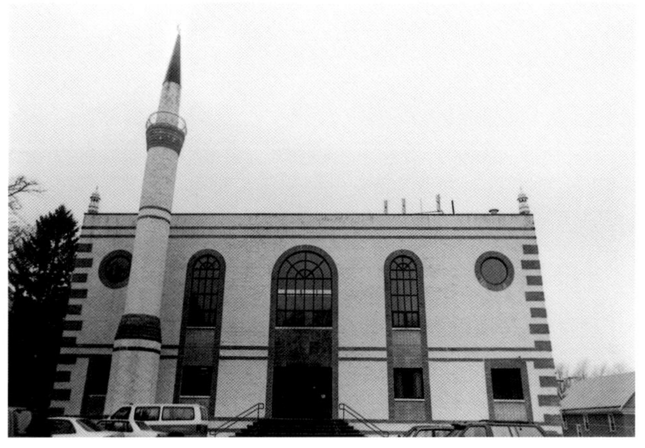

Albanian Islamic Cultural Center, Staten Island

entering at first find themselves facing the theater's former stage, which has become a gallery for the women of the congregation, but they must turn their backs on the stage to face the qibla, the direction of prayer.[29]

It is in turning to face Mecca that one's experience of this reinvented space is completed: a mural of painted Iznik tiles transforms the qibla wall with Ottoman arabesques, floral interlace patterns, and bold, cursive inscriptions. This rich and luminous decoration, so anomalous to Sunset Park's patchwork of faded classical structures and newer cool, prosaic commercial ones, reorients the building, and gives it an ethnic heritage to match its Islamic function. At the center of the wall is the Mihrab; to its right an elegant Turkish Minbar, or pulpit, reaches into the room with a narrow stairway over which a skin of the same tiles is stretched. Their lively, complex, interwoven ornament is posed against an otherwise hushed, empty space. The streets of Brooklyn evaporate.

When asked how the mosque determined to add these tiles to the reused theater, the Imam would only say, "It was not a particular wish or decision of the mosque community. A generous member of the congregation gave them to us. He paid to have them installed."

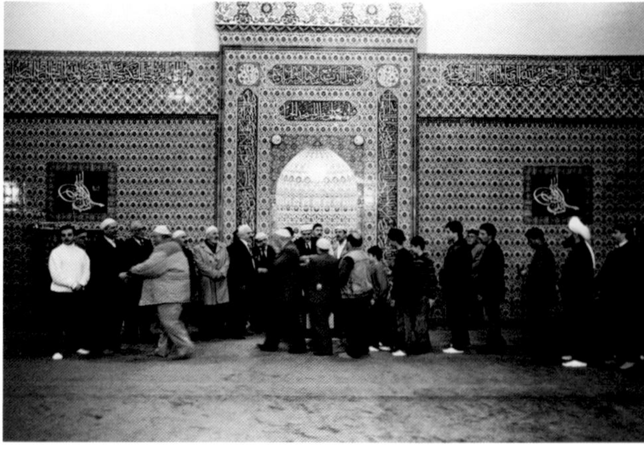

Fatih cami, Brooklyn

In evoking the traditional arts of Ottoman Turkey, the tiles could be seen as providing a focus of common identity for this primarily Turkish Muslim community, creating an alternate visual world that would remind these integrated Turkish Americans of their common identity in this complex city. In interviews, however, I could find no sense of imperiled identity, or fear of over-assimilation that this architecture might be meant to defy. Primarily middle class and urbane, this congregation includes a large number of professionals and a significant proportion of second and third generation Turkish-Americans, as well as a growing population of Muslims from a wide swath of varied traditions.

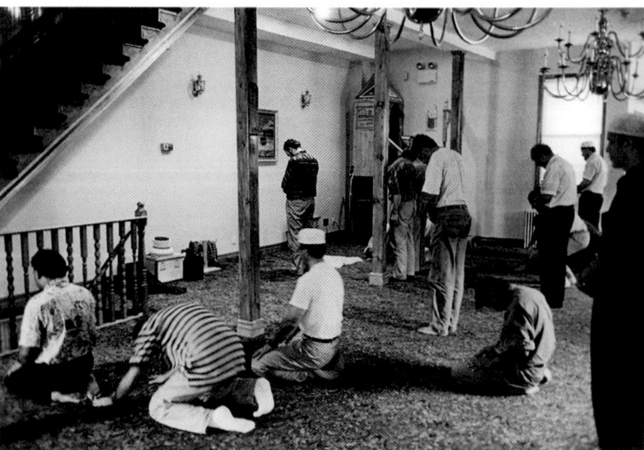

Ali Pasha Mosque, Queens

In fact, the leadership of Fatih Cami has been particularly resolute in not drawing its identity from the past, or from a particular ethnic tradition. On most Fridays, the Khutbah is given in three languages. As is the case with many New York mosques, the traditional Arabic Khutbah is repeated in the language of the founding group of the mosque, the group that represents the largest part of the community: in this case, Turkish. But at Fatih Cami, the Khutbah is also repeated in English, to be understandable to the growing non-Turkish component of the congregation. "There were two weddings here this weekend," Imam Akdag pointed out one Monday, "a Pakistani couple, and a Turkish bride and groom. Of course we are all Americans really, but this is a very international congregation in its cultures." A message popped up on Fatih Cami's web site sometime last spring: "We are not a Turkish Mosque. We are a Muslim Mosque."[30]

Far from an embattled refuge to a pure ethnic past, the tile decoration of Fatih Cami might be seen rather as a kind of stimulus response on the part of a congregant to North America's touristic attitude towards ethnicity, an attitude reflected in New York by a kind of reverent eclecticism.

The magazine published by the mosque, *Fetih*, includes community news, articles concerning issues of faith and Islamic life, as well as illustrated features concerning historical monuments from Turkish-Islamic culture. It is possible that traditional architectural form at Fatih Cami reflects the attitude of that part of the congregation whose entitlement to American cultural identity is fairly well established, so that it can extend to the nostalgic exteriorization of an ancestral home.

Two other mosques displaying historical tradition in a conscious way are the Albanian Islamic Cultural Center and the Ali Pasha Mosque. The Albanian Islamic Center, a monumental block in Staten Island, is flanked by an elegant cylindrical tower minaret, designed like those that dotted war-torn cities in news headlines during the Kosovo wars. Architect Brent Porter found that the predominantly Albanian community preferred not only Balkan style Ottoman windows, but the slim tower that is "a traditional Balkan variant" of the minaret. The community's commitment to the survival of Albanian culture in the face of its purposeful destruction in Kosovo is clear and direct. And yet, this investment in history does not exclude the present American experience. The Albanian Islamic Cultural Center believes it has something to offer relatives in Europe as well. Their desire to help rebuild the Kosovar mosques of Lypjan and Drenice, and to "transplant the idea of a community center" to Kosovo reminds us that as their notion of ethnicity and tradition is strengthened, it grows nevertheless from a demonstrably American Albanian community identity.

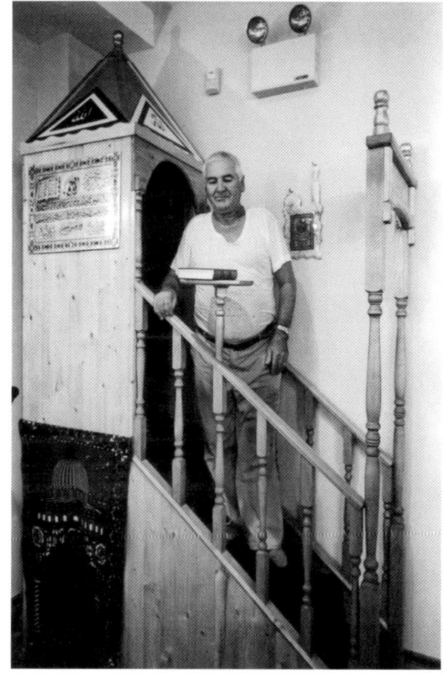
Ali Pasha Mosque, Queens. Hamo Hurla

The Ali Pasha Mosque, a former two family home in Astoria, Queens, was decorated by Bosnian and Hercegovinian-American carpenters to approximate a traditional Bosnian timber interior. Led by an energetic board that includes businessmen, computer specialists, and carpenters, the renovation produced a prayer hall and cultural center with meeting rooms, lodging for the Imam and students, and a garden where congregants meet. Two floors have been cleared for prayer, and in each plaster partition walls have been replaced by stained wooden columns and exposed beams, while all of the interior's original wood supports and details were stripped and finished by community members. Hamo Hurla made a lacquered Minbar and Kursi (a reading stand for the Qur'an) in the forms of examples he had seen "at home."

There is certainly a search for tradition at the Ali Pasha Mosque, and it could be said to be a resistant one. But it is not posed against assimilation into American culture, Shura members explained. Rather, the life of Bosnian tradition here resists its obliteration in a culturally cleansed Bosnia. The genocidal acts that obliged the founding core of this congregation to immigrate spurred the desire to re-seed in New York an imperiled cultural tradition.

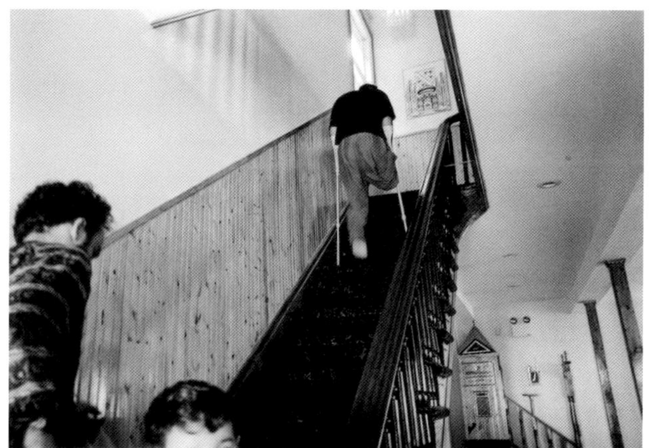
Ali Pasha Mosque, Queens

"First you need a place to pray for everyone, not just for Bosnians," Imam Bayram Mulic explained, "but then, if you can, it is important to make the mosque nice; maybe even traditional. We have lost so much." The Imam wants in particular to reach Bosnian immigrants and refugees who grew up in the former Republic of Yugoslavia, and were raised as part of a secular state. "They believed they could have Bosnian tradition without Islam. But there is no artistic or architectural tradition, no cultural Bosnian tradition without religion. There is no secular tradition that you can separate from Islam. And in the end there is only Allah."

Founded as the "Bosnian Cultural Center," the congregation changed the name to the Ali Pasha Mosque in the mid-1990s, in order to emphasize its inclusiveness for a community that rapidly grew in diversity. As at Fatih Cami, the mosque's leadership wished to reaffirm its identity with the larger Islamic community. "We are a place for all Muslims," Mulic affirmed. "You need a place where your soul can be protected."

Ethnic identity in New York's mosques does not seem to have been conceived to resist New York's messy, interactive present, or to remain linked to a frozen, traditional past. New York's immigrant Muslim communities have moved dynamically into New York's burgeoning landscape; they exhibit all of the growth and ambivalence inherent in the displacement and grafting of divergent identities to create a third, new one.

ARCHES AND DOMES

"Those domes? Really, this architecture does not concern us. It has nothing to do with the past; it does not reflect any idea or decision. The dome was the choice of the man who paid for the renovation. That is all." [Mr. Sattur, Masjid Al-Abidin]

"Somehow the dome became symbolic of the mosque...over a period of time such things just happen. It could have been anything..." [Dr. Rashid, Masjid Alfalah]

"This building was conceived to receive visitors," Imam Osman of the Islamic Cultural Center pointed out in a matter of fact way. "We are in America now, where people are interested in judging people through their architecture. This is not really our way. But I think that this can be seen as a new era for the mosque. Since this is America, the mosque should be made in an architectural language that Americans understand. But that has nothing to do with Islam."

"The Dome," Imam Osman added, unprompted, "has no meaning."

"One of the only things we really stipulated that we wanted was the dome," Ziad Monayir, a representative of the Cultural Center's building committee told me pointedly. "We just thought there ought to be a dome; that here the dome was the form by which Islam might immediately be recognized in New York."

There are no universal architectural forms understood by all Muslims to represent Pan-Islamic tradition. In Islamic countries throughout the world, the dome has not stood, throughout history, as a universal sign for Islam. Its wide-scale use, and in particular, the Euro-American association of the dome with Islam, can be traced to its prominence in the great empires of Safavid Iran, Mughal India, and Ottoman Turkey: the Islamic empires that had the most extensive interaction with early modern Europe. But even in those places, domes were often understood to distinguish monuments that carry the names of powerful rulers or patrons, and bear the mark of their personal piety and authority. Traditional neighborhood mosques in these and other countries only sporadically employed the dome, using instead a variety of local architectural typologies; and for a number of the countries represented in the community of the Islamic Cultural Center, the dome does not occur as a traditional form in mosque architecture.

The notion that the dome might be a universal signifier for Islam has been conceived in a number of different places, one of which is the European and American Orientalist tradition. Since the 18th century, Orientalists saw the domed, curvilinear skyline of Istanbul or Isfahan as other to the rational urban profile with which many European cities, and New York, had begun to imagine themselves. In this fictive polarized view, the dome becomes mysterious and irrational, opposite a rational European and American rectilinear identity.

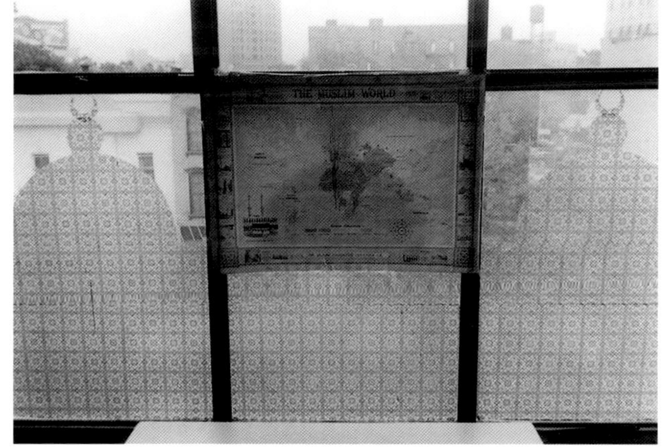

Al-Farouq Masjid, Brooklyn

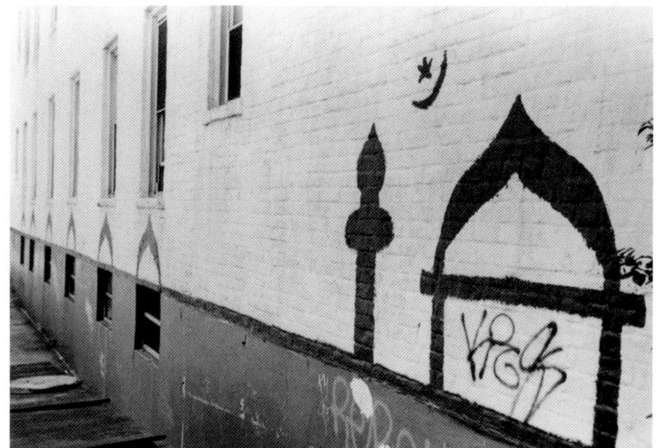

Masjid Baitul Mukarram, Queens

Irrationality is, of course, not an intrinsic property of domes, in Islamic countries or outside them. Here, at the Islamic Cultural Center, the massing of the dome owes much to the clear, rational massing of Ottoman architecture, though the architects generally attribute its geometry to universal modernist values: "The dome isn't Mughal, or Safavid, or from any specific culture of Islam," asserts Mustafa Abadan, project architect for Skidmore, Owings & Merrill during the mosque's construction. "We made it half a sphere, which is not the most felicitous form, but it was pure geometry, so it could not be associated with any one national or cultural group." The dome of the Islamic Cultural Center was conceived, then, as a rational form in the modernist sense—a universal form whose construction is revealed with a kind of austere lucidity through the juxtaposition of glass and opaque support. It is this modernist gloss on a traditional theme that seeks to reinvent the dome for this new American community, this new audience. But the Islamic Cultural Center is unusual, and unique among all the mosques studied here. Its powerful international patrons hoped to represent the presence of Islam in New York, and the use of the dome was calculated to be a sign, a marker informed by the expectations of Americans, Muslims and non-Muslims alike.

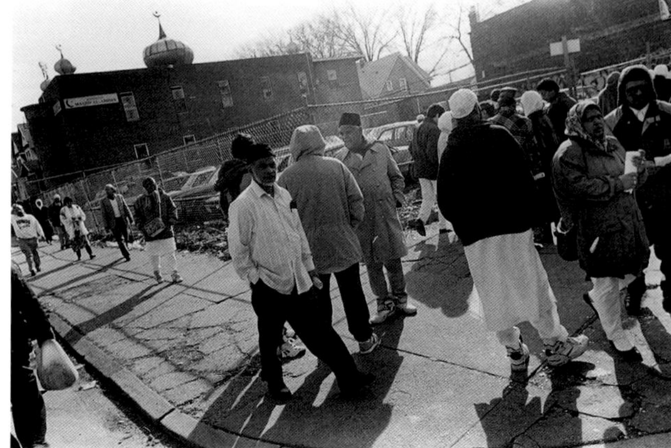

Masjid Al-Abidin, Queens

But the dome has also become the favored expression of such "landmark" new-built mosques internationally. Holod and Khan have noted that "even when the client has stipulated a modern design, this has been accompanied by a clearly expressed desire to offer an 'Islamic' image." Domes and minarets are seen by such official clients as carriers of these meanings that can be integrated into a modernist language. Architects who are used to working "in a totally contemporary idiom" now find they have to turn to "historic models" for "validation" of their designs to clients.[31] Or consider the words of Gulzar Haidir, North America's most reflective mosque designer: "I brought to my encounter with this American landscape an architectural ambivalence of my own, articulated as the draw of 'modernity' against 'tradition' at every sphere." He speaks of "dome and minaret envy" in relationship to his designs which have resisted typological and historical reference.[32]

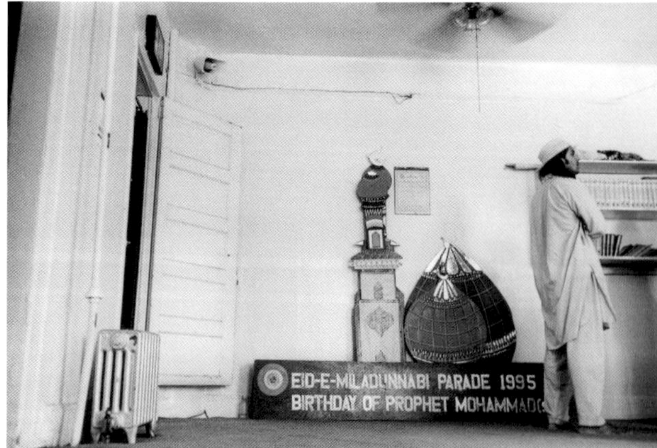

Gawsiah Jame Masjid, Queens

Are these all images configured for the non-Muslim gaze, outward looking, without particular meaning for the mosques' primary patrons? To understand how these meanings are made, I think it is necessary to explore not only official "landmark mosques," or the new-built mosques of mature, established communities, but also mosques that might be argued to represent the interests of American and immigrant Muslims at different social and economic stages in their community histories.

In many growing communities in New York City, a series of more layered, complex meanings are being formed around the dome. Indeed, makeshift, ad hoc versions of the dome are rapidly becoming the marker for mosques in the five boroughs, regardless of the ethnicity of the community. At Gawsiah Jame Masjid in Astoria, a silhouetted dome cut out of plywood once marked the

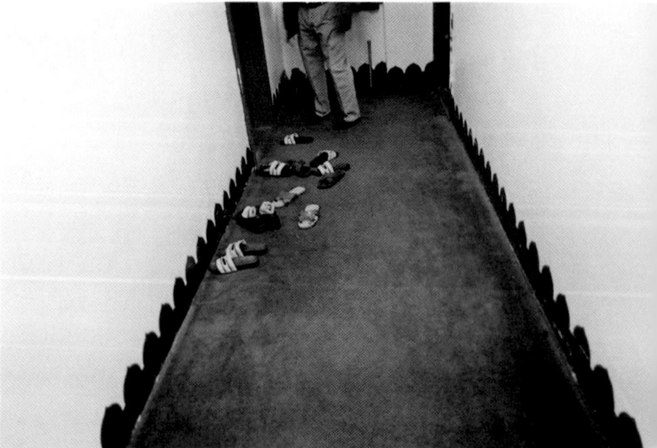

Masjid Taqwa wa-Jihad, Bronx

door of a mosque housed in a small commercial building. Masjid Baitul Mukarram, in Queens, is signaled only by a green dome and minaret painted on the alley wall, which serves as its entrance. These same pointed, curved, green arches, which suggest both a dome in two dimensions or a kind of exoticized arcade, can be found on the facades of Masjidul Aman in Ozone Park, and at the Islamic Congress in Astoria. They were created in three dimensions out of sheet rock for the interior of the renovated Madina Masjid in Manhattan, where a more substantial version in relief marks the mosque's new entrance. A frieze of domes runs along the base of the wall at Masjid Taqwa wa-Jihad in the Bronx, and Al-Farouq Masjid's bare loft windows glow with a frieze of little translucent contact paper domes, which mark the direction of the qibla.

At times, a new renovation is marked by a false dome—one appended to a building exterior. Such is the dome at the Al-Khoie Islamic Center on the Van Wyck Expressway and the Musa Mosque in the Bronx. And increasingly, as communities grow and prosper, and feel the ability to exercise the financial and social confidence necessary to construct a new building to house their mosque, the dome is the form chosen to distinguish it within the community. At Hazrat-i-abu Bakr, in Flushing, Queens, the recently constructed new-built mosque and community center at 32nd Avenue was conceived as a domed building from the beginning. The Shura council planned the construction of the domed mosque for some time, consulting first with an engineer, and finally with an architect. The blocky building mass is crowned by a blue onion dome, over which an interlacing pattern of white lines sweeps like a wind-blown net. "The idea of the dome grew from the community. We believe it makes the mosque more beautiful, more remarkable. You see it, and you know it is a mosque," Imam Sherzad of Hazrat-i-abu Bakr explained with great feeling.

The dome takes on meaning for New York mosques in incremental ways in their interaction with the city. At Masjid Al-Abidin, in the Richmond Hills section of Queens, a single family home became the initial mosque to serve this community of recent Guyanese immigrants. In the course of about a decade, the adjacent house was purchased, and a permit was obtained to expand the first building. Three separate enlargements occurred in the course of 16 years, as the Guyanese community became a growing and prosperous presence in Richmond Hill.

Today five domes crown the mosque's residential profile. Four tiny domes anchor the corners of the rectangular roof, while the largest, at its center, creates a pocket of interior space filled with a chandelier in the mosque's principal prayer hall. The domes are swelling and onion-shaped, like the Guyanese mosques in the community's Islamic calendar.

In an interview with Shura council members, I asked why they had included the domes. Were they meant to evoke the swelling domes of Guyana in New York? "Really," came the response, "this architecture does not concern us. It has nothing to do with the past; it does not reflect any idea or decision. The dome was the choice of the man who paid for the renovation. That is all."

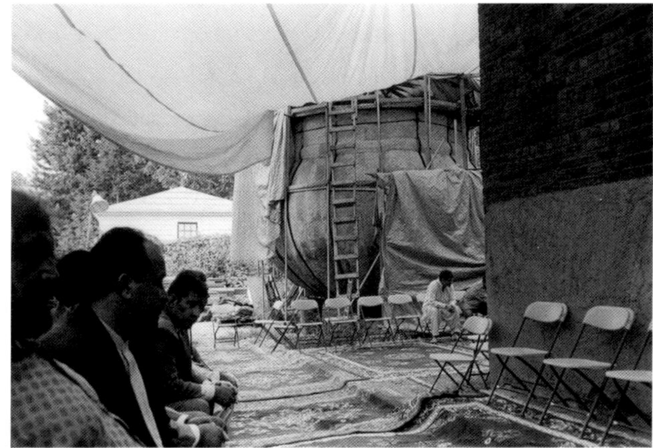

Masjid Hazrat-i-abu Bakr, Queens. New Dome under construction

A few weeks later, on one of a number of subsequent visits to Masjid Al-Abidin, a member of the Shura spoke to me after prayer and said, in passing, "We were talking about your question. The dome, if it has to mean anything, perhaps it could mean the Dome of the Rock."

Like the Kaaba, the Dome of the Rock and the Mosque of the Prophet in Medina are buildings that belong to, and have meaning for, all Muslims. They appear in posters that adorn nearly every mosque in New York. They are also the subject of the only floats in the Muslim World Day Parade; evocations of a community which must be represented, as Susan Slymovics has observed, through spaces and ideas rather than people and narratives.[33] There is no doubt for the congregants of Masjid Al-Abidin that the association of their domes with these buildings was an afterthought; perhaps even a response to my question. But their response was also part of a willingness to enter into the discourse which sees architecture as possibly reflecting a collective identity, and, most importantly, part of a repossession and reinvention of their domes.

I wonder if what we are seeing is the emergence of a series of new meanings for domes in New York, meanings that are both layered and dynamic. The dome, emerging from ethnic traditions or from the Euro-American imagination, is slowly being recoded in certain New York communities, through reference to monuments like the Dome of the Rock that have meaning for all Muslims. Perhaps in the 1990s, we witnessed the invention of a tradition meant to accomplish something that was not necessary in the Islamic countries of origin of many of these immigrant communities. The use of the dome in community mosques is not the result of a naïve insertion into a western urban landscape, or an obsequious pandering for the Euro-American gaze, but rather an empowered, creative response to an internal need to develop a language of forms that expresses the shared experience of integrating Islam into American life, of marking out a new kind of identity for a community while it weaves itself into the fold of New York's urban fabric, economically and socially. The dome has come to represent Islam for New York Muslims, whose links, as Americans and Muslims, supercede national identities. "Muslims from different countries," community leader Dawud Assad said over twenty years ago, "are finding that in America they can establish ties around their religion rather than their nationality."[34] "Any new masjid, any community in New York, wants to have a dome," Imam Sherzad of Masjid Hazrat-i-abu Bakr declared; "the dome means Muslims in America."

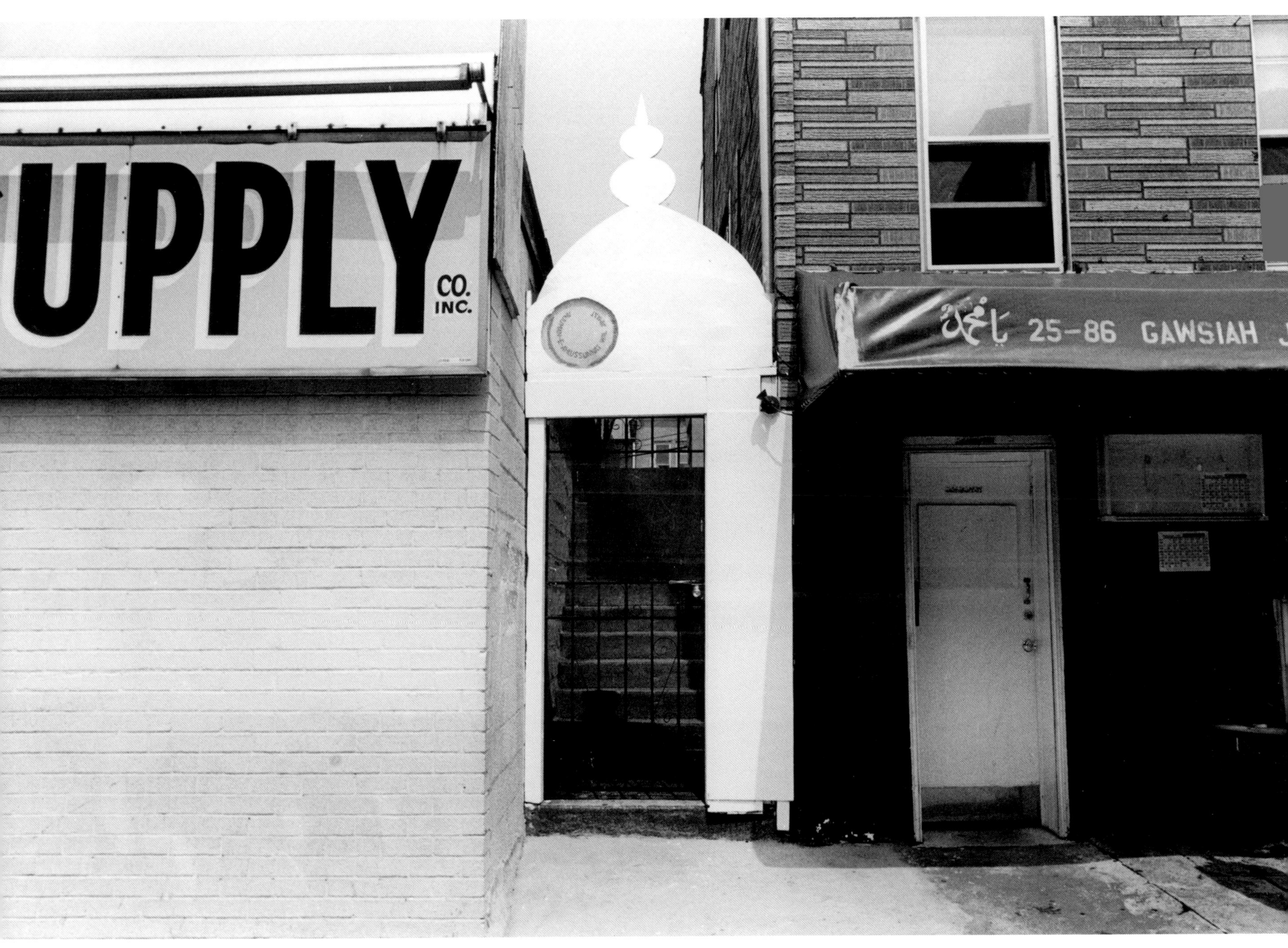

Gawsiah Jame Masjid, Queens

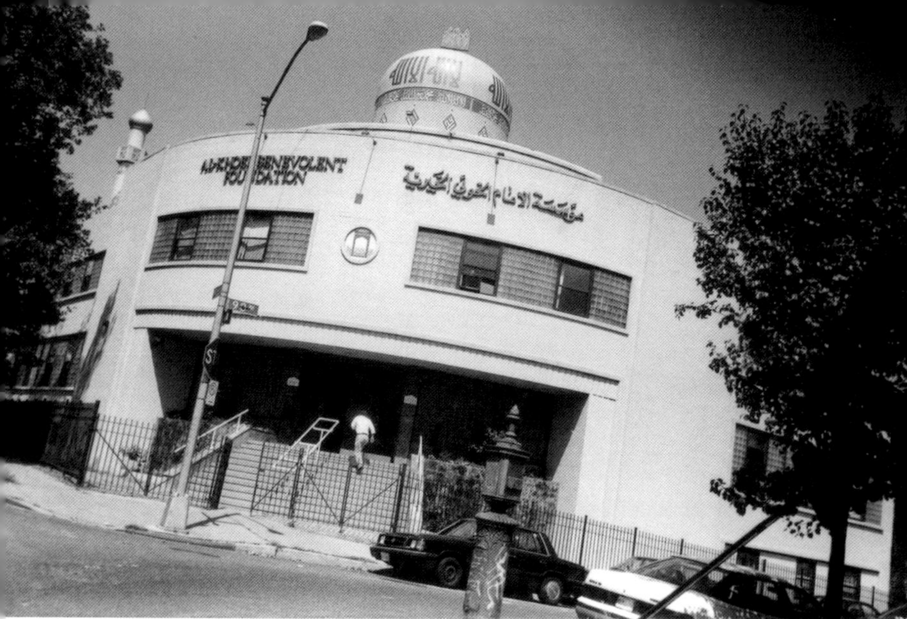

Imam Al-Khoei Islamic Center, Queens

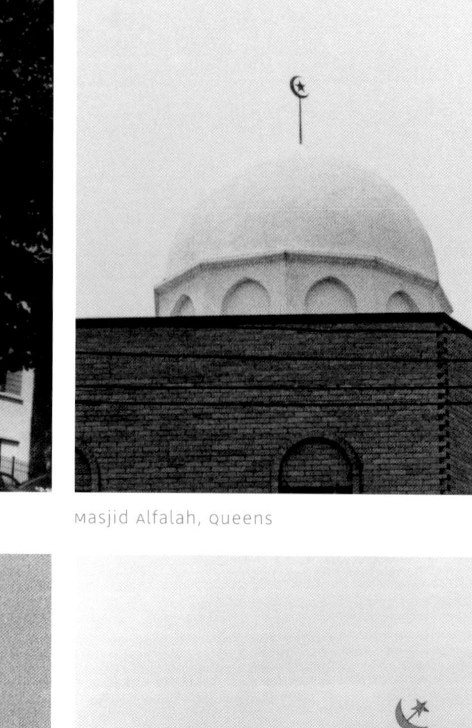
Masjid Alfalah, Queens

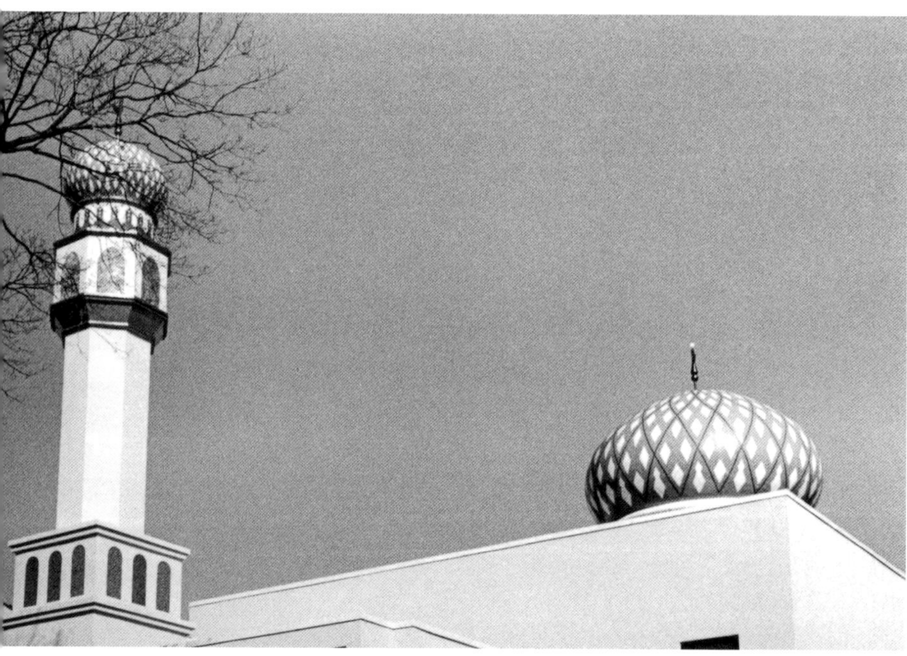
Masjid Hazrat-i-Abu Bakr, Queens

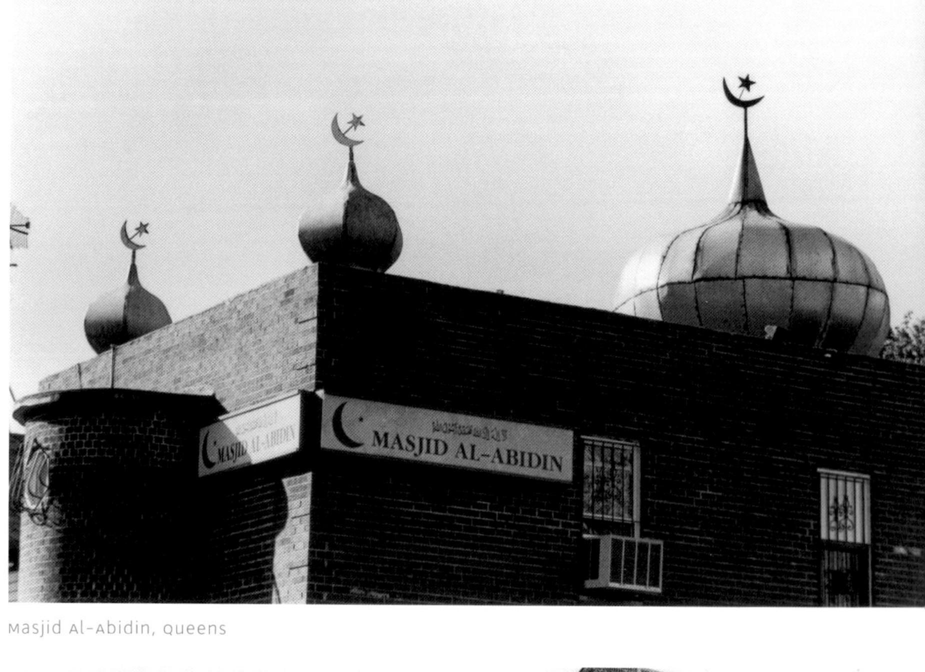

Masjid Al-Abidin, Queens

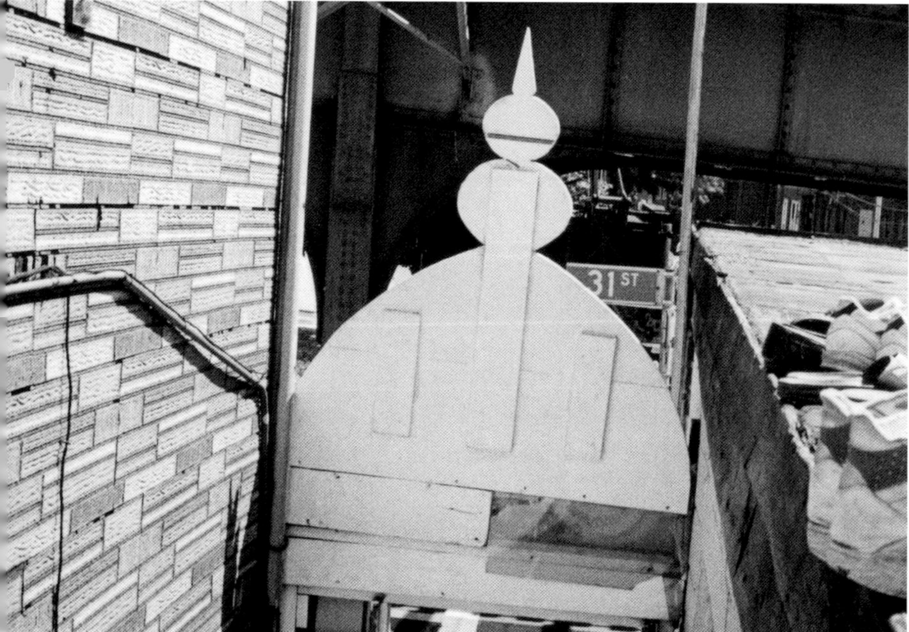

Gawsiah Jame Masjid, Queens

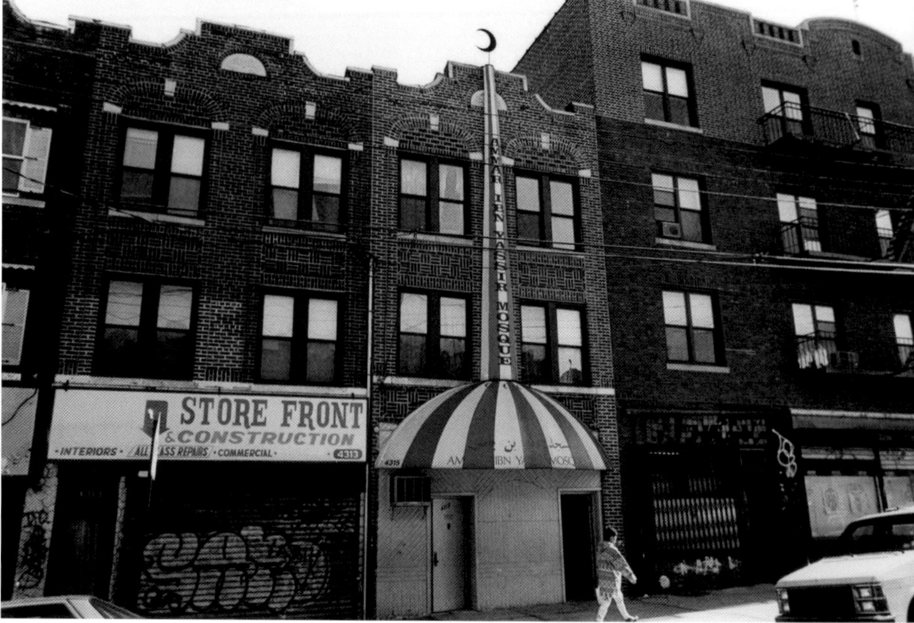

Ammar Ibn Yassir Mosque, Brooklyn

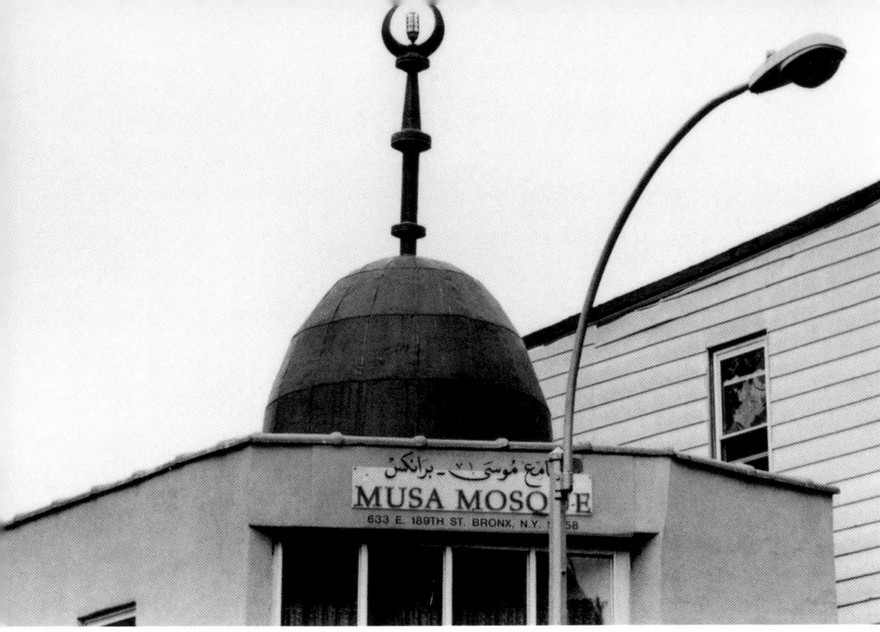

Musa Mosque, Bronx

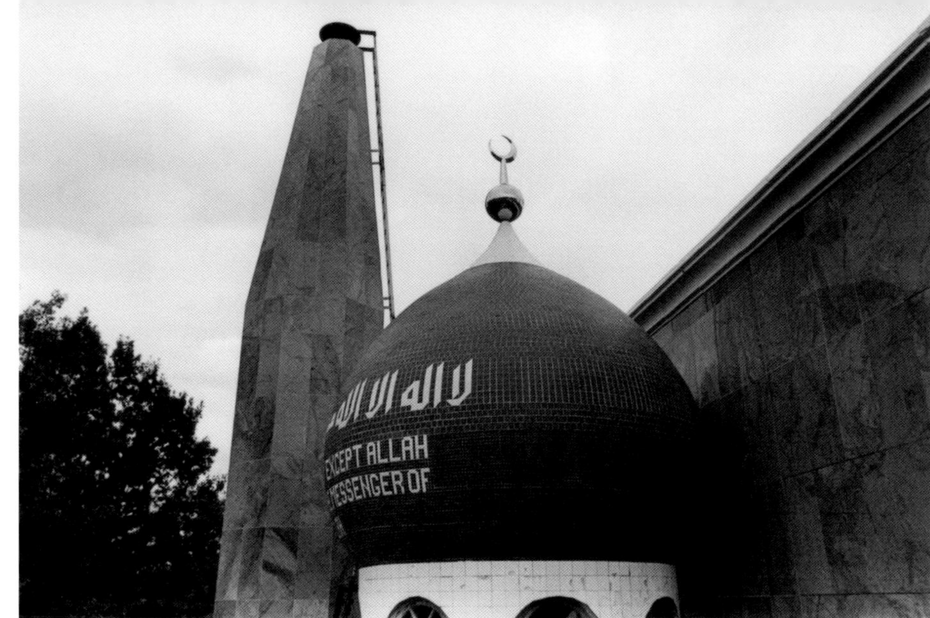

Muslim Center of New York, Queens

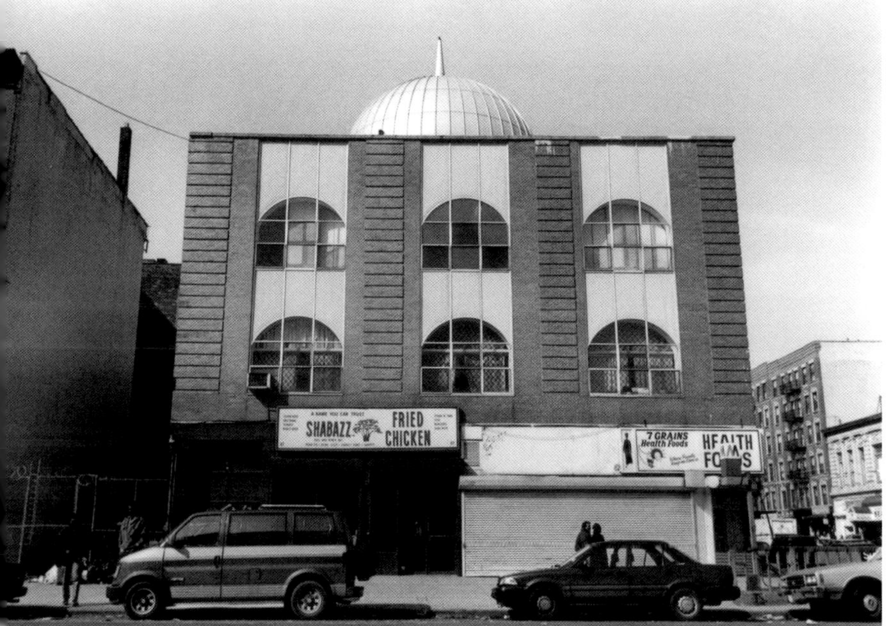

Masjid Malcolm Shabazz, Manhattan

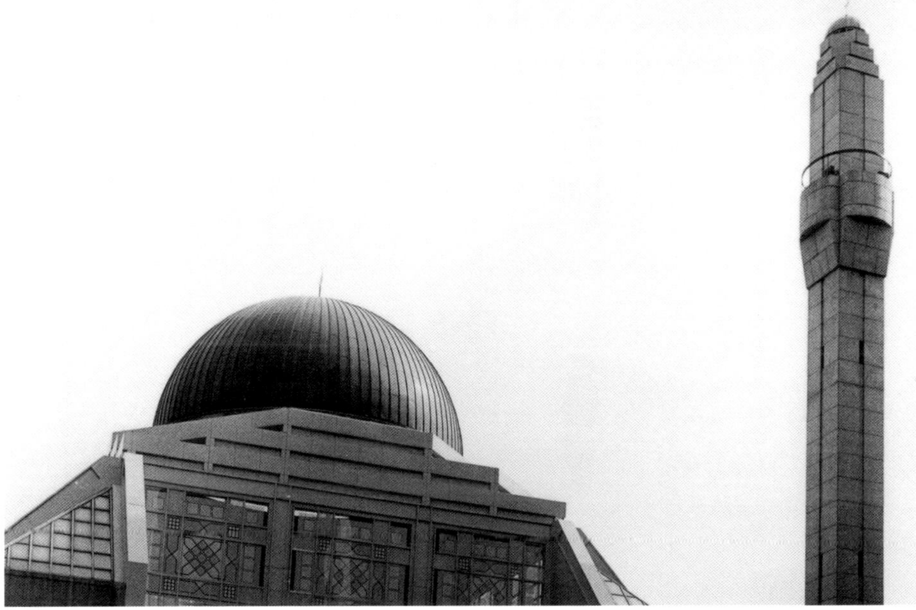

Islamic Cultural Center, Manhattan

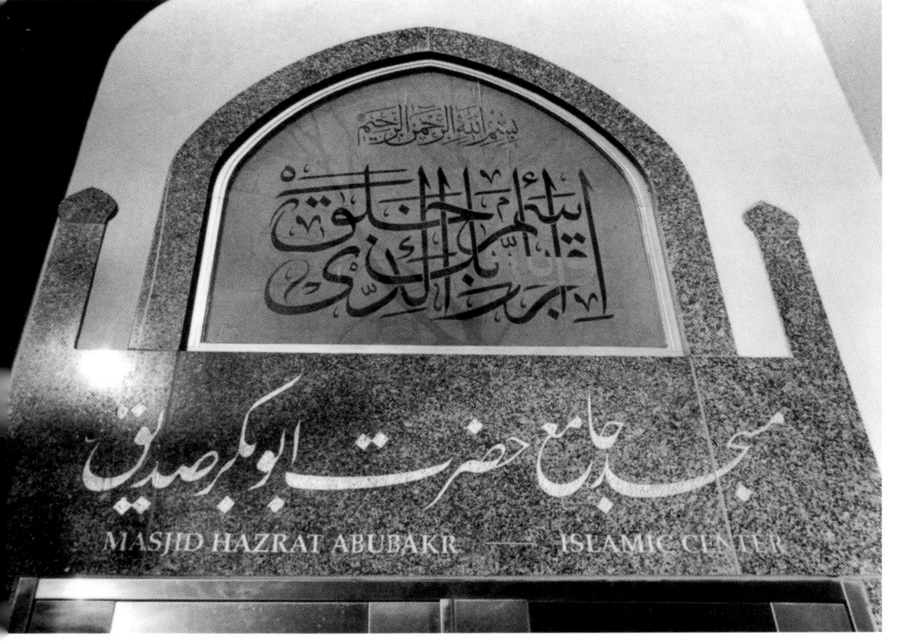

Masjid Hazrat-i-Abu Bakr, Queens

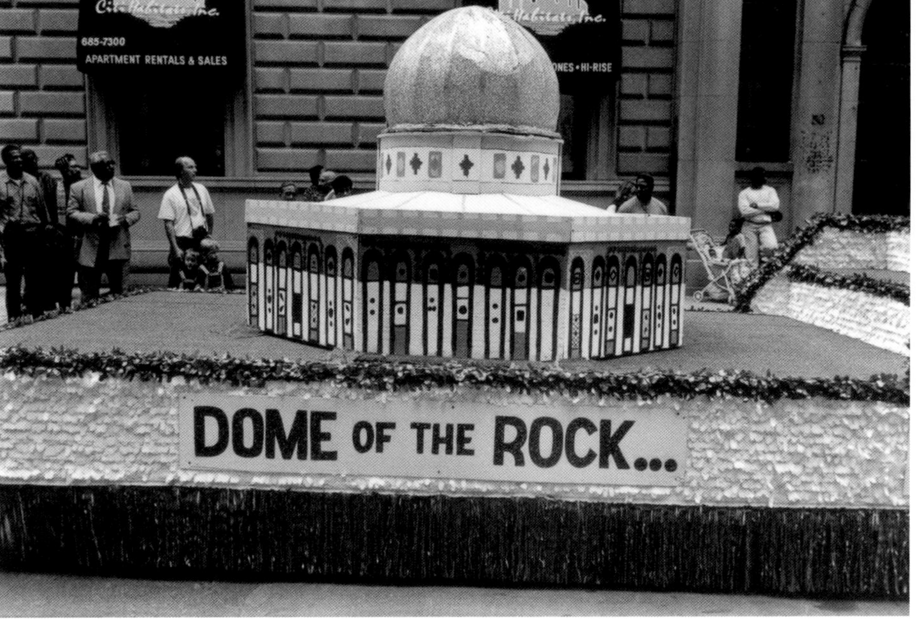

Muslim Day Parade, Manhattan

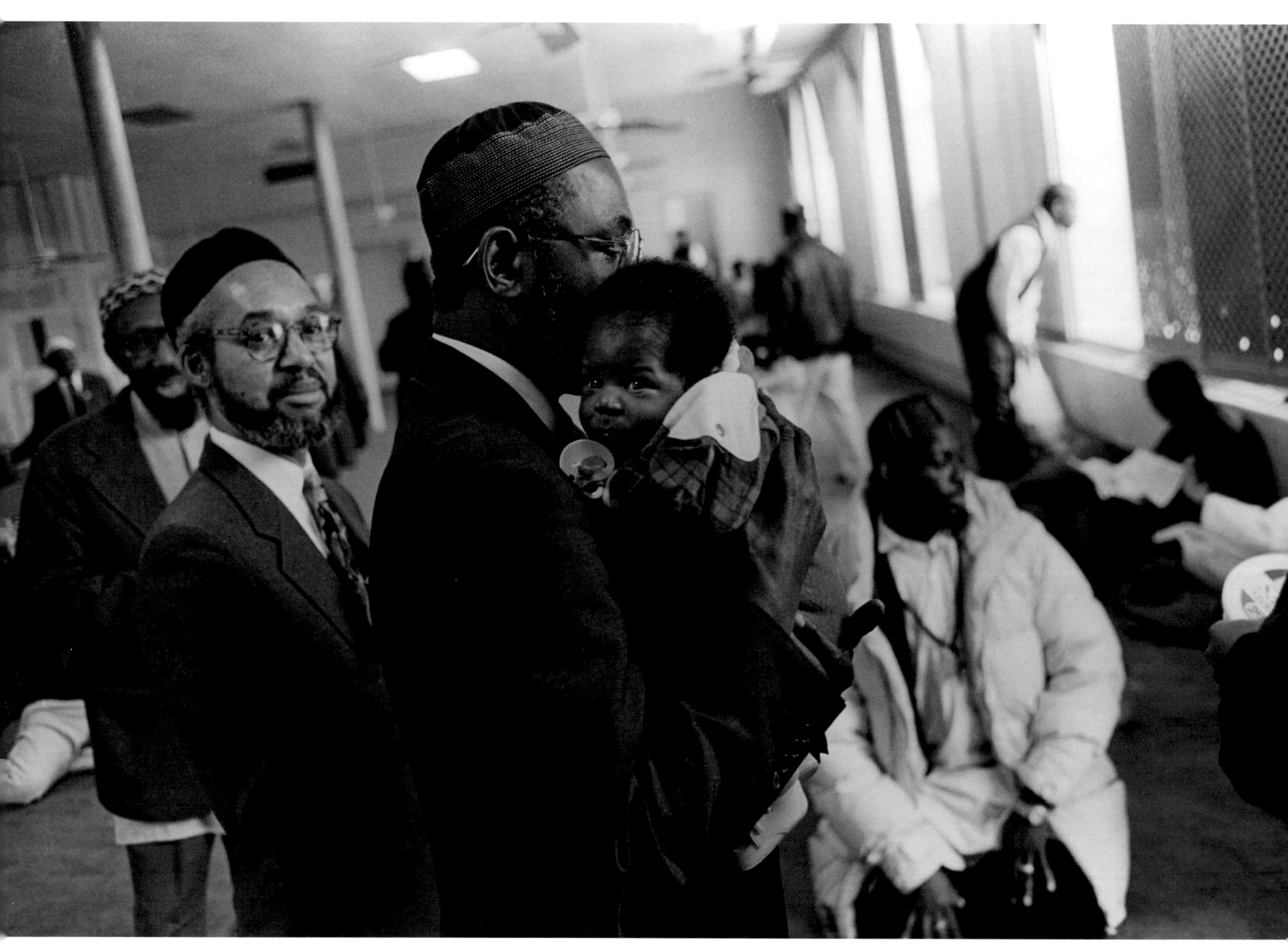

Masjid Malcolm Shabazz, Manhattan

ANOTHER DOME

"sometimes a real down-and-out type will come down Lenox Avenue, dragging his feet, his shoulders hunched; maybe he's got a bottle in a paper bag...but then he'll catch sight of our mosque, and he'll remember how much pride the Muslims have in this neighborhood, and you'll see him straighten right up; for a block or two he'll walk tall as he passes the Masjid." [Assistant Imam Kareem Shakur, Masjid Malcolm Shabazz]

Divergent histories and experiences create converging interpretations, so that the dome itself enters New York's skyline from a variety of experiences. One of New York's earliest and most distinctive mosque profiles is the dome of Masjid Malcolm Shabazz, on the corner of Lenox Avenue and 116th Street in Manhattan.

This traditional Sunni Muslim mosque, with an international community, is a particular point of pride for the Sunni Muslims of Harlem. Masjid Malcolm Shabazz occupies the former site of Lenox Casino. The casino had been reused, until 1965, as Muhammed's Temple of Islam, a center of worship for adherents of the Nation of Islam. Destroyed after the death of Malcolm X, it was rebuilt in its present form under the direction of the architect Sabbath Brown, and continued to serve as a temple. Its present history began in 1975, under the leadership of Warith Deen Muhammed, when the congregation converted to Sunni Islam, and so became part of New York's orthodox Islamic community.

Masjid Malcolm Shabazz is the center of a lively Ummah which supports a private parochial school, the Sister Clara Muhammed School, as well as a number of community and social services that serve families, children, the sick, and the elderly of the neighborhood. Leaders of the mosque, among whom is its principal Imam, Izak El Pasha, have also been instrumental in developing urban renewal initiatives in the neighborhood, spurring the construction of public housing and housing for the elderly which, it is hoped, will contribute to the economic revitalization of the area.

The mosque occupies a three-story corner building constructed in brick and faced with panels that frame two floors of large, arched windows. Its plump, carnivalesque onion-shaped dome occupies the roof with a certain amount of authority, despite exhibiting a character and materials that are anomalous in the neighborhood. It is in fact the incongruence of the dome and arches that give them a kind of prominence: they are potent reminders of the presence of Muslims in the neighborhood, of Islam as a divergence from the hopeless norm, of a rectilinear street wall until recently pocked with the cavernous windows of abandoned housing stock. There is a strong feeling in the community that the presence of the distinctive mosque building in a torn and wounded urban context is part of the mosque's healing role.

For community members, this broad dome interrupts the conventional but bruised profile of the blocks that stretch from Lenox Avenue, and suggests hope in a neighborhood that has in the past

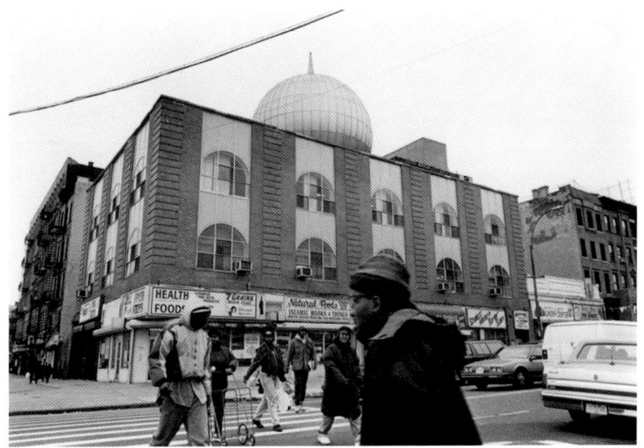

Masjid Malcolm Shabazz, Manhattan

been rent with the architectural signs of urban despair: empty lots and abandoned and deteriorating buildings. Purposeful architectural anomaly becomes a declaration of the congregation's capacity to transform and heal the very urban fabric of its surroundings.

As much as this might be the case, Imam Karem indicated a changing attitude towards the mosque's dome. He explains that it "reflected what people used to think Islam was about. (Domes) have more to do with an old-fashioned American interpretation of what Islamic architecture looked like, or with Ottoman architecture, than with Islam in general."

"We have lately become interested in an architectural style that reflects the African heritage of many in our community," Imam Izak El Pasha explains, as he reveals plans for housing the mosque he hopes to help develop in the neighborhood. "This dome has served us well, but we are thinking that in our next mosque we might turn to West-African Islamic architectural style," Imam Kareem adds. He showed us an architect's drawing of a pavilion-like structure with multiple supports...and no dome.

The process of creating an American Muslim identity, one that is not polarized, is similar at Masjid Malcolm Shabazz and at the mosques built for immigrant communities. It is only that the use of architecture—meanings given to architectural forms like the dome—are simply different in divergent times and places. At Masjid Malcolm Shabazz, an American Orientalist dome was exploited as a subverted image of marginality, just as early African American Muslims subverted the conventional image of black inferiority until divergence became a point of pride. In time, the community is reaching beyond this reductive image of otherness quite specifically for architectural forms that can articulate a more particular—but less polarized—identity. At Masjid Al-Abidin, in the same city, a dome initially drawn by a patron, perhaps as part of traditional forms from a Guyanese homeland, is also reinvented in time, so that it comes to represent a new common identity for American Muslims.

The cavernous rectilinearity of New York's skyline, only sporadically relenting, imbues its multiplying domes with singularity. But the meanings of these domes, whether traditional allusion, common identity, or Orientalist reduction, can be irrepressibly divergent in the New World marriage of Muslims and New York.

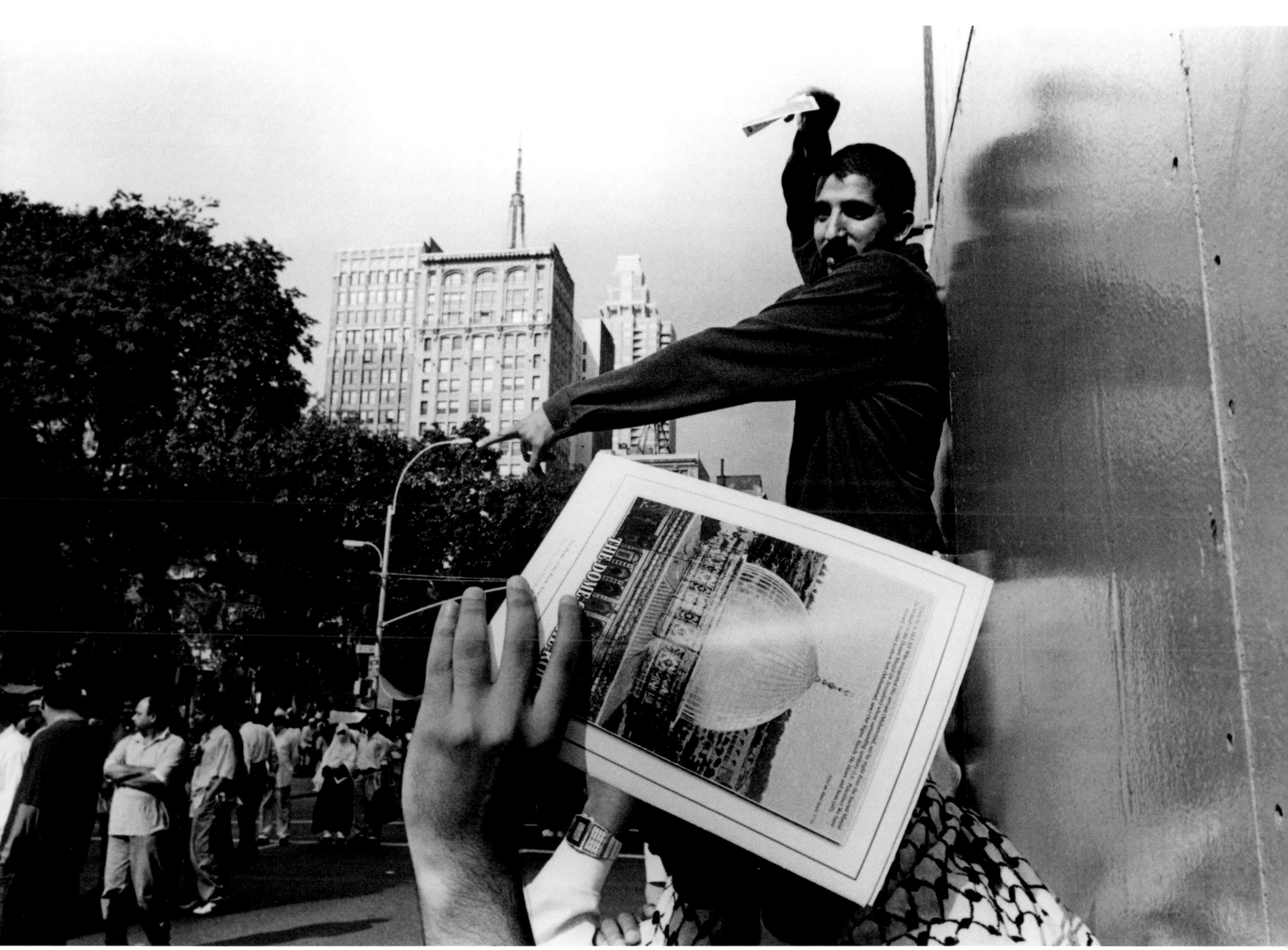

Muslim Day Parade, Manhattan

Ali Pasha Mosque, 1994

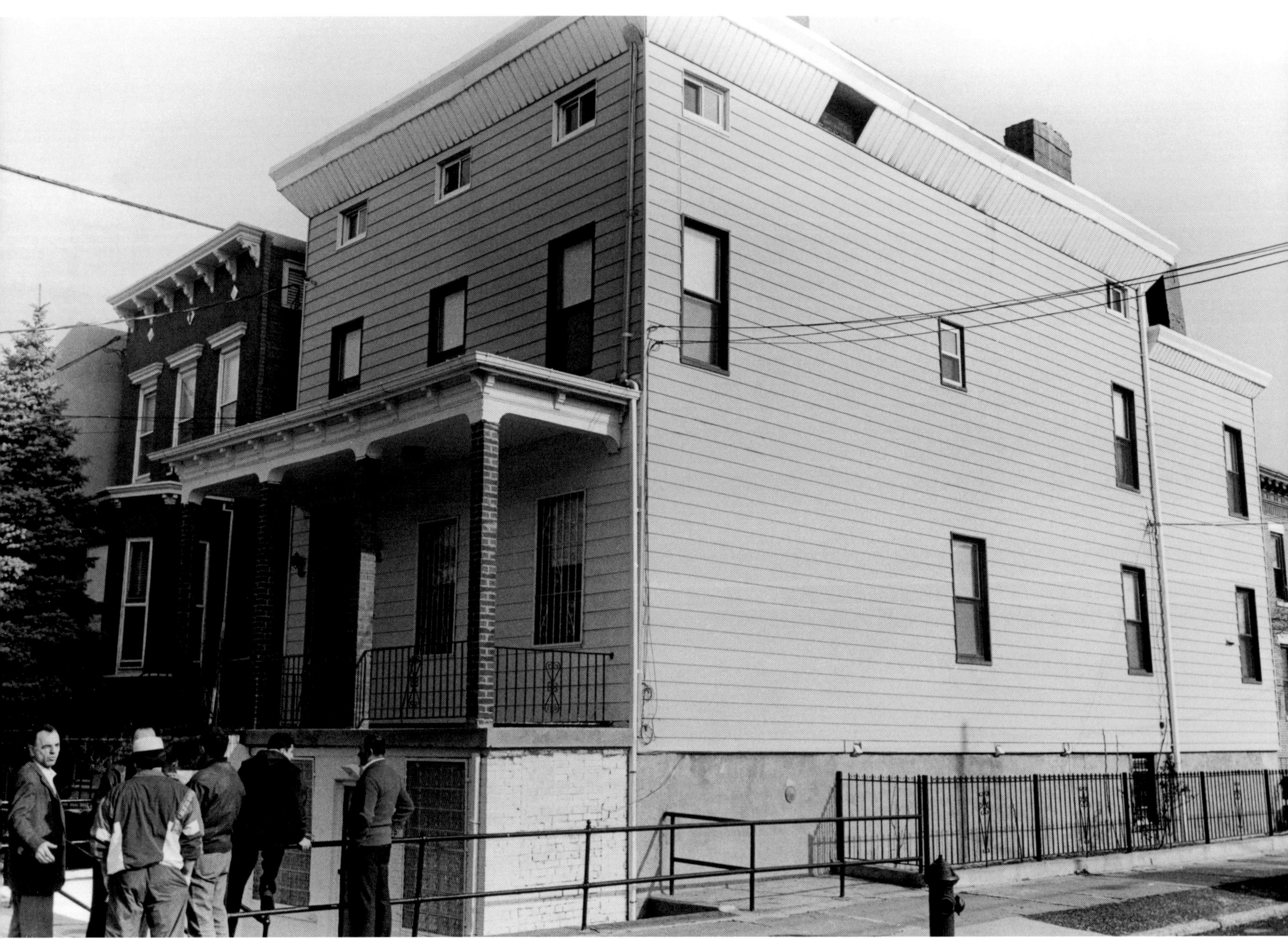

Ali Pasha Mosque, Queens

Ali Pasha Mosque, 2000

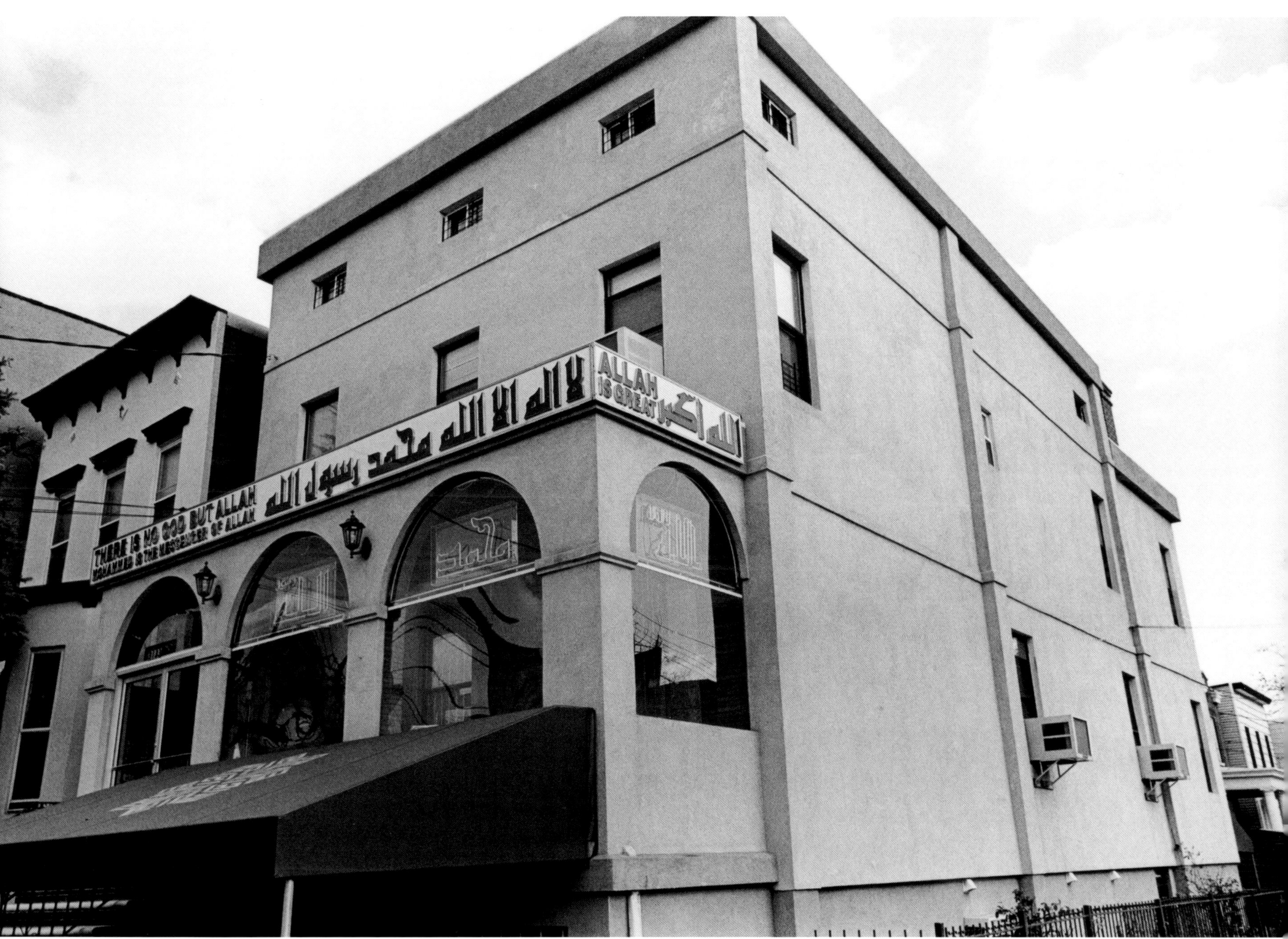

Ali Pasha Mosque, Queens

Masjid Hazrat-i-abu Bakr, 1995

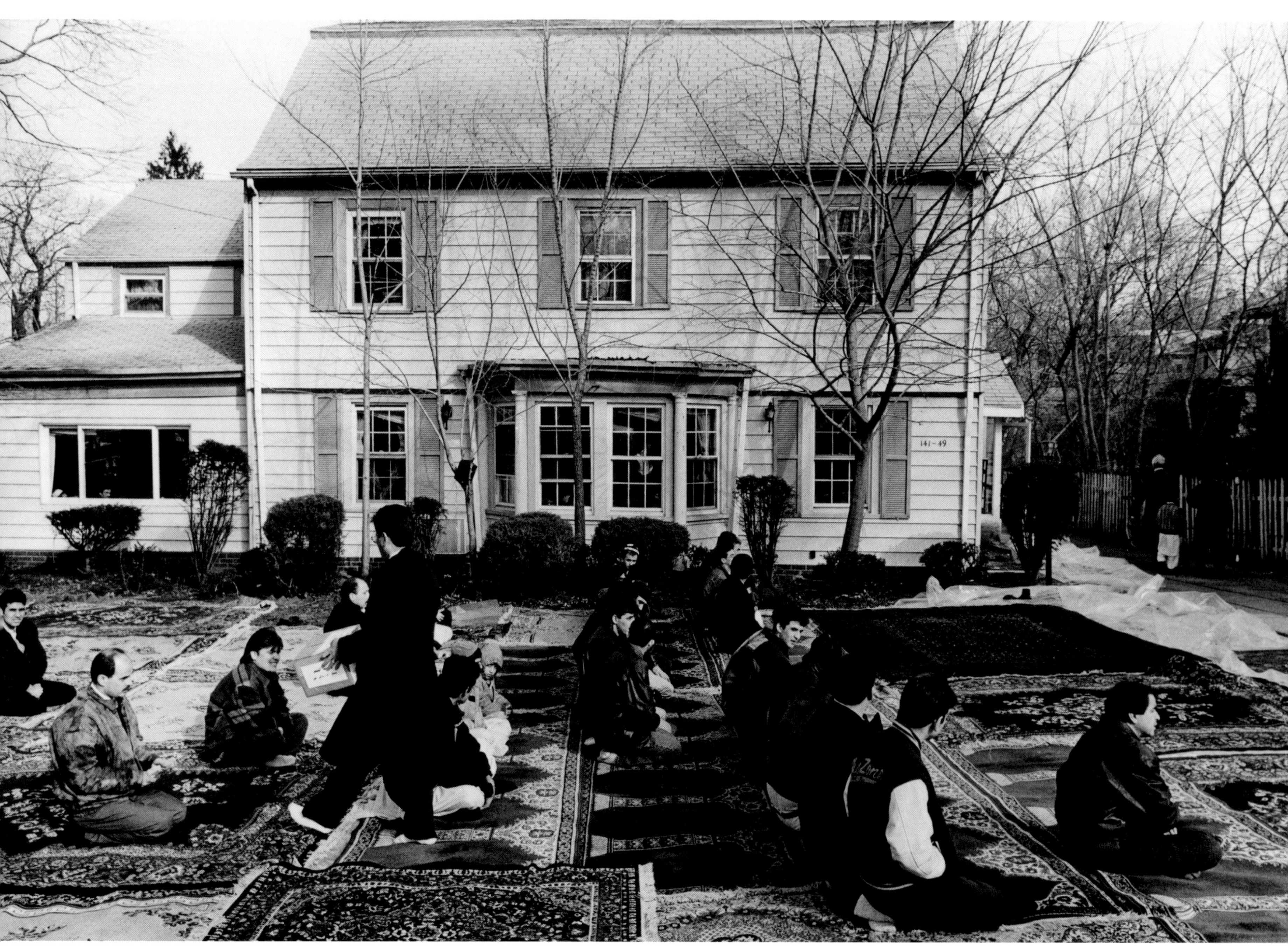

Masjid Hazrat-i-abu Bakr, Queens

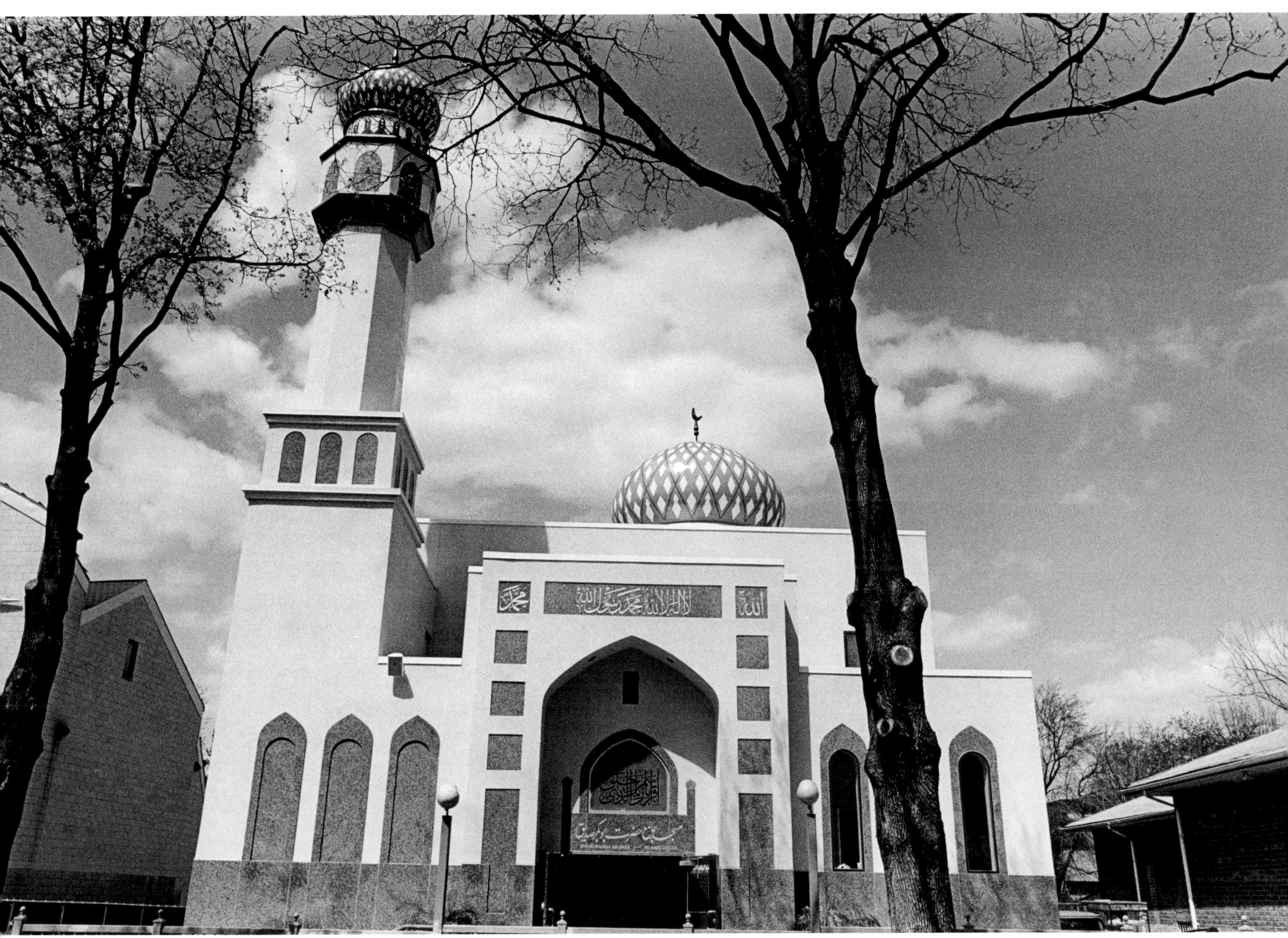

Masjid Hazrat-i-abu Bakr, Queens

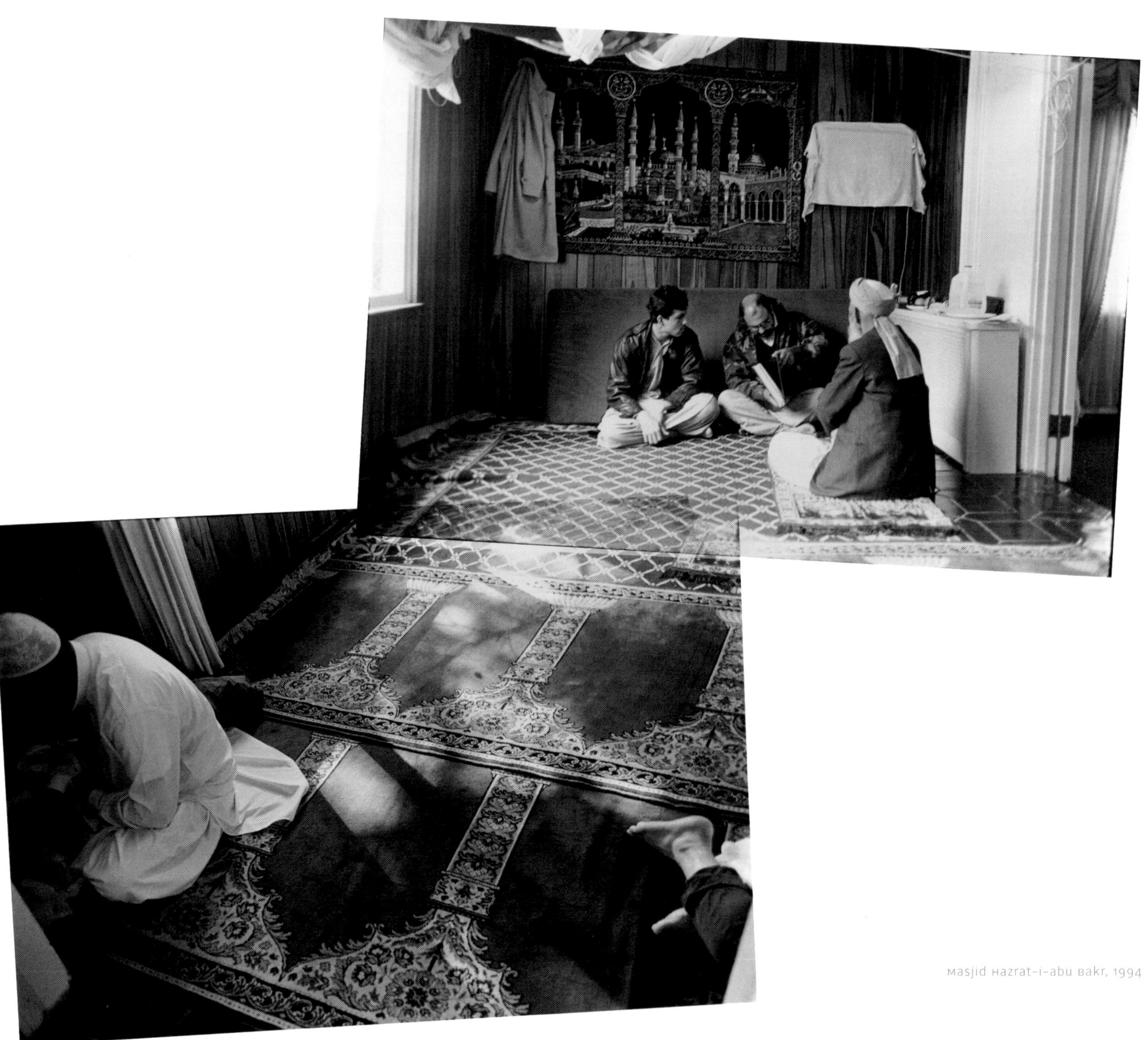

Masjid Hazrat-i-abu Bakr, 1994

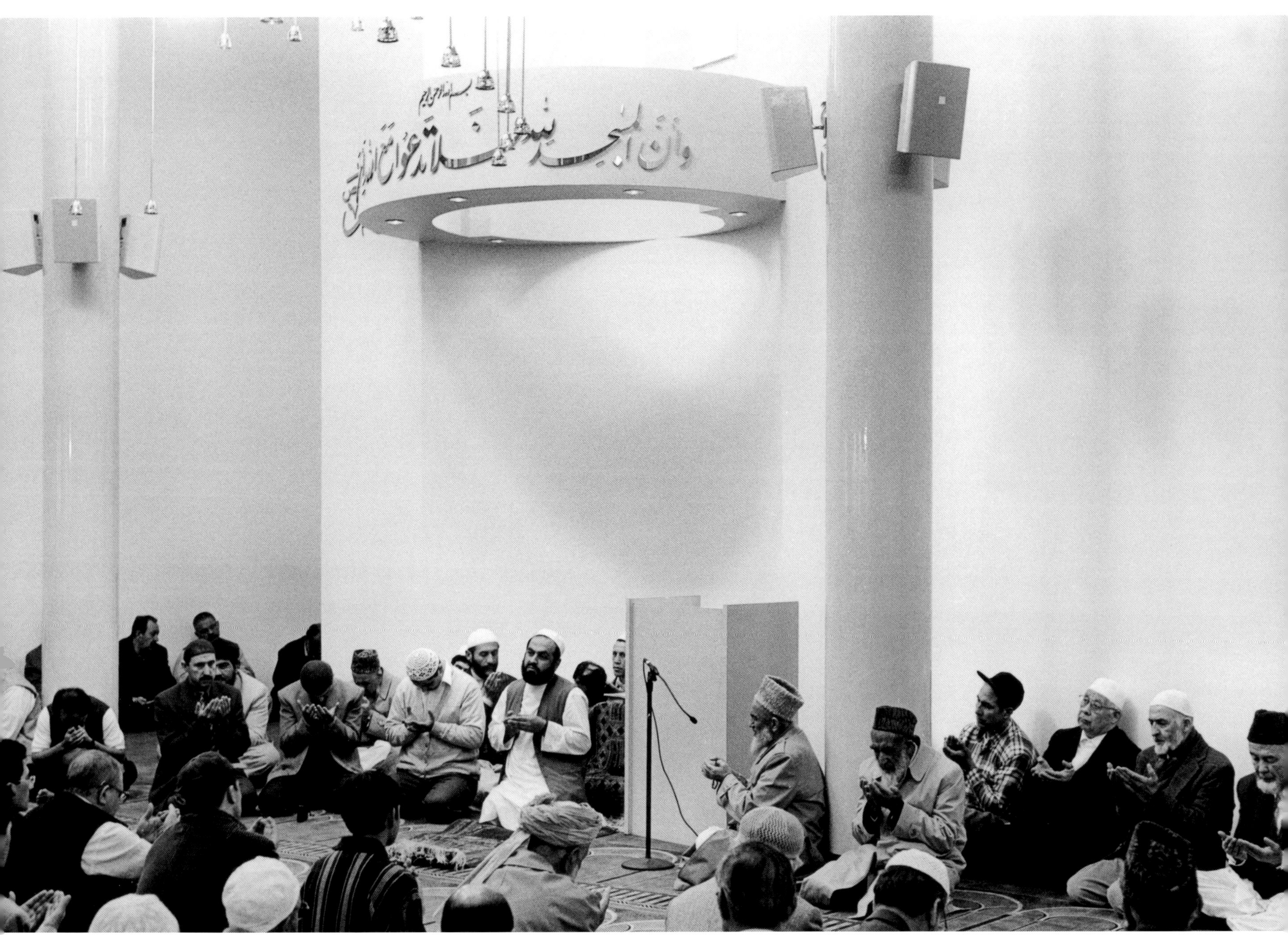

Masjid Hazrat-i-abu Bakr, 2000

Madina Masjid, 1994

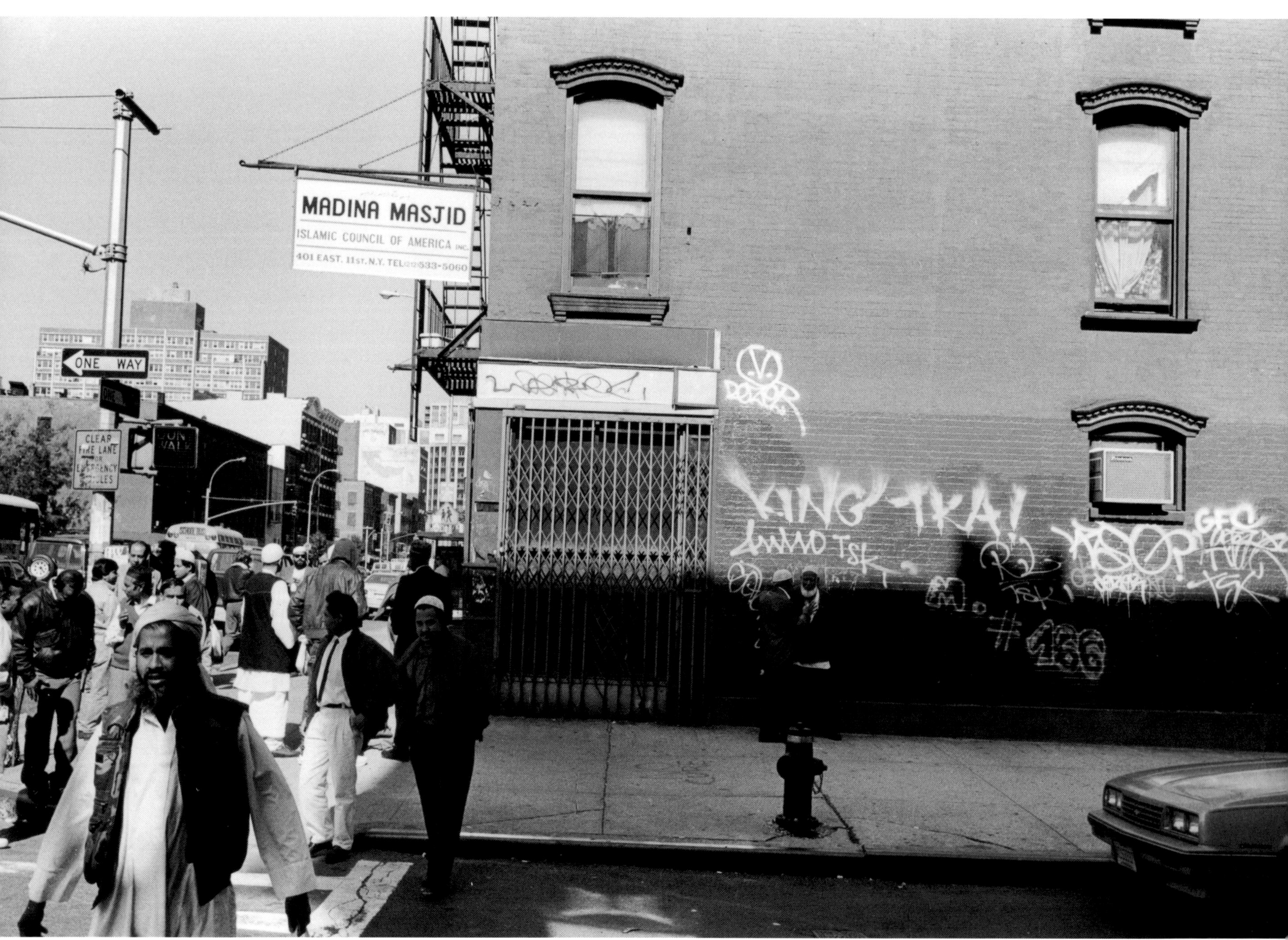

Madina Masjid, Manhattan

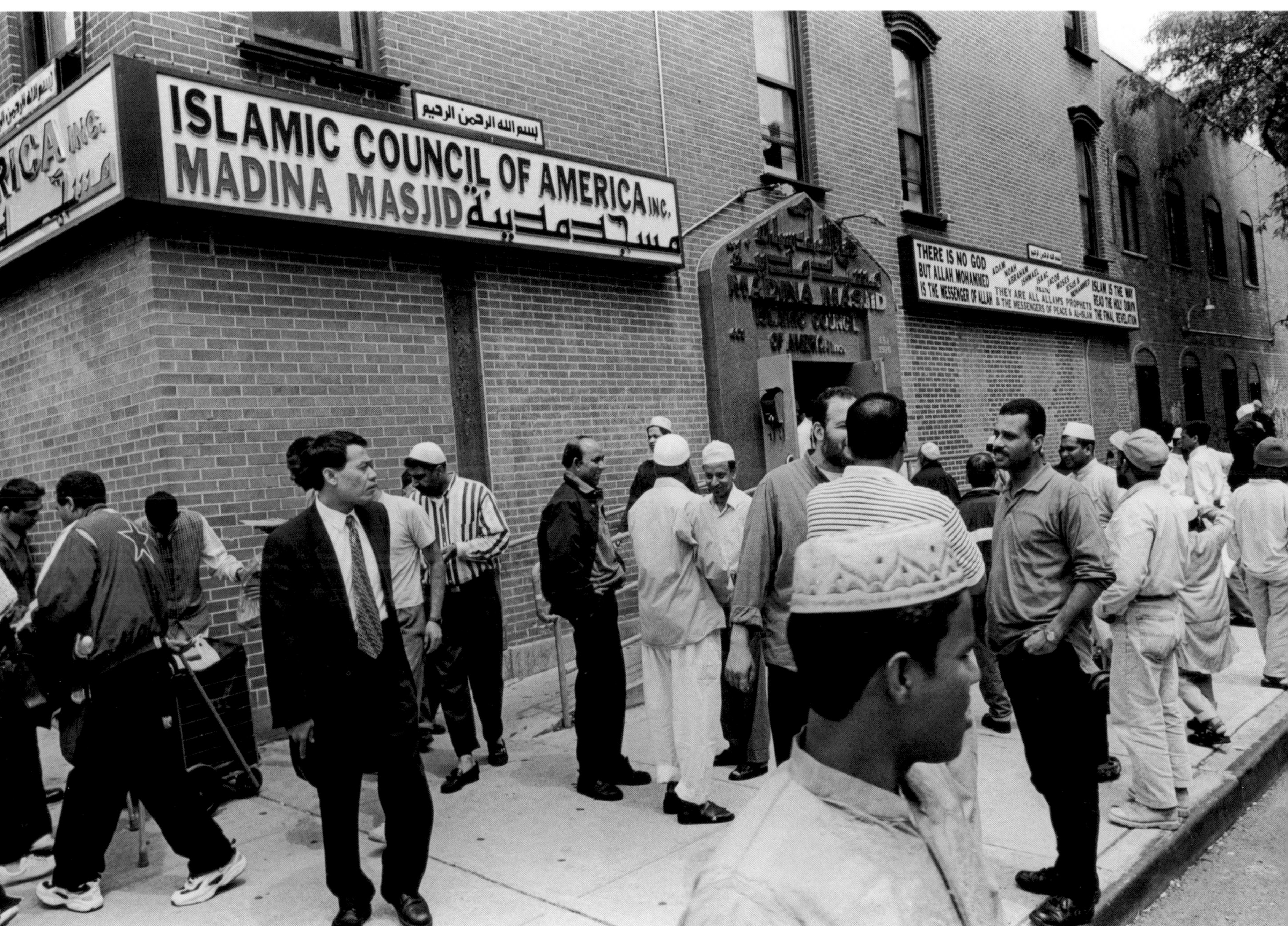

Madina Masjid, Manhattan

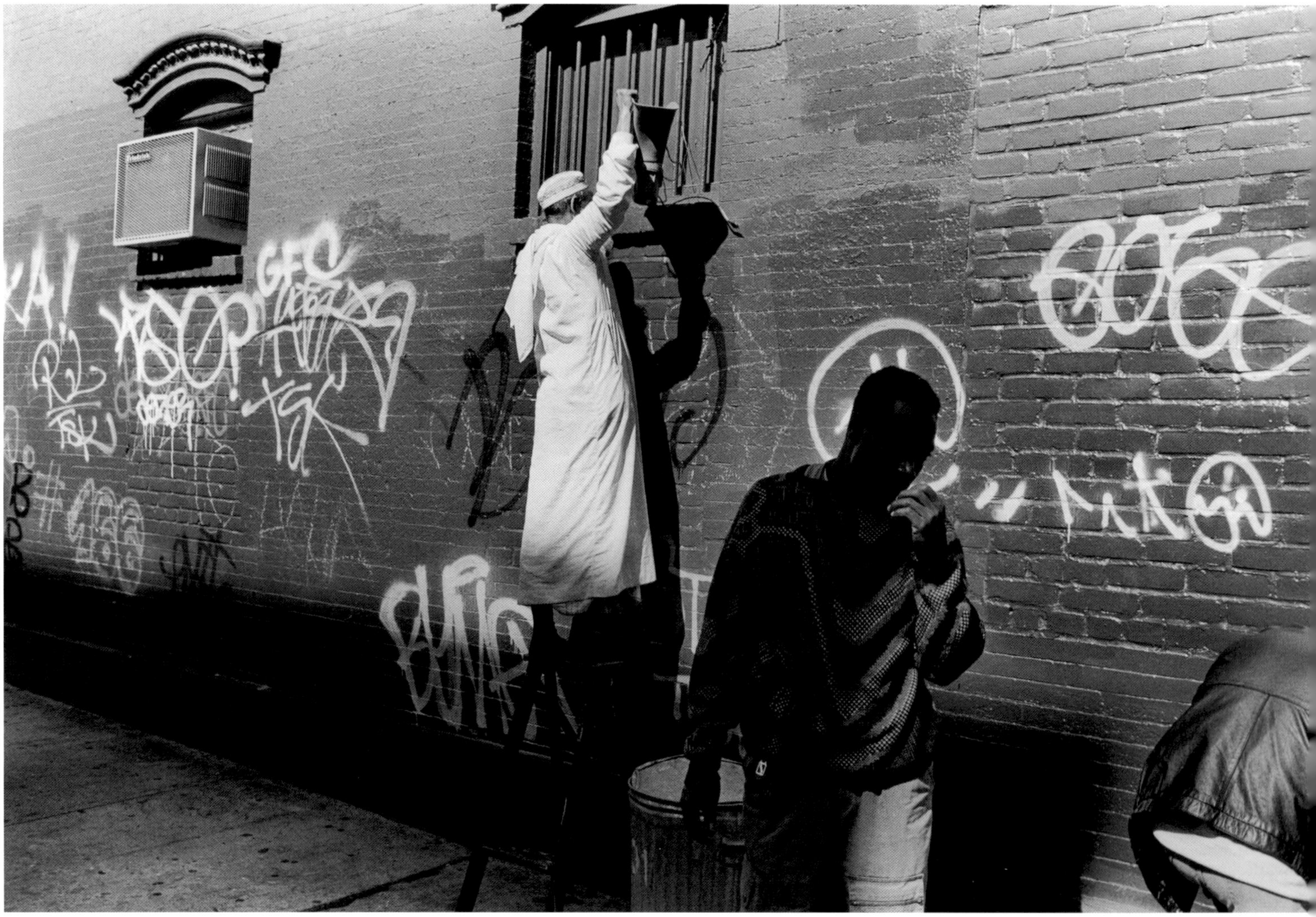

Madina Masjid, 1994

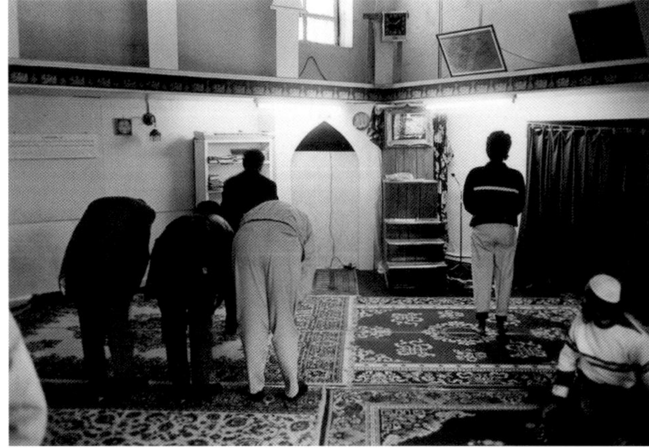

Madina Masjid, 1994

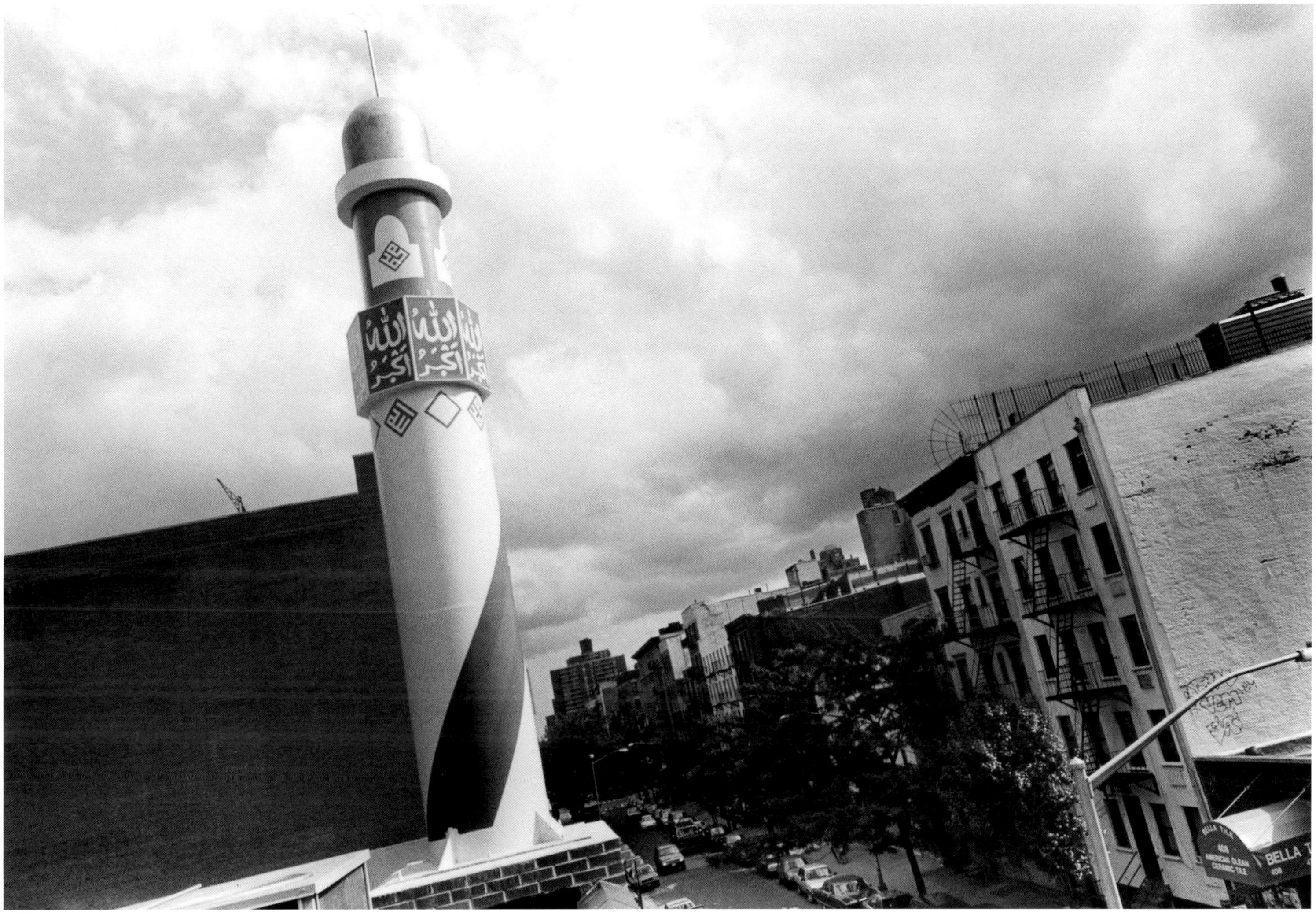

Madina Masjid, 1998

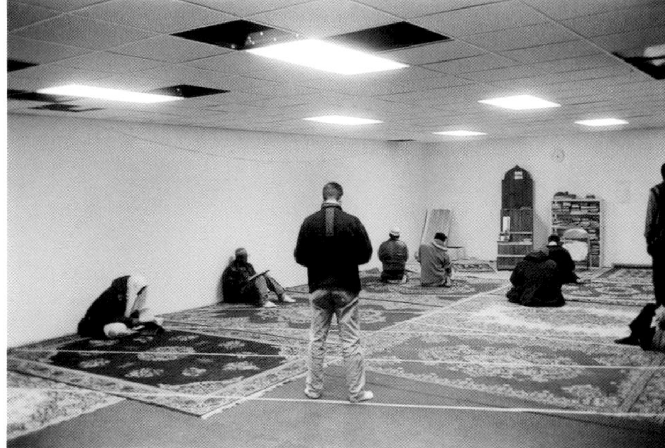

Madina Masjid, 1998

Masjid Al-Abidin, Queens

ISLAMIC NEW YORK

"Liberation as an intellectual mission has shifted from the settled, established, and domestic dynamics of culture to its unhoused, decentered, and exilic energies...between domains, between homes, and between languages." [Edward Said, Culture and Imperialism][35]

"When we first acquired the building, we wanted the exterior to remain unimposing. We did not want to become a target. But now we are like old tenants in the neighborhood. People trust us, so now I believe it is time to start thinking about a sign for the mosque." [Dr. Abdul Rehman, Masjid Al Noor, Staten Island, 1996]

Islam has never been other to New York; it has, from the beginning, been part of the city's dynamic, plural life. But in the past decade Muslim communities have begun for the first time to trace their presence visually on the face of the city. The process began tentatively, and was frozen in a kind of breathless quiet immediately following the media reaction to the 1993 World Trade Center bombings. Now, in the first years of a new millennium, we are witnessing the emergence of New York's vibrant Muslim minority as a public collective in the city—a significant shift from the dispersed, quiet integration of the early 90s.

Three developments might be seen as creating catalysts to the emergence of New York's mosques as salient public architectural statements. The first is demographic: the important increase in Muslim immigrants since 1965 and the establishment of stable communities by earlier immigrant groups have developed a significant population density that has integrated and assimilated into established neighborhoods. Such a critical mass creates a secure environment for the tentative architectural gestures we have chronicled here. The second has to do with precedent: exterior forms, in particular arches and domes, were evident in a few mosques before the 1990s, but it is possible that the construction of the Islamic Cultural Center, New York's first monumental mosque and a symbolic presence as well, provided a kind of license (though not a model) for the exterior expressions of identity which are emerging more frequently today. Finally, selective public resistance—including the organized intervention of Muslim organizations—to the destructive media coverage that followed the 1993 World Trade Center bombings gave way, in the course of the 1990s, to positive attempts in the news media to understand the experience of American Muslims. This, in turn, might have provided some communities with a motive and the freedom to emerge as a public visual presence in the city.

Still trembling in the wake of the destruction of the World Trade Center and its 3,000 souls, we are today, as a city, stunned. We cannot yet say how these events will effect the Muslims among us, many of whom lost loved ones in these attacks, nor how they will effect their relations with those New Yorkers who see them as different. In the days following the World Trade Center attacks of 2001, death threats were made to children attending the school of the Islamic Cultural Center in Manhattan, and bias crimes against Muslims were reported in several neighborhoods.

There is nevertheless the sense of a new city emerging from the dark mist of New York's shattered autumn, one whose relationship with its own Muslim minority has been subtly transformed since 1993, when Islam and terrorism were linked so destructively in the popular imagination. In the wake of 9/11, Mayor Rudolph Giuliani repeatedly warned against the reductive coupling of New York's Muslims with those who had attacked the city, and among the most impassioned religious leaders at the city's vast memorial service in Yankee Stadium was Izak El Pasha, Imam of the Malcolm Shabazz Mosque. A surge of public interest in Islam has been charted as non-Muslim New York struggles to separate the rhetoric of terrorists from the religion practiced by its many Muslim neighbors.

There is a sense, in fact, that the integration of Muslims into New York's visible social and cultural matrix will not be undone by the events of September 11th; that these acts, by their violent and inhuman nature, defy the kind of apathetic and passive assumptions of sameness that have led non-Muslim New Yorkers to link all Islam and terrorism in the past. And there is a sense, as well, that the tentative new visibility of New York's Muslims plays a strong role in the creation of a new space: the space in which Muslims become Americans, and America embraces Islam.

The result is an Islam that can no longer be visualized in America through the glass of an opulent palace in Kuwait, through televised videos of the night sky in Iraq, or through the domes of Disney's "Agrabad." The between 600,000 and 800,000 Muslims of New York, whether prosperous or poor, assimilated or insular, are participating actively in the rebuilding of the city's urban fabric. At this moment, we are all part of the collaborative expansion of a vision that continues the creation of our city and of the dynamic transformation of our urban setting into one which takes into account visual identities which are both American and Muslim.

Jerrilynn D. Dodds

The Muslim Day Parade, Manhattan

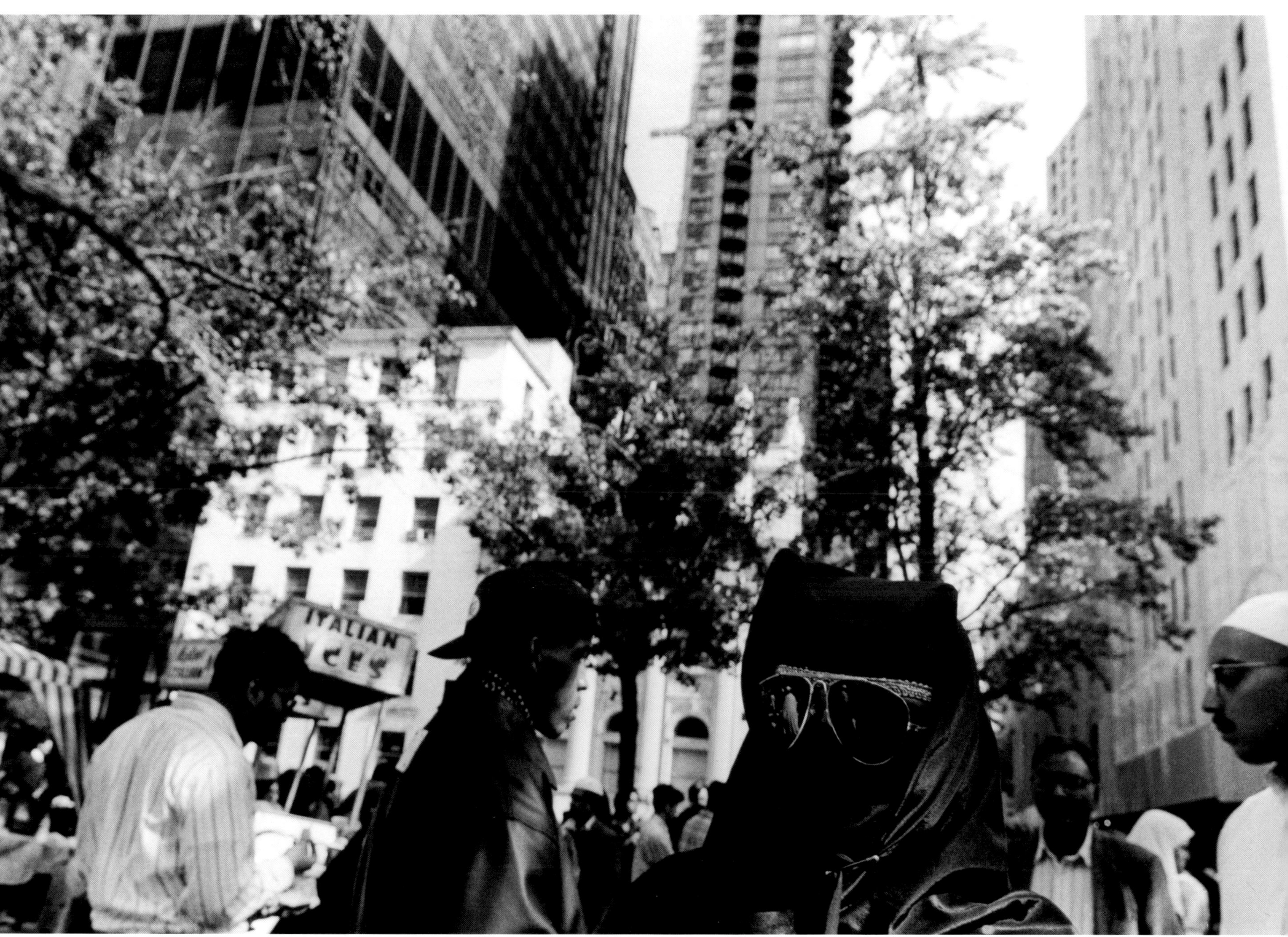

Muslim Day Parade, Manhattan

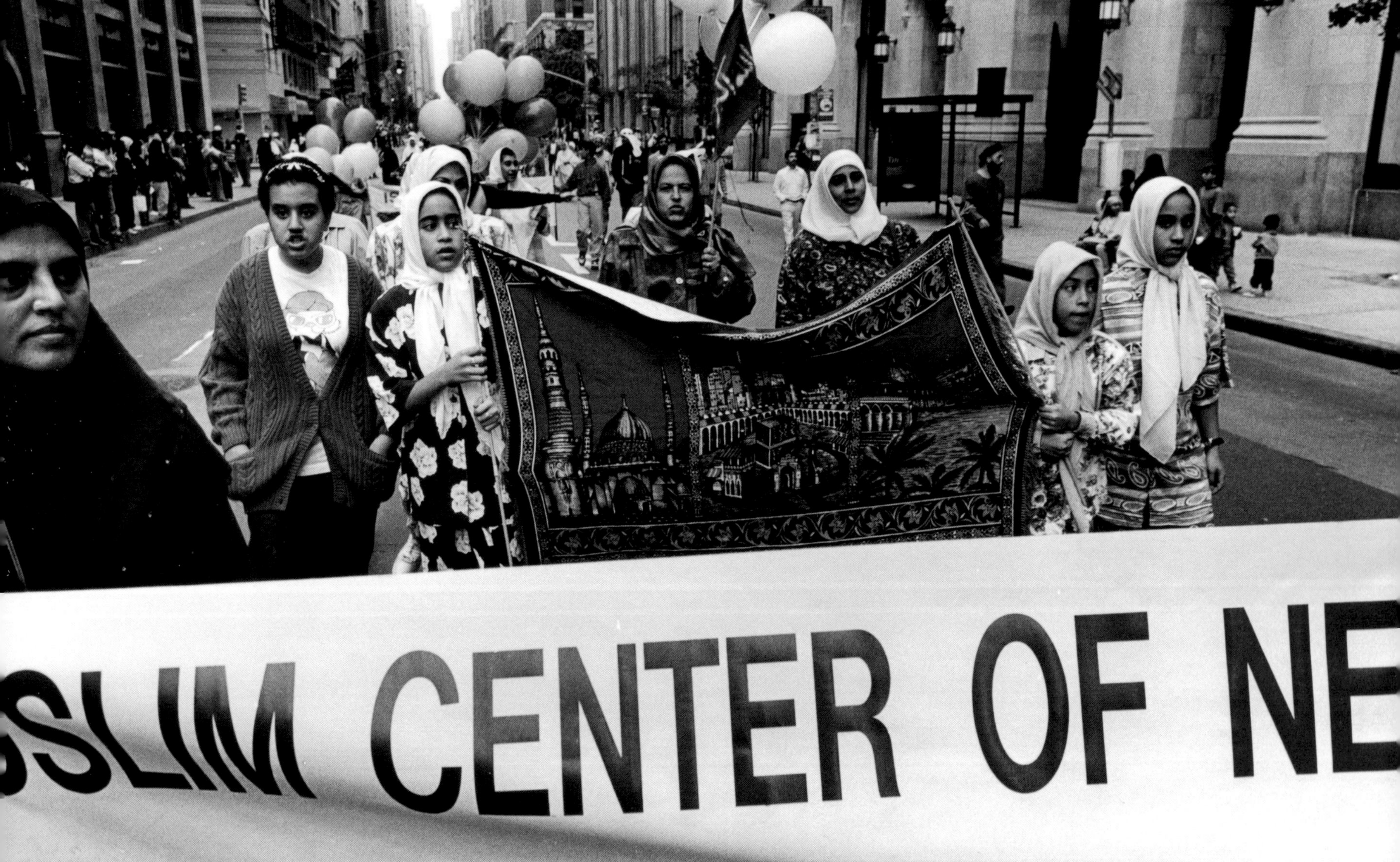

Muslim Day Parade, Manhattan

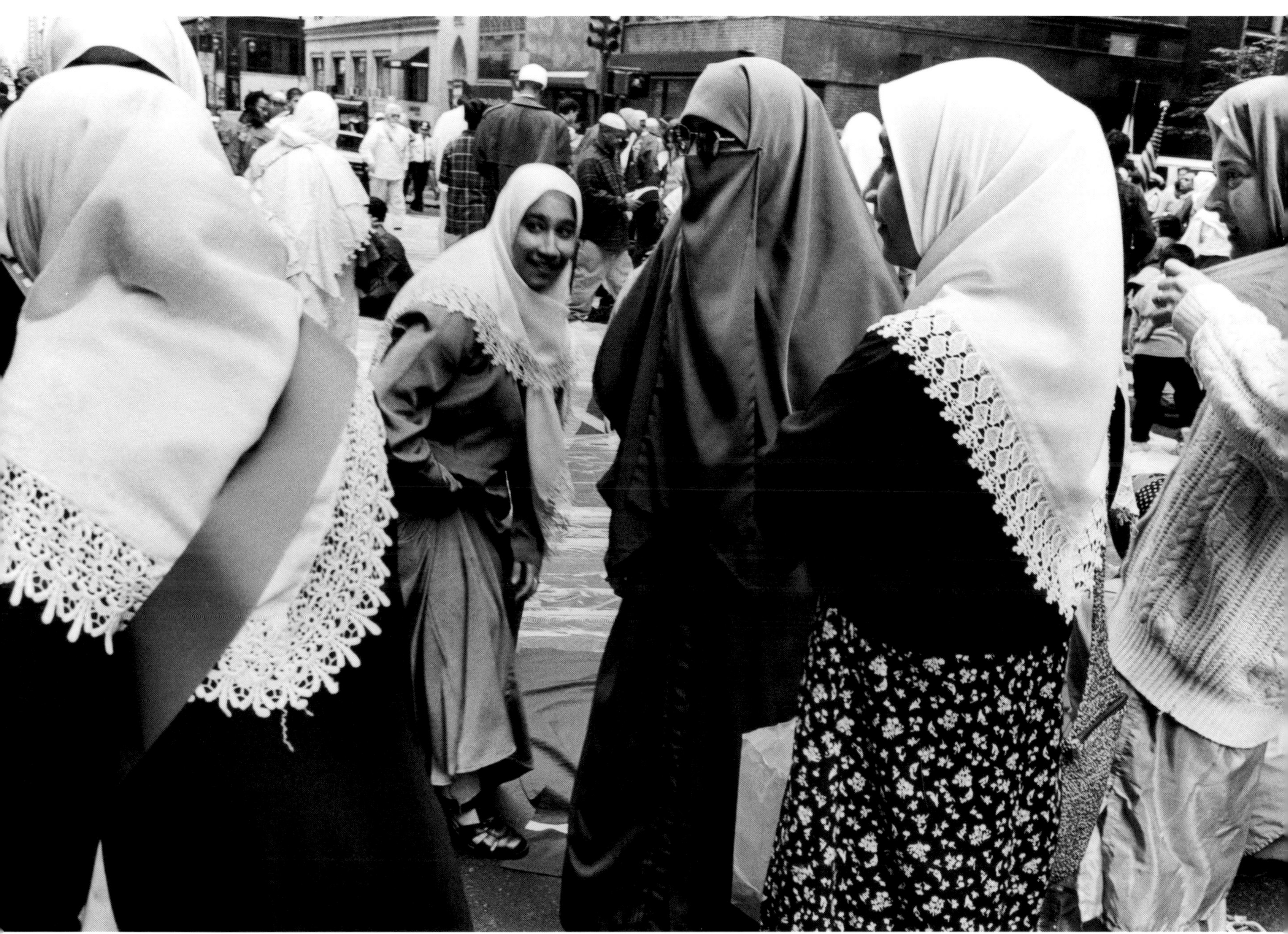

Muslim Day Parade, Manhattan

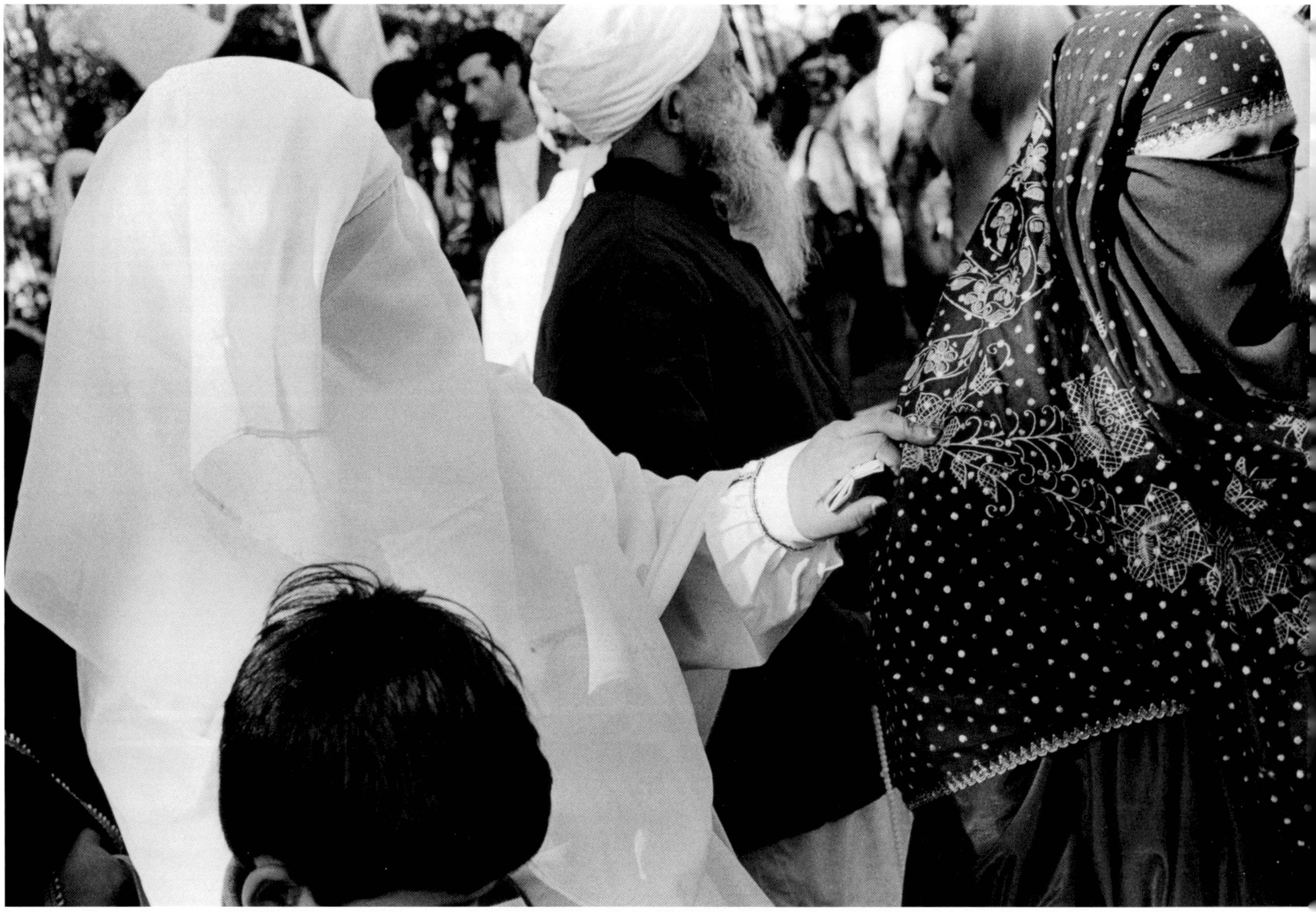

Muslim Day Parade, Manhattan

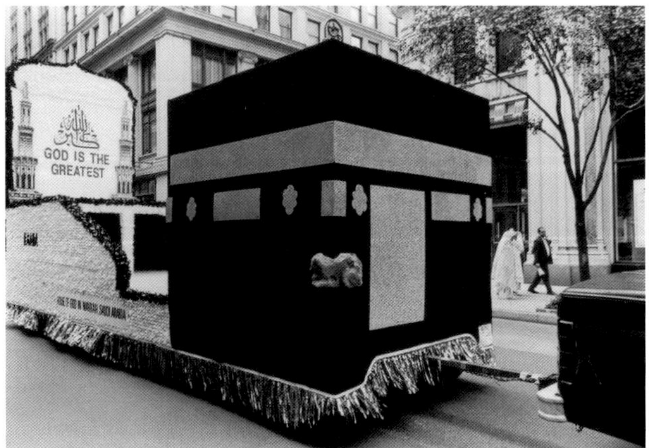

Muslim Day Parade, Manhattan

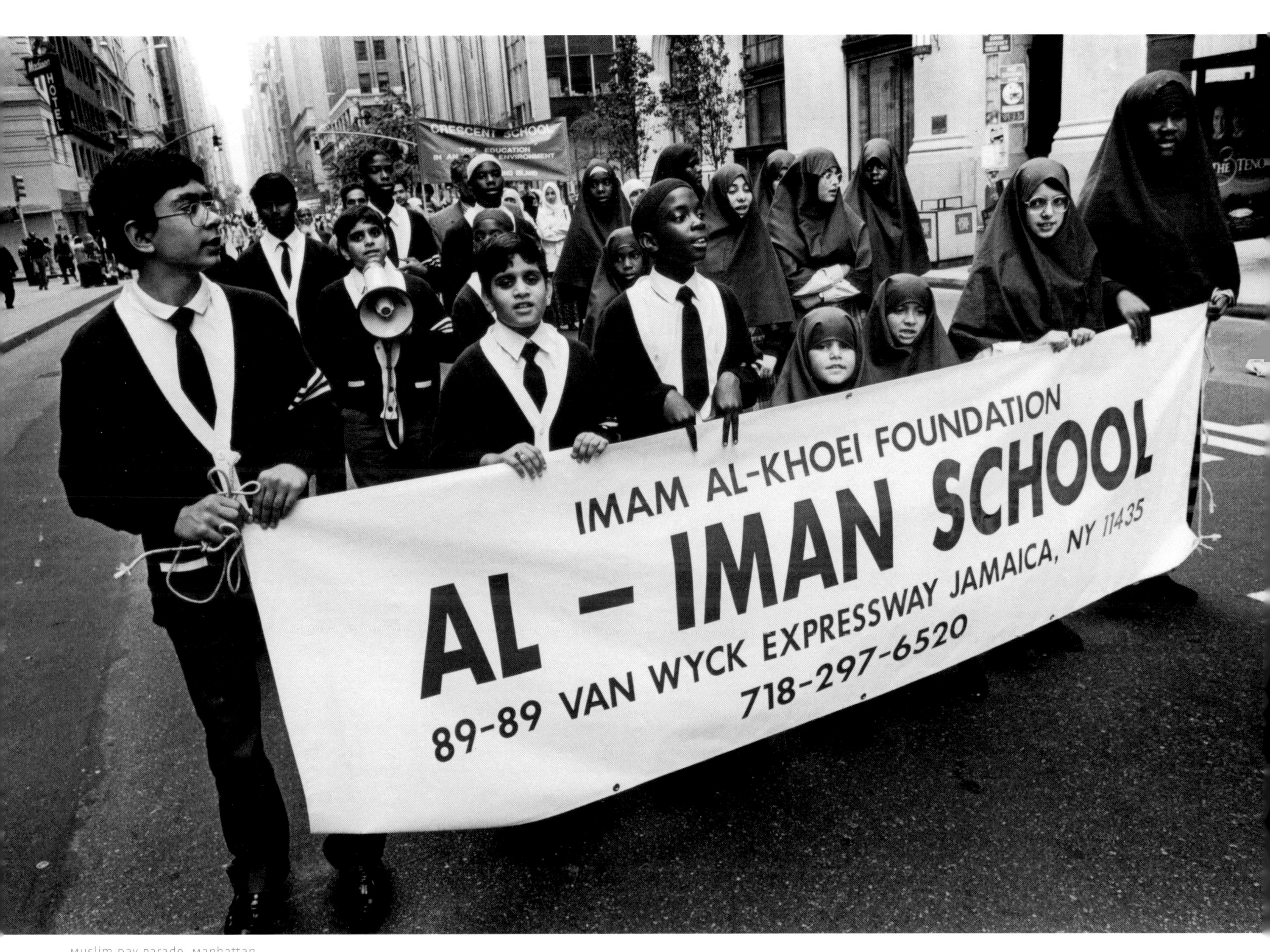

Muslim Day Parade, Manhattan

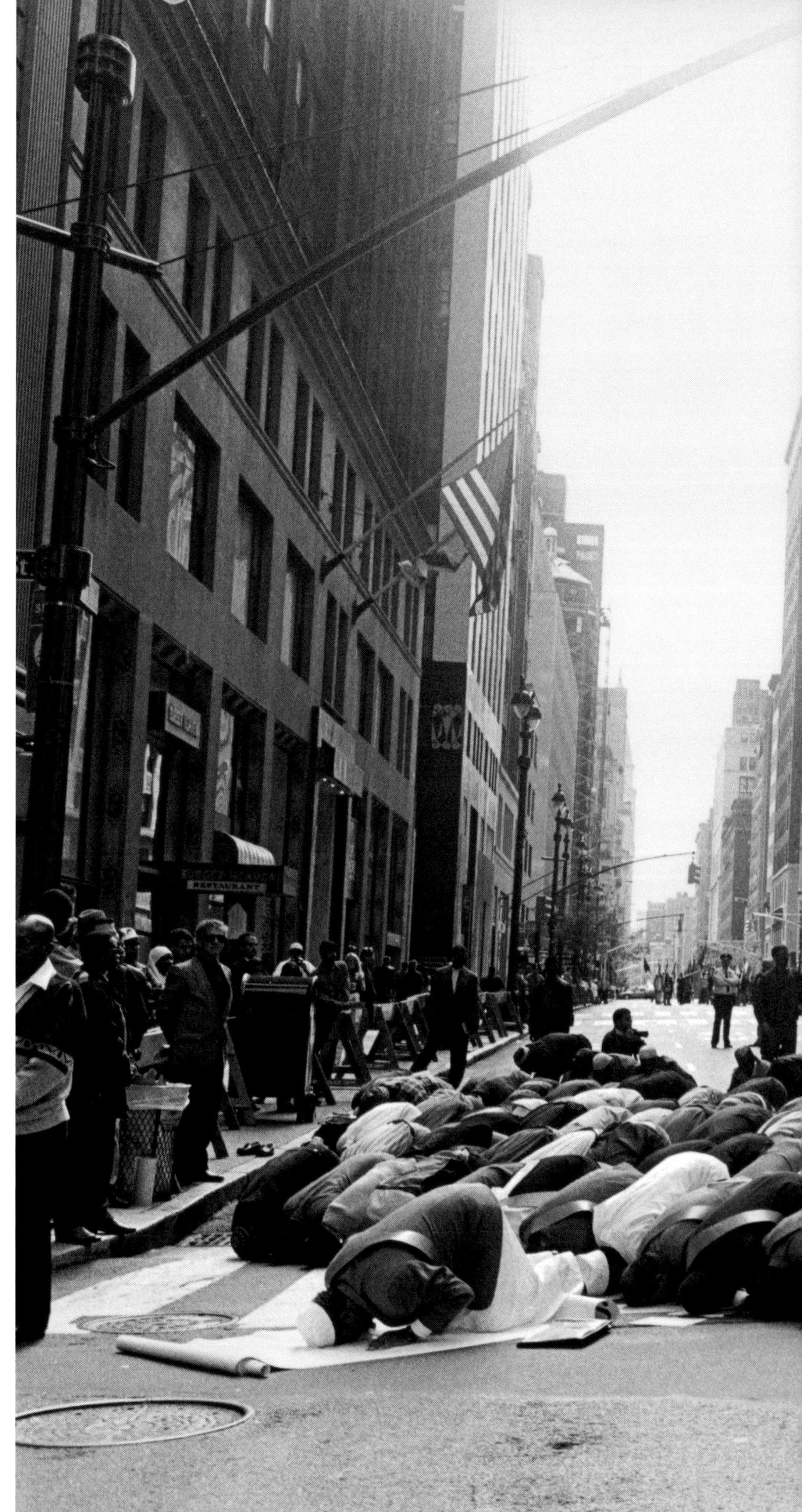

Prayer before the Muslim Day Parade, Manhattan

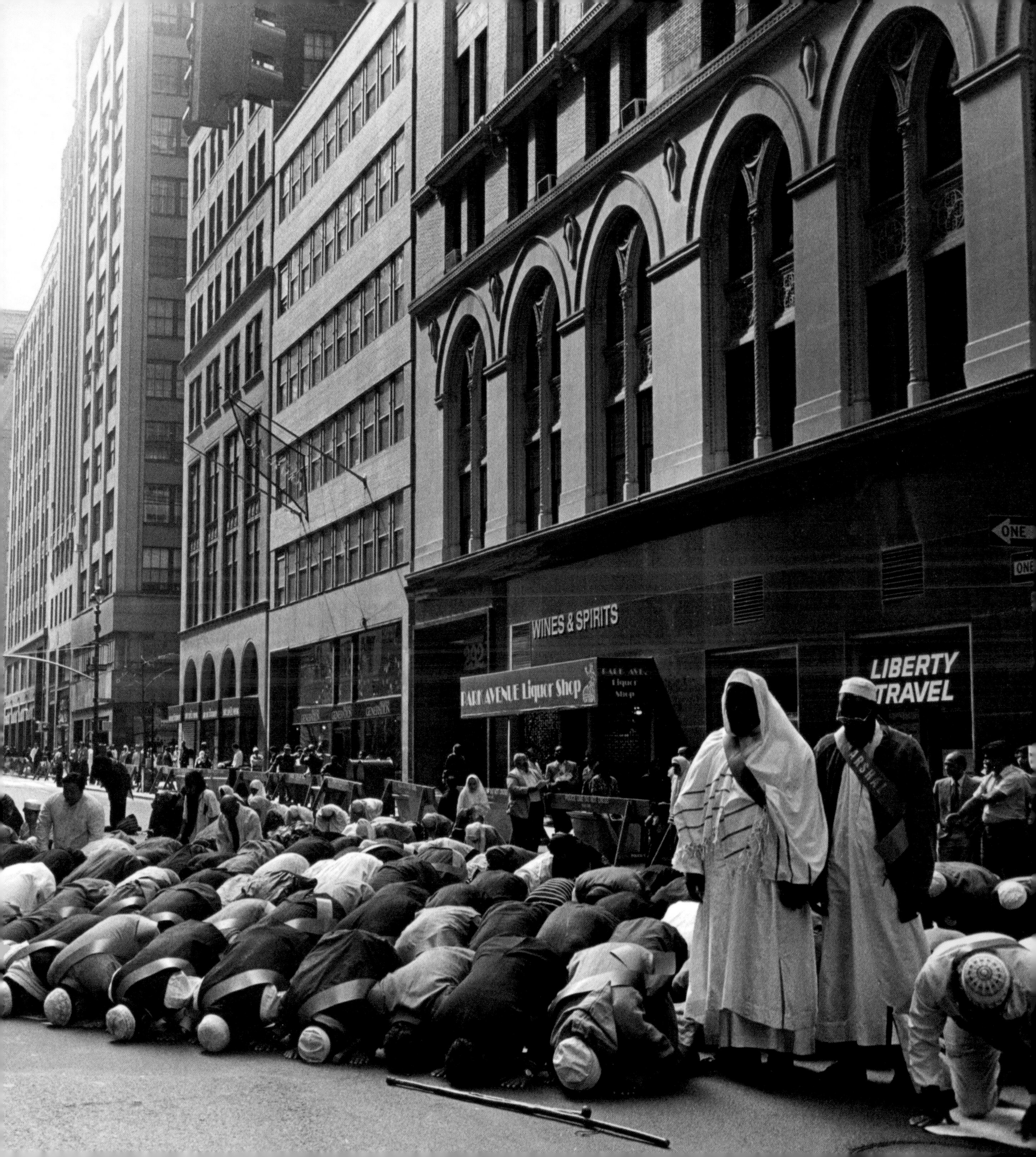
WINES & SPIRITS
PARK AVENUE Liquor Shop
LIBERTY
TRAVEL
ONE

ACKNOWLEDGEMENTS

Very important to the initial years of this project were students of the School of Architecture, Urban Design and Landscape Architecture of City College. During seminars and fieldwork, they uncovered and visited mosques, conducted their own interviews and quests, and kept us engaged in the impassioned plural discourse which makes City College the most exciting educational environment imaginable. When the project became an exhibition at Storefront for Art and Architecture in 1996, six gifted alumni became valuable collaborators: Khader Humied was administrative coordinator (and project philosopher); Khidir Abdalla, Layla Bahbahani, Numreen Qureshi, and Justin Weiner conducted fieldwork, research, translation, and documentation. Their presence created a passionate, stimulating dialogue, and their mark can be felt in many parts of this text. This short study is indebted as well to the extensive, groundbreaking work of those who came before: in particular the publications of the legendary Dr. Yvonne Yazbeck Haddad, and the brilliant and humane Dr. Susan Slyomivics; to the extensive research of Marc Ferris; and to both the scholarship and wisdom of Dr. Mustafa Bayoumi.

At Storefront, the creativity and commitment of Shirin Neshat and Kyong Park made the mosques visible and public, and the courage and generosity of many writers brought their message to an even wider audience. In recent times, Columbia University's important "Muslim Communities in New York Project"—a collaboration of Columbia's Middle East Institute and its Center for Urban Research and Policy—has incorporated and continued the work begun here. Thanks are due its visionary director, Dr. Reeva Simon, to Dr. Lorraine Minnite, project coordinator, and especially to Louis Abdellatif Cristillo, co-principal investigator, whose studies of the Muslim communities in the five boroughs have been invaluable, and who has generously shared his research with us.

At powerHouse Books, the support of Daniel Power has been enormously important, together with the collaboration of Susanne König, Craig Cohen, and Sara Rosen. Juliet Wiersema and Susan Bell copyedited the manuscript with amazing dispatch. We are especially indebted to the sensitivity and intelligence of Sophia Murer, whose design nurtured the meanings of the book.

Ed Grazda wishes in particular to thank Chris Killip at Harvard for introducing him to Jerrilynn Dodds; Jerry Poynton for his recommendation of Sophia Murer as a designer and his support for this project; Alice Rose George and Howard Stein/Camera Works Inc. for their continued interest and support of this project; and Jerrilynn Dodds, whose energy and insight made it all happen.

Jerrilynn Dodds wishes to thank Sandy and Theo Gifford, who have been patient, loving, smart, critical, humorous, and humane throughout the work for this book, which has lasted more than half their lives. And thanks to Ed Grazda for an amazing collaboration, for wonderful photographs that unlock new meanings and teach academics new tricks, and for loyal collegiality and friendship.

Fieldwork, research, and presentation of this material were generously funded by the National Endowment for the Arts, the New York State Council for the Arts, the Graham Foundation for Advanced Studies, The PSC-CUNY Research Award Program of the City University of New York, and the School of Architecture, Urban Design and Landscape Architecture of the City University of New York.

We are above all indebted to all the communities and individuals documented here, who opened their doors to us, told us their stories, and taught us as well. Among them we wish, in particular, to acknowledge Aisha Al-Adawiya of the Schomberg Center for Research in Black Culture; Nisar Zuri, editor of *Ayendah E-Afghan*; Imams Kareem Shakur and Izak El Pasha and Sister Khadija of the Masjid Malcolm Shabazz in Manhattan, Imam Abdel-Rahman Osman and Mohamed Younes of the Islamic Cultural Center of New York, Imam Hilmi Akdag of Fatih Cami in Brooklyn, and Imam Bayram Mulic of the Ali Pasha Mosque in Queens.

J. Dodds and E. Grazda

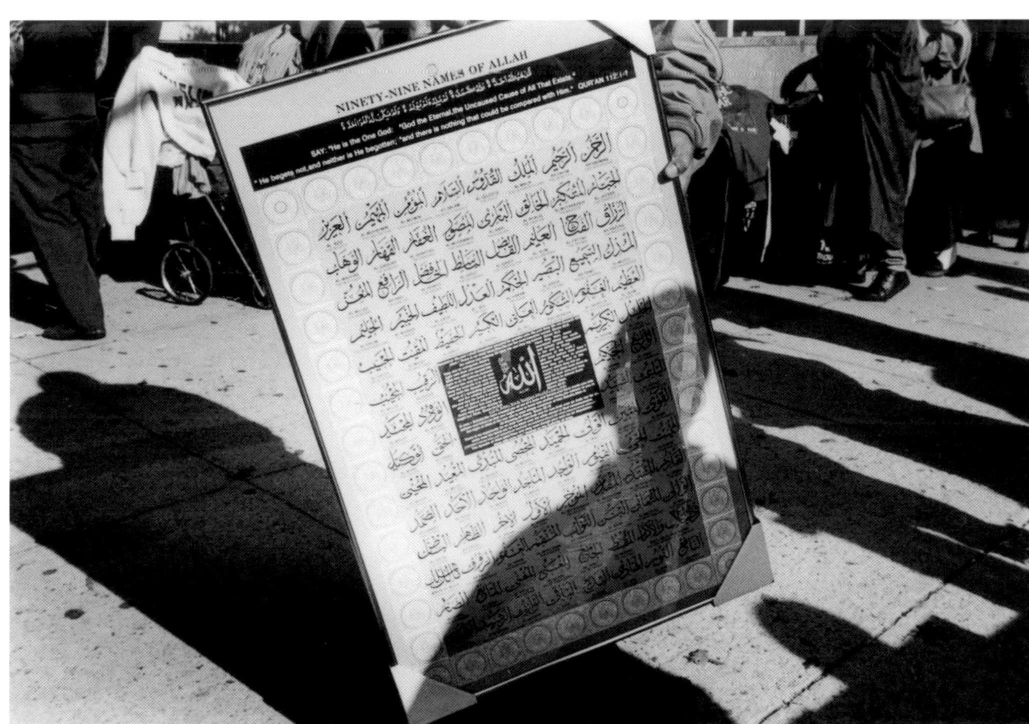

Notes

1 see also: Edmund Gjareeb, Split Vision: The Portrayal of Arabs in the American Media, Washington, 1983; Edward Said, Covering Islam: How the Media and the Experts Determine How We See the Rest of the World, New York, 1981. Also of interest here is Ella Shohat and Robert Stam, Unthinking Eurocentrism, New York, 1994.

2 James Brooke, "Attacks of U.S. Muslims Surge Even as Their Faith Takes Hold. Survey of Mosques Documents the Hate Crimes," The New York Times, August 28, 1995, 1.

3 See: "AMC Discusses Anti-Muslim Stereotypes with Warner Bros," (in) The AMC Report, Vol. 6, No. 4, April 1996, 1.

4 Our thanks to Columbia University's "Muslim Communities in New York Project"—a collaboration of Columbia's Middle East Institute and its Center for Urban Research and Policy. We are indebted to Louis Abdellatif Cristillo for sharing these and other important statistics with us.

5 According to an empirical field study conducted by the "Muslim Communities in New York Project."

6 Marc Ferris, "To Achieve the Pleasure of 'Allah: Immigrant Muslim Communities in New York City 1893-1991," (in) Yvonne Yazbeck Haddad and Jane Idleman Smith (eds.), Muslim Communities in North America, Albany, 1994, 209-10.

7 Allan D. Austin, African Muslims in Ante Belum America: Transatlantic Stories and Spiritual Struggles, New York, 1997; Mustafa Bayoumi, "Moorish Science," Transition #80, Vol. 8, No. 4; Sylziane A. Diouf, Servants of 'Allah: African Muslims Enslaved in the Americas, New York, 1998.

8 Marc Ferris, "To Achieve the Pleasure of 'Allah" 210.

9 Marc Ferris, "To Achieve the Pleasure of 'Allah" 211-2.

10 Marc Ferris, "To Achieve the Pleasure of 'Allah" 216; see also: Y. Haddad, J. Voll and J. Esposito, The Contemporary Islamic Revival: A Critical Survey and Bibliography, New York, 1991.

11 See: Clifton E. Marsh, The Lost Found Nation of Islam in America, New York, 2000.

12 When this research began, in 1993, there were approximately 70 mosques documented in the five boroughs of New York City. The growth of the number of mosques in more recent years has been mapped by Columbia University's "Muslim Communities in New York Project."

13 This study is limited to orthodox Islamic communities—both Sunni and Shiite, and includes no discussion of mosques founded by the Nation of Islam or by other groups whose basic ideologies diverge from those of conventional Islam.

14 Quoted in Randy Kennedy, "Jews and Muslims Share a Piece of Brooklyn," The New York Times, August 17, 1995, 1.

15 Delivered at the Islamic Congress of America, June 3, 1994.

16 Concerning loans and interest, see: Yvonne Yazbeck Haddad, and Adair T. Lummis, Islamic Values in the United States: A Comparative Study, New York, 1987, 99-102.

17 For instance, at the Ali Pasha Mosque and the Albanian Islamic Cultural Center.

18 Susan Slyomivics, "The Muslim World Day Parade and Storefront Mosques of New York City," (in) Barbara Daly Metcalf (ed.), Making Muslim Space in North America and Europe, Berkley, 210.

19 See: Jonathan Bloom, Minaret: Symbol of Islam, New York, 1988.

20 For a wider discussion of youth and Islam in America see: Nimat Hafez Barazangi," Parents and Youth: Perceiving and Practicing Islam in North America," (in) Earle Waugh, Sharon Abu-Laban, and Regula Qurseshi (eds.), Muslim Families in North America, Edmonton, Alberta, 1991, 132-153.

21 For an interesting study of changing attitudes as regards gender and Islam among American Muslims, see: Haddad, and Lummis, Islamic Values in the United States, 134-44; and Marilyn Robinson Waldman, "Reflections on Islamic Tradition, Women, and Family," (in) Waugh, Abu-Laban, and Qureshi (eds.), Muslim Families in North America, 309-325.

22 Interview with Imam Hafiz and Dr. Rashid, January 1994.

23 When a student working on our project, who was also a member of the mosque, asked leaders to give us an interview, they expressed fears that the project was a CIA cover-up.

24 Booklet published by "The Forum for Islamic Work" entitled: This is Our Destiny: Let Us Make It.

25 Imam Rahman, Masjidul Aman, November 1994.

26 On the interaction of indigenous values and life in New York City, see also: Haddad and Lummis, Islamic Values in the United States, 71-3.

27 See: Earle Waugh, "North America and the Adaptation of the Muslim Tradition: Religion, Ethnicity and the Family," (in) Waugh, Abu-Laban, and Qureshi (eds.), Muslim Families in North America, 68-95, especially "Islam and the Issue of Western Intellectual Bias," 68-70.

28 Though the architects of the Islamic Cultural Center acknowledge the inspiration of Ottoman forms in the design of that mosque, it was not with the intention to evoke a particular ethnic tradition. Rather, the Ottoman dome was thought to lend itself to modernist, pan-Islamic formal values. The issue of the relationship between religion and ethnicity is a complex one. In New York, as in many places in North America, Hannerz has argued that identity boundaries change as groups interact with each other (cited in Waugh, "North America and the Adaptation of the Muslim Tradition: Religion, Ethnicity and the Family," (in) Waugh, Abu-Laban, and Qureshi (eds.), Muslim Families in North America, 88.)

29 Susan Slyomivics, "The Muslim World Day Parade and Storefront Mosques of New York City," 210-11.

30 Thanks to Louis Abdellatif Cristillo for drawing this to my attention.

31 Renata Holod and Hasan Uddin Khan, The Contemporary Mosque: Architects, Designs and Clients since the 1950s, New York, 1997, especially 13-4. See also: Gulzar Haidir, "Muslim Space and the Practice of Architecture. A Personal Odyssey," (in) Making Muslim Space in North American and Europe, 31-42 and Jerrilynn Dodds, "The Dome and the Grid: Mosques of New York City," Aramco World, Nov/Dec 1996, Vol. 47, No. 6, 30-39 with photos by Edward Grazda.

32 Gulzar Haidir, "Muslim Space and the Practice of Architecture. A Personal Odyssey," 32-3; 38.

33 Susan Slyomivics,"New York City's Muslim World Day Parade," Peter van der Veer (ed.), Nation and Migration: The Politics of Space in the South Asian Diaspora," Philadelphia, 1998; see also: "The Muslim World Day Parade and Storefront Mosques of New York City."

34 The New York Times, April 28, 1987, cited in Marc Ferris, "To Achieve the Pleasure of 'Allah" 220.

35 New York, 1993, 332.

New York Masjid: The Mosques of New York City

Published in the United States by powerHouse Books,
a division of powerHouse Cultural Entertainment, Inc.
180 Varick Street, Suite 1302, New York, NY 10014-4606
telephone 212 604 9074, fax 212 366 5247
e-mail: masjid@powerHouseBooks.com
web site: www.powerHouseBooks.com

First edition, 2002

Library of Congress Cataloging-in-Publication Data

Grazda, Ed, 1947-
New York Masjid : the Mosques of New York City / Edward Grazda, photographs; Jerrilynn D. Dodds, text.
p. cm.
1. Mosques–New York(State)–New York. 2. Mosques–New York (State)–New York–Pictoral works. 3. Architecture_New York (State) New York–20th century. 4. Muslim_New York (State)–New York. I. Title: Mosques of New York City. II. Dodds, Jerrilynn Denise. III. Title

NA4670 .G73 2002
297.3'5741_dc21

2001058799

Hardcover ISBN 1-57687-135-5

Separations, printing, and binding by Artegrafica, Verona

A complete catalog of powerHouse Books and Limited Editions is available upon request; please call, write, or come to our web site.

10 9 8 7 6 5 4 3 2 1

Printed and bound in Italy

Book design by ddny, Sophia Murer, New York City

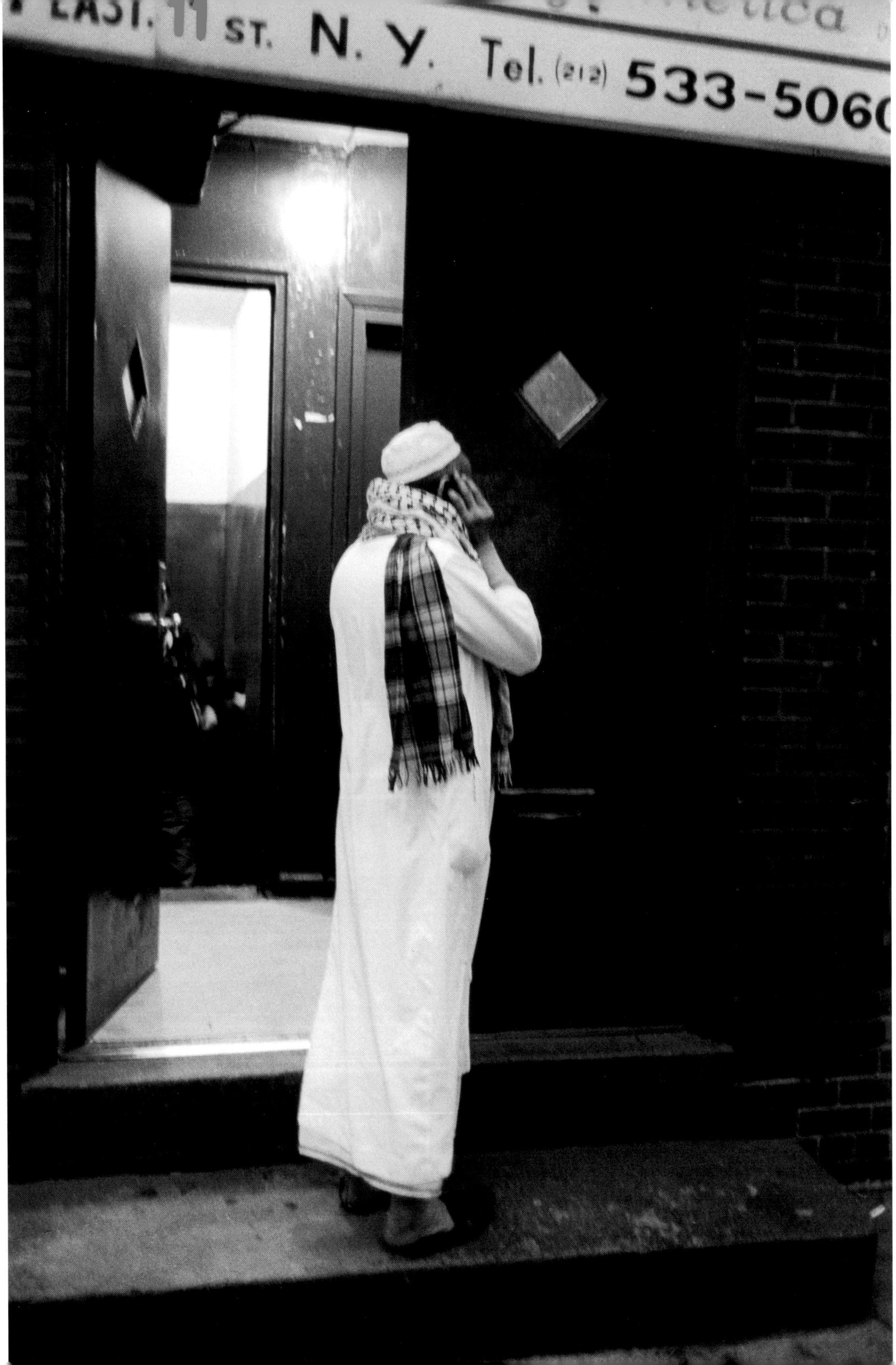

ST. N. Y. Tel. (212) 533-506